For my dear
friends, Hans or
Denise
with love Lilly

Also by Lilly Barnes

A Hero Travels Light (a series of interrelated stories, told
by the same narrator), Oberon Press, 1986
MARA (a novel), Variety Crossing Press, 2010
Journey (poetry), Inanna Publications, 2015

Lilly Barnes received a Gemini Award for her Outstanding
Body of Work writing scripts for the children's television show
Mr. Dressup for the Canadian Broadcasting Corporation.

THE ADVENTURES OF
GOLYGA

in the Realms of Spirit

by

Golyga as told to Lilly Barnes

BALBOA.PRESS
A DIVISION OF HAY HOUSE

Balboa Press books may be ordered through booksellers or by contacting:

Balboa Press
A Division of Hay House
1663 Liberty Drive
Bloomington, IN 47403
www.balboapress.com
844-682-1282

Because of the dynamic nature of the Internet, any web addresses or links contained in this book may have changed since publication and may no longer be valid. The views expressed in this work are solely those of the author and do not necessarily reflect the views of the publisher, and the publisher hereby disclaims any responsibility for them.

The author of this book does not dispense medical advice or prescribe the use of any technique as a form of treatment for physical, emotional, or medical problems without the advice of a physician, either directly or indirectly. The intent of the author is only to offer information of a general nature to help you in your quest for emotional and spiritual well-being. In the event you use any of the information in this book for yourself, which is your constitutional right, the author and the publisher assume no responsibility for your actions.

Any people depicted in stock imagery provided by Getty Images are models, and such images are being used for illustrative purposes only. Certain stock imagery © Getty Images.

Print information available on the last page.

ISBN: 978-1-9822-5353-0 (sc)
ISBN: 978-1-9822-5355-4 (hc)
ISBN: 978-1-9822-5354-7 (e)

Library of Congress Control Number: 2020916219

Balboa Press rev. date: 09/21/2020

Gratitude to all the teachers in my life, including
Ion Soare, Diana Muenz Chan, Martin Roher,
JeannetteMcCullough, Harvey Freedman, Freyda Isaacs,
and, of course, Golyga.
And to our editor, Stuart Ross.

For Martin Roher

Prologue

Once upon a time, there were stories to tell and tales to spin, but no one around to listen to them. So the Great Storyteller in the Sky created some ears. Ears could listen, of course, but they were incapable of reacting in a manner pleasing to the Great Storyteller in the Sky. Which led him/her to create yet another feature. No, not the mouth, but the diaphragm. He/she gave the gift of breath so the listener might be able to respond with a more complete response, whether it be the sharp intake, the repeated short exhale—as in giggling—or the horror-struck, long-held breath that—sorry to tell—seems the one humans are often all too fond of and make, some of them, into a lifelong habit.

Now, the reason for telling you all this is as follows: the Great Storyteller in the Sky became bored after a while with these Breathing Ear Listeners, and he/she—henceforth referred to as he for the sake of brevity...

LILLY: That's what they all say. One more letter and it's "she" for the same reasons of simplicity and elegance.
GOLYGA: Finally, an acknowledgement. All right then, it's "she."

...decided that what she really wanted in the way of listeners was a greatly complex being capable of the maximum number of—and the subtlest possible—responses to any given tale she chose to tell, and so were created what are now known as the Human Beings. And to make sure the attention of these human beings—humans for short—would not be flagging at any time whatsoever, she made them into the characters in her stories. In other words, they became the active participants, so they couldn't very well decide to take a break or an intermission and be back for the next part of the stories and tales told by the Great Storyteller in the Sky. And whether or not they enjoyed the stories and tales was decidedly up to them—to their enthusiasm in participating, their dedication to playing their part well and with conviction, and, above all, their capacity for enjoyment.

GOLYGA: *What do you think, Lilly dear?*
LILLY: *I love it. More, more.*

Introductions

LILLY

When Golyga first began whispering into my ear, I was astounded and not sure I wanted to join those who are "odd" or "weird" or otherwise outside the norm. However, since I had never really been part of any norm, I was soon happily engaged in listening to and writing down the tales about delightful characters and the lessons and blessings they demonstrated—always to my edification and with the purpose of sharing them as widely as possible.

Which meant a book.

And while this book has been a long time in its completion, there was never a moment's doubt that it would one day delight many readers while also leading to many a satisfying "Aaah!"

GOLYGA

Dear Reader,

The short intro above gives you an idea of the ride you'll be taking if you decide to read on: most of it easy and delightful, some of it puzzling until you come to realize its point, and some of it just plain "directions for travel" in this world of yours.

The main purpose of the journey you are undertaking is to provide you with interesting landscapes that nevertheless hold some "Aha" and "Oh, I see" for your enlightenment about living on this Earth home of yours.

You'll also be encouraged to follow some ridiculously easy changes of perception that will make for more joy on your journey.

All of this will happen by way of entertaining stories, parables, and interspersed bits of direct teaching, which, of course, you can choose to ignore.

(NOTE: Since the beginning of our connection and co-writing of this book, Lilly and "I/we" have enjoyed an easy partnership, which will become evident to the reader. And because we have always followed strict and immutable laws—such as "do no harm"—and have always been fully aware of Lilly's physical incarnation, the book took longer to complete than we had anticipated. Not that this made any difference to us, dwelling in a timeless condition as we are, but there will necessarily be an entry or two that are less applicable in the factual sense. There is, however, enough value in them in the larger sphere, and so we retained them as they were.)

Now, lest you get impatient, dear Reader, we'll begin by introducing our main characters—your fellow travellers on this journey.

Once upon a time, neither long ago nor far away, there was a Being we'll call Golyga.

GOLYGA: Yes, yours truly, but I intend to tell the tale in the third person, so we can more easily bring in characters of various sorts and make them part of the story. If the tale were told in the first person, all these characters would have to be explained in terms of the knowledge the first person has of them and, let's face it, I am not God Almighty him/herself, so you can see that telling it in the third person will give more verisimilitude to our tale.

Once upon a time, then, neither long ago nor far away, there was a Being we'll call Golyga. Golyga, for the sake of our tale, will be male.

GOLYGA: It seems that Lilly has a fondness for males and male heroes, and yet, and yet...there will come a major surprise that will delight her and bring her a new recognition of herself as heroine, so that henceforth her past experiences with malevolent females will fall away like so much flour dust, and she will emerge a fully gorgeous goddess. How's that now?
LILLY: Sounds wonderful, but is this part of the story?
GOLYGA: Oh, indeed it is. Makes it more interesting, too, I'll tell you. Wouldn't you agree?
LILLY: Yes, I would.

Now, Golyga, a Being of Light, has always been in the habit of travelling. Galaxies, planets—at least those of interest—and dimensions that have no known equivalent or analogous existence on Earth. I am going to tell about the first of his travels that is of interest to earthlings, and that is the journey to the faraway dimension of—I'll spell it—G-y-r-a-g-y-r-a.

In the dimension of Gyragyra, there are several interesting features that brought our Hero Golyga much joy: there, everything is beautiful, and everything is freshly created with every thought that arises. Thus Golyga could create for himself an environment of such unsurpassed delight that he didn't think he'd ever want to leave this dimension. Also, in the dimension of Gyragyra, every entity has the ability to create itself in the image it prefers. Golyga immediately created himself in the image of a very tall tree, overlooking the surroundings as far and wide as he pleased. Soon thereafter, however, it occurred to him that a tree is rather stationary, by choice, and he preferred to keep moving, so he became a bird. Needless to say, a large and powerful bird with the capacity for covering vast distances and staying aloft for eons at a time.

In the shape of a giant bird, then, Golyga set out to discover all the possible regions of this dimension and soon came to roost on a mountaintop as high as the Himalayas, and there he decided to create for himself a family of beings that would be his companions as well as his challenges. Because, you see, Golyga was getting bored with the ease and delight with which he lived every moment of his life in Gyragyra.

The companions included a mate, called Lillykins.

LILLY: Are you serious?
GOLYGA: Of course not. Just having fun—aren't you? All right. The mate's name was actually Carey. Is that better?
LILLY: No.
GOLYGA: Nuff said.

So the mate Lillykins was created, and soon thereafter a group of friends, the foremost of whom was Hylie. Hylie and Lillykins were brother and sister, in fact, and they had the sibling's habit of understanding each other all too easily. Golyga found that he had to develop telepathic skills that he had not possessed until now, and so he did, and he also found that he had to change his shape often to keep up with the various doings of his mate and his best friend. They, you see, aspired to being angels.

In the pursuit of angeldom, those two would dash off to other domains to be helpful in various ways, and each time their absence became longer and more burdensome for Golyga. So he started following one or the other of them and, to do so, he often had to change shape. Here is one such change and its subsequent adventure.

Lillykins took off from the mountaintop that was not unlike the Himalayas and, changing herself into a vastly amusing clown, dove right into the middle of an epidemic, trying to cheer up the multitudes who lay dying of some plague-like disease.

GOLYGA: Do not ask me about places or times, please. They are largely irrelevant and certainly not my forte.

Lillykins the clown became a beloved source of light and delight among the children—both healthy but bereft and also those afflicted and dying—and they appreciated her clowning and her gift of laughter. But the adults in this domain were a dour lot. They decided that laughter in a time of harrowing suffering was not to be tolerated, so they decided to apprehend and kill this clown.

Lillykins, innocent of the knowledge of danger, was doing a high-wire act above a town, carrying a cat around her shoulders. The cat's tail stuck straight up into the air, and Lillykins used it as the balancing fulcrum for her journey across the wire. The cat suddenly saw a procession with torches coming toward the high-wired street, preceded by a horde of children shouting, "Run, Lillykins, run!"

The cat let out a disgusting screech, jumped straight up and off Lillykins' shoulders, and ran off into the clouds. Lillykins looked down, saw the danger she was in, but had no idea how to avoid being roasted alive. So Golyga, watching the entire scene from high above, on the wing, descended in a great whoosh of wings to rescue his mate.

Well, Lillykins wasn't having any. No big bird or any other Being is going to come whooshing in to the rescue, so just forget it, she said. Which left Golyga no choice but to change shape, become a very tiny tick, and bite her ass, repeatedly, to get her into action mode.

"Eeech, uuugh, ouch!" yelled Lillykins, and she commenced to scratch and jump on the high wire until, suddenly, she fell off. And would have landed right in the arms of the torch- bearing torturers but for Golyga's swift and heroic actions. Changing himself into a cloud, he flew beneath the falling clown, his mate, and as she landed on the soft, engulfing fluff, he carried her off and away—far away from the crowds of vengeful creatures below.

Now, you would think this action would have been welcomed and elicited appreciation from Lillykins, but no. Yelling and berating, she raised her voice in horrible noises, until Golyga had enough of it and dropped her into a lake.

More anon.

LILLY: This is a lot of fun, just like you promised.
GOLYGA: Good. We aim to please. More than that, too, of course, but we'll sneak that part in all unbeknownst to you and others until: oh, my goodness, we're wise! Not yet, though.
In the meantime, this better be it for today.

* * *

GOLYGA: Where were we?
LILLY: You dropped her into the lake.
GOLYGA: That was a rhetorical question, actually, but thanks.

Lillykins, as she was falling, yelled out a long farewell because she fully expected to drown. Not that drowning presented a fearful fate to her; rather she intended, in the moment of drowning, to grow gills and become a fish, but such was not her fate-to-be. Golyga, in the moment before Lillykins hit the water, once again came whooshing down. This time he had taken on the form of a raindrop and landed on Lillykins' nose.

LILLY: What's up, I'm not getting a smooth dictation—is it me?
GOLYGA: Yes. You are anticipating/commenting in your mind. Stay out of it, please, until we're done.
LILLY: Sorry. I'll try again. Where to resume?
GOLYGA: The raindrop landing on Lillykins' nose. Okay.

Lillykins stuck out her tongue, expecting more raindrops, but none came. Instead, the one on her nose grew larger and larger and floated her off to an island in the lake. Here it pulled her ashore, and now the two of them—huge raindrop and Lillykins—sat side by side and tried to come to an agreement: either they would resume their partnership and work in tandem or else they would go their separate ways, to do the work they aimed to do on their own.

What exactly is the work you aim to do? asked Golyga. I haven't been getting any clear idea of what you want, please tell me.

Lillykins was immediately taken aback. Clear idea? she said. Clear idea? Why does it have to be a clear idea? A vague and warmly fuzzy idea is one I usually prefer for my direction and feel-good thoughts and encounters of every kind. Why not follow the fuzzy-warm feel-good path in work? Do I absolutely have to have a clear idea?

Golyga stopped to think about this. A new notion to him, he found. But not entirely absurd. After all, many a good piece of work was the result of warmly fuzzy.

Okay then, said Golyga, give me a general idea—not clear but warmly fuzzy. A very general idea of what you have in mind for your work.

Making things better, said Lillykins. Making things better for people, especially children, for the Earth, especially trees, and generally adding to the positive energies of the world.

The Earth? said Golyga. Is this a place I have known? Let me think. The Earth...a planet, right?

Right, said Lillykins. Very beautiful. About three degrees off the main route when you're travelling on the grid continuum you usually zip around in.

I'll have to visit this planet Earth, said Golyga, and see why you have taken a special interest in it.

Do that, said Lillykins. And then you'll have some idea of what the work is I want to undertake there. Believe me, the needs and opportunities are endless.

At this point, a large cloud went sailing by above and, seeing Golyga the raindrop and Lillykins, still in her clown incarnation, sitting side by side on the island, dropped down to the shore. There it changed into the brother of Lillykins, best friend to Golyga, and joined them in the form of a giant ant.

Have you been looking for us? asked Golyga. Your sister here has been absolutely adamant that I not come whooshing to her rescue, although she keeps engaging in foolhardy and dangerous deeds. Speak to her, for heaven's sake.

What's the worry? asked Hylie. She can change shape as well as we can. She can rescue herself any time she wants to, remember?

Oh, shoot, said Golyga, I forgot. So what exactly is my role here, as the mate of such a creature?

Oh, for goodness' sake, said Lillykins. What exactly is my role, for that matter? If it's roles you want, how does a raindrop come to be asking questions of a clown? Roles, indeed.

Forget roles then, said Golyga. Let's talk relationship.

Lillykins groaned, not once but several times. Please, she said. I hear enough about that stuff when I'm on Earth. Relationships, relationships, relationships. As though the bottom line for every one of them isn't exactly the same: Is there love? Is there enough love? Period. I can't tell you how utterly boring it is to have to sit and listen to earthlings and their endless talk of "relationships." When you think what-all they could be enjoying instead. Like sitting on the shore of an island, talking to raindrops and clouds and ants.

I see what you mean, said Golyga. Nevertheless, I wish to be able to describe, at least to myself, in what way exactly we are mates. How do we differ from any other pair of relating entities?

That's for me to know and for you to find out, said Lillykins, and off she flew, clown suit and all, like a balloon trailing not a string but a voice calling: Find out…find out…find out.

Golyga and Hylie looked at each other.

Well, yes, said Golyga. I will have to follow her and find out, sometime. But right now I need a break. How about a little adventure on the planet Viberion?

You know, said Hylie, changing himself into a very large bird. The last time you and I went to Viberion, we nearly had our feathers ruffled. But come on, let's do it.

Golyga, too, changed himself into a large bird, and the two of them took off, side by side, soon landing on the silver planes of Viberion.

LILLY: I have some niggling doubts that this material will be of interest to adults. Not that shape-shifting isn't "in," but it's usually treated either with more solemnity or as children's stuff.

GOLYGA: Never you mind what is niggling. Keep going and we'll soon reveal to you what this is in aid of.

LILLY: Are you going to tell me later this is just preparation?

GOLYGA: No. But on the other hand, this isn't the final version of the tale. This is the dictation of material that will become a springboard and outline, so to speak. How we go about getting it into the final version you'll have to leave until later. Let's continue for just a bit longer today.

Golyga and Hylie, in the form of two big birds—and I mean big: the size of mountaintops—descended, landed, and immediately were spotted by the inhabitants of Viberion. No wonder, you'll say, the birds' size being what it was, but then the size of the inhabitants of Viberion is not negligible either. Each had not only enormous ears and feet, like earthling teenagers, but also a huge belly, tiny head, bristling with a furry cover, and the best darn Hockenstocks in the universe.

   More anon.

LILLY: You certainly know how to do cliffhangers.

GOLYGA: I told you it'll be entertaining. Now let's go over today's instalment.

LILLY: Okay...

...

LILLY: Having just gone over it, I take back all my niggling. It's funny and thought-provoking, and I apologize profusely for doubting any of it.

GOLYGA: You are welcome, my dear. And do please include these bits with the rest, okay?

* * *

GOLYGA: All right. Now we go back to the Tale of Golyga and his mate Lillykins and his best friend—and Lillykins' brother—Hylie.

Hylie was becoming a bit of a nuisance on the subject of the weather. He couldn't decide whether he liked the sunshine, the rain, or the ever-ready hurricanes that blew on the planet Viberion. He missed, in fact, the calm and balmy delights of his home planet, Hesperus. Yes, there are many names of planets unknown to humans except by way of somebody's creative imagination. Hesperus, however, was one big yawn to Golyga, and he refused to go there, so Hylie took off on his own.

LILLY: Wait a minute. Did nothing happen on Viberion before Hylie went off?
GOLYGA: Nothing relevant to our story at this time. But you'll find out more about Viberion even without the presence of Hylie, never fear.

All right. Hylie went off, quacking like a duck in heat, and Golyga went in search of adventure. The kind of adventure he liked best: not knowing what was around the next bend but determined to encounter it with great courage and his famous sense of fun. Well, what turned out to be around the next bend was a feather. A feather flying, or rather gently sailing in swoops, on the breeze that heralded yet another hurricane to come.

Golyga caught the feather and stuck it among his own, under the right wing. There, he said. You'll have a safe haven from the coming hurricane. Snuggle in and be warm, and I'll let you sail on after the hurricane has blown over.

What Golyga neglected to notice was that the feather was a rather unusual one: it had the markings of a king's royal crest and the colours of a sand star. It was, in fact, a royal message to the rulers of Viberion from the King of Saltbar Island. Golyga knew none of this, nor did he anticipate what that feather message under his wing was about to cause him in the way of chafing and calibration.

Now we want to go back, briefly, to Lillykins and her sojourn back on the planet Earth.

GOLYGA: You have surely guessed by now that we were talking of just that planet, though as experienced by beings of another dimension?

Lillykins was sitting cross-eyed with huffiness, mumbling to herself about the likes of would-be rescuers who just took off whenever they weren't allowed to do their hero act. She eventually got up and started jogging around the island, idly glancing at the horizon or into the bushes and forest undergrowth, not expecting to see anything much but alert to every possibility.

Suddenly, a huge snake appeared in her path, rearing its head in her direction. Lillykins stopped jogging.

The snake started swaying, its head moving from side to side on an elegant neck, and its eyes never leaving Lillykins' jogging shoes. Lillykins, if you remember, was still in the outfit of a clown and her shoes looked amazingly appropriate, but they interested the snake because of their potential for becoming airborne.

How high can you bounce on those? asked the snake.

Oh, I'd say about two feet or so. Bouncing, that is. Jumping would be much higher.

Let's see you, said the snake.

Lillykins started bouncing. Soon she was easily reaching two feet with every bounce, and when she started jumping, she managed four or five, without expending much energy doing it.

Excellent, said the snake. I've been looking for something like that. I need to send a message to the King of Saltbar Island, and a message wearing shoes just like that should get there at the right time for my planned undertaking. Will you lend me your shoes?

Lillykins didn't hesitate. She took off her jogging shoes, handed them to the snake, said her goodbyes, and jogged on, barefoot.

The snake, meanwhile, inserted the message in one of the shoes and sent it off, jogging toward Saltbar Island. With the other shoe, the snake created two large bifocal but rimless attachments for its eyes, which looked, from a distance, quite a lot like those baker's doughnuts, but when seen up close turned out to be binoculars of the finest order.

The snake, you see, was a scientist and fond of turning something meant for one thing into something else altogether and then calling it a "new discovery" or "invention." Yes, the snake scientist, who we'll meet again, is a trickster to be watched and watched with care.

Lillykins, meanwhile, was jogging barefoot, and before long, she stepped on a burr. Ouch, she said. This isn't going to be much fun without shoes. Think I'll change shape. Never did enjoy jogging, anyway.

And so Lillykins changed herself into the shape of an elongated, hairpin-shaped Galapagos of islands, connected below the waters and ever ready to submerge various parts of herself in order to have some fun with the tourist excursion boats weaving their way around the islands.

Her favourite sport was to submerge a foot-island, say, and then, when a luxury cruise ship was riding over it, lifting the foot so the boat was high on her instep and dry, and all those aboard started yelling and shouting, "Earthquake!" and then she would resist all temptation to play soccer with the ship and would gently lower her foot back into the water and, with the barest shove of her big toe, send it on its way toward her knee.

Now, you might think it was childish of Lillykins to engage in such pranks, and I would agree with you, except that in total secret and from well-hidden positions, I actually delighted in the playfulness and gentle hilarity of my mate Lillykins. This said, I must point out that, being Golyga, I am able to be here, there, and everywhere at once, there being no sequential time, and so am able to watch Lillykins have her little bouts of fun while also pondering the fact, on Viberion, of a skin irritation under my wing caused, I was becoming sure, by the feather I had casually tucked away.

But more about all of this anon.

LILLY: *Thanks for the fun, Golyga. I can feel my imagination expanding.*
GOLYGA: *We aim to please.*
LILLY: *And to sneak the lessons in.*
GOLYGA: *And what have you learned?*
LILLY: *That I would like to be able to live life as a dance.*
GOLYGA: *It's your life.*

* * *

GOLYGA: *Yes, we are ready to work, and even eager for it, but we have to warn you, this session will be like no other. We are planning a little diversion, branching off into another realm, and you had better be prepared to travel far and wide, all in a moment. Here we go…*

As soon as Golyga had reached Viberion, he also arrived at a conclusion: this place was no place for him or anyone close to him. Why is that? you might ask. And we shall be happy to tell you. Golyga was turned off by Viberion because it had a greenish light. Yes, that was all. But just imagine a greenish light wherever you happen to be. Trees in a greenish light? Lakes in a greenish light? Skyscrapers in a greenish light? Not very attractive, wouldn't you say?

Well, that all depends, said Lillykins later on, when Golyga told her about it.

On what? Golyga suspected that Lillykins just wanted to be contrary, or perhaps unique in her opinion. It depends on what?

On the colour of whatever it is that green light shines on. Say it was—oh, purple. Purple trees, purple lakes, purple skyscrapers. How would those look in a green light?

Golyga shuddered. He thought they'd look even worse than they did now, and, after picturing it, Lillykins laughed and agreed.

Well, never mind, she said. You don't *have* to go to Viberion, do you?

That's true, said Golyga. But I hate the thought of being kept from any place in the universe on principle. I want to be able to roam freely anywhere at all, and a pocket of somewhere not open to such roaming bugs me.

It's open, Lillykins pointed out. You're the one who isn't. You've decided you don't like the green light and won't go for that reason. It's not the limitations of the place, it's you.

Golyga had to admit that Lillykins was right and decided forthwith to return to Viberion and see whether he could persuade himself to have a different opinion of the green-lit planet.

Golyga landed right at the foot of a giant ladder. A greenish-looking ladder.

A ladder, Golyga always thought, is meant to be climbed, and climb it he did. At the very top, he found that the ladder was leaning against the chest of a giant. Golyga grabbed a fistful of chest hair and pulled himself up closer to the giant's head, until he was perched just under his chin. Now what? The giant had no beard and so there was nothing more Golyga could hang on to to get higher up and perhaps see this giant's face. Snorting in frustration, Golyga caused the giant to be tickled under the chin. The giant lifted one huge hand to scratch the tickle and encountered Golyga, whom he had not hitherto seen or felt or heard.

Argh, said the giant. What is this? What kind of pest are you?

Golyga really objected to being referred to as a pest and, there being no other means of communicating this, he bit the giant's little finger. The giant rubbed it with his other hand and said: Stop tickling me, you little pest. What do you want, anyway? I know everybody and everything wants something from me. What is it *you* want from me?

Golyga was astonished. Want something from the giant? Phew. All he wanted right now was to get released from his grip, put safely on the ground, and be free to go about his business. Which was what again? Golyga couldn't remember what exactly he had been doing when he encountered the ladder and became curious about where it led. How, he wondered aloud, to make the giant understand him, since the giant seemed incapable of hearing anything.

What makes you think I can't hear you, asked the giant, astounded at the talking pest in his hand. I can certainly hear you perfectly well, want to or not.

You didn't hear me when I was climbing up your chest, did you? Or feel me either.

Well, I was fast asleep, you little pest, said the giant. Do you hear every little pest around when you are sleeping?

All right, all right, said Golyga. And since you can hear me, let me tell you that I really object to being called a pest every few seconds. I am nothing of the kind.

What kind are you? asked the giant. And what are you doing here, anyway? Shouldn't you be somewhere else with all the others who are scared to come near me even though I put a ladder out so they can come close enough to see I'm nothing to be scared of? It's my size that has everyone scared, and I can't seem to find a way to show them I'm actually quite kind and understanding and gentle.

Hm, said Golyga, let me think about this. But you'd better put me down before you accidentally squeeze me to death in your kind and gentle hand.

The giant bent forward and put Golyga on the topmost rung of the ladder. Then he bent backwards and lowered himself to the ground so that Golyga was, in fact, standing on the giant's middle and could walk around on him, like one of those Lilliputians of literary fame. Golyga started pacing and thinking and he came up with this idea:

If you, giant, were to lie here all peaceful and smiling, and if I, Golyga, brought everyone from their hiding place to come and see you, and I climbed up on your body again and demonstrated how safe it is to be in your company, would you say that might work?

Well, of course it would, said the giant. I've been hoping and waiting for somebody to come close enough to take this message of safety to everybody. Off you go, and tell them I'm a sweetie, would you?

Where exactly are these "everybody" hiding from you? asked Golyga. Do you know?

The giant snorted so hard that Golyga was almost blown right off his body.

They're in a cave, he said. My own giant's cave, as a matter of fact. I have not been able to go home and have a good night's sleep—which is why I was sleeping right here when you first came. I don't want to scare them literally to death by going there, so I'm hanging around, waiting for them to come out, and it's been too long. Go get them out. The cave is 3,000 miles that way.

The giant pointed to the west, and Golyga thought: Three thousand miles? What's that? Never mind. He knew the direction and it sounded far, so he turned himself into a flying catamaran and took off. As soon as he arrived at the cave, he told everyone there how gentle and kind the giant claimed to be and that he, Golyga, had actually found him not at all scary.

The people in the cave hooted and laughed their heads off. They didn't look a bit scared. They looked greenish, of course, but that was not their fault.

We're not scared, said the leader of the cave dwellers. We are finally feeling safe and enjoying this enormous cave, having shelter and a good place to chisel paintings on the wall. We're not scared at all, we're just glad that huge giant is out of here. Tell him to find another place to live because this is ours now. And you, piss off. Or we'll give *you* something to be scared about.

Golyga was astonished. At the giant's misreading of the situation, at the cave dwellers' effrontery, at their appropriating the cave and telling him to piss off, and at the way the greenish light on Viberion seemed to rob him of his intuitive understanding of anything and everything going on. On the other hand, even the giant had misread the cave dwellers's actions, so what *was* going on?

Back he flew to the giant and told him what he had found out. The giant was amazed.

They want to stay in *my* cave? Without even a "may I" or "do you mind"? Well, we'll see about that!

And next thing he knew, Golyga had been grabbed by the neck and stuffed into the giant's pocket, and the giant had taken a few steps and reached the cave, where he let out a mighty bellow right into the entranceway. It was so loud that all the walls trembled, and when he stomped his feet once or twice, the ground shook as in an earthquake, and, as you can imagine, all the cave dwellers shook in their skins and turned a ghastly colour in the green light. Out they came, squeezing past the giant as fast as they could—out, out they came, in a long stream, and every one of them looked shell-shocked and terrified.

Okay then, said the giant when the last of them was gone. I thank you, little visitor, and I'll be forever grateful to you, but now you had better be off. I'm going to have my first good long sleep in a while, and if those usurpers find you around here, they'll slaughter you like a piggy-went-to-market. Thanks, and away you go.

The giant went into his cave, curled up comfortably, and was asleep before Golyga could say a word. Perhaps because he was rather slow in finding a reply. What in the world was he to make of this reversal? A kindly giant turns fierce and frightening. Arrogant cave dwellers become frightened refugees? And all this in a greenish light?

Golyga decided that he needed time to ponder all this and that he wanted to do it somewhere else. Anywhere else, in fact. And so, off he flew and landed on his favourite island, and there he sat and pondered.

LILLY: I have a feeling that's it for today. Will there be an addendum?
GOLYGA: We believe you already have one in the manuscript.
LILLY: All right then. I'll find it.
GOLYGA: Good work, Lilly dear. Read it over again later, and enjoy the day.
LILLY: Thank you. Beeswax, is it?
GOLYGA: Yes, indeed. Though we dare say you'd be more comfortable with a dignified sort of name for us, Teachers of Light that we are.

LILLY: Yes and no. I like having my notions challenged and my thinking expanded, and at the same time, "Beeswax" does ring a little frivolous. And then there's "None of your Beeswax."

GOLYGA: Amazing and confusing. Almost as though bathed in an unfamiliar greenish light.

LILLY: Aha! I know the addendum: Confusion is the state from which growth is possible. Certainties prevent growth. Am I right?

GOLYGA: Yes you are, you clever thing. So now you have just added the addendum and we're off. Until soon, my dear.

LILLY: Thank you, Beeswax.

* * *

And so it came about that the most High and Delightful were sent to the planet Viberion to rescue once more all the various forms of life that existed there because they were all in danger from the machinations and vicissitudes of fate. Fate in the form of the venerable Golyga, that is.

We have seen how the first of his trips came about, when his mate Lillykins was indicating he had better get himself elsewhere quickly or be harangued and beset upon, and then we saw him once more voyaging in the universe, seeking adventures and delight as well as enlightenment. Well, the last came soonest.

Looking around Viberion, Golyga noted that most of the creatures were winged ones, and some had enormous wings, at that. Also enormous beaks and talons. What could be the purpose of such large numbers of large winged beasts? Golyga asked himself, and immediately received an answer in the form of a journey.

One of the winged creatures, the largest he had ever seen, took Golyga by the scruff of his not inconsiderable neck and transported him to a mountaintop where he showed him a long long valley, an iridescent river snaking along its bottom.

This valley, said the huge Bird, is the valley of our destruction unless a way can be found to reduce the iridescence therein. You see, the water contains a vast amount of mercury—dropped here not by the planet of the same name but by some unscrupulous space travellers—and as we partake of the water—whether directly or in the form of plants that drink of the waters—we grow huge. Unfortunately, the larger we grow,

15

the more we must partake of the water. Soon we'll be too big for this planet to support us and then we shall have to move to another one. Not easy for us because we are not only attached to this one, we have yet to discover another that supports life forms such as ours. So, please, can you help us?

Golyga sat on the mountaintop and thought. What immediately came to mind was the planet Earth, where pollution was also coming close to causing the extinction or departure of its inhabitants. What solutions, he wondered, are they coming up with on the planet Earth?

I'll have to go to the planet Earth, Golyga told the huge Bird. Perhaps I can find solutions for your problem in their analogous situation and their grappling with this problem. I'll be back as soon as I have found out something useful.

As it happens, Golyga was gone for a long long time because the planet Earth didn't yet have anything useful worked out on a large scale. Little groups were finding local solutions and fighting the larger problem as best they could, but there was no overall will or plan to solve the mammoth, disastrous developments on the planet Earth. Golyga did, however, find a number of intriguing creatures there.

GOLYGA: Lilly dear, I can feel your mind running interference. Please remember, you don't have to make an effort to come up with intriguing characters for this tale. This one will be populated with creatures that I, Golyga, find intriguing.
LILLY: Great. I'm intrigued. Tell on.

The first of the intriguing characters was a huge tower. Sticking up like a needle into the sky, doing not much of anything.

What are you about? Golyga asked the tower, who turned out to be rather laconic and not exactly up on self-knowledge.

Um... said the tower. About height and standing up straight, even in the wind, and about being pointy at the top with some flashing lights.

Fascinating, said Golyga. For about a minute. But there must surely be a hidden meaning to your existence. Let me try to find out what that is.

Well, if you find out, said the tower, let me know, will you? It's getting damned boring standing here, and I really wouldn't mind knowing there's more to me than I know.

Golyga went off to try and find out what the tower meant to other creatures around it. A shiny blue building nearby wasn't in the mood to talk at all. In fact, most of the concrete and glass creatures had little of interest to say. So Golyga started listening to the small creatures that scurried in between those big solid ones. The ones called humans.

And he did, finally, hear some of them talking about the tower.

"Used to be the biggest free-standing structure in the world."

"You can eat in a restaurant that revolves way up there."

"On a clear day, good view of the city's downtown."

And: "I understand it's a relay tower for radio and television."

Well now, I'll have to tell tower all about that, Golyga said to himself. But even that isn't going to keep tower thrilled about life for very long. What else could be the meaning of this pointy thing? The children of a giant race at play in a sandbox? Experimenting with what will stand up for how long? In that case, where is the giant race? These humans I see are pretty small—yet they seem to be the ones who built this thing. But they're so small, could it be that some aliens came from another planet and built this?

Golyga was more determined than ever to find out the secret meaning of this tower. In he went, up an elevator and down again. Then he went up to the various levels and looked out and around. Finally, he came upon a child sitting beside a telescope, crying.

What's up? said Golyga in the shape of a seagull.

My mother's gone, said the crying child. She was going to get change for the telescope and she told me to wait here, but she hasn't come back and it's been a long long time.

Suddenly, Golyga and the child heard loud noises from below.

Sirens, said the child. Police sirens and ambulance sirens. Let's go see.

The child led Golyga to the other side of the tower, and when they looked down, they saw a tiny body being carried into the ambulance. It was the child's mother, and she had managed to jump off the tower to kill herself.

Oh, Jesus have mercy, thought Golyga. How do I tell tower about this one?

Then he couldn't even think about it because the child started wailing away so hard that something had to be done.

Come with me, said Golyga, turning himself into a huge seagull, big enough to carry a child. Hop on and I'll take you where you'll be safe and happy.

The child didn't believe a word of this, but what else was he—a boy child, yes—to do? He hopped on the seagull's back and Golyga flew him down to ground level. The ambulance could be heard driving off on the other side, but Golyga didn't stop to point that out. He flew low along the ground until he came to a tunnel, where he quickly turned himself into a bat, flew the child through and out the other side, and then altogether off the planet Earth and over to where Lillykins was sitting, on her island.

What's this? Who is this? Lillykins yelled. Well, actually, she wasn't yelling. She was surprised and intrigued, so it came out with enthusiasm and high energy. Lillykins liked children—of every kind—and here was a little boy landing beside her feet.

Can you take care of him for a while? asked Golyga. I have to go back to the planet Earth and find out the meaning of a tower there.

No way, said Lillykins. You do not dump a child beside my feet and take off. You want this child taken care of, you'd damned well better do at least some of the caretaking, so quit looking like a bat caught in sunshine and find something for this child to eat. As for the meaning of the tower, I can tell you its meaning.

Have you ever even seen this tower? Have you been to the planet Earth and seen the one I'm talking about?

Oh, for heaven's sake, said Lillykins. If you've seen one tower, you've seen them all, and their meaning is all the same, too. If you want to know the meaning, just change yourself into a woman for a while and you'll be clear as rain about it in no time. It's embarrassingly simple and hardly worth mentioning. It's a cliché, for goodness' sake.

Golyga shook his head, trying to find some spot in there that would come up with the cliché Lillykins was referring to, but nothing emerged. So he changed himself into a woman.

Oh my, sighed Lillykins. Not here, Golyga. Do it on the planet Earth! There aren't any of those silly towers here on the island, are there? Do it on Earth, but first get some food and shelter happening for this child. I'm busy at the moment and can't be doing everything myself.

What are you so busy with? asked Golyga.

If you really want to know, said Lillykins, I'll tell you. Anon.

LILLY: Did you forget about the feather tucked under Golyga's wing that was irritating his skin?

GOLYGA: Not at all. Did you?

LILLY: I had, actually, it being a while since we worked, but I did have the feeling something wasn't connecting right.

GOLYGA: What makes you think the feather isn't still there, still bothering Golyga our hero?

LILLY: Just that he didn't mention it.

GOLYGA: Our hero is not one to talk of a skin irritation when there are planets and their inhabitants in danger of extinction, let alone an abandoned child to take care of. Do you mind?

LILLY: Sorry to have been so presumptuous.

GOLYGA: Judgmental, you mean. Editing is all well and good in its time and place. This ain't it.

LILLY: Sorry again. Unless of course you forgot about the feather and are just now covering your—er, wing—with a lofty explanation.

GOLYGA: Having been so quick to catch me up, you'll never know, will you?

LILLY: Okay, I give up. I'll send my editor way out of the way henceforth—as much as I can.

GOLYGA: Thank you. We'll both be calling on your editor soon enough. Meantime, enjoy!

LILLY: I will. I do. Thank you.

* * *

GOLYGA: To work, says our beloved Teacher MarTee, but not for long. We can but obey.

LILLY: Are you sorry to have chosen such a poor body for your channel?

GOLYGA: Feeling sorry for yourself, I see.

LILLY: That, too. But I do wish I had energy for more of this, more regularly.

GOLYGA: We know that. And MarTee is helping you to get there. As for me, I'm happy to be in touch and working with you whenever it happens. Time is simply not involved here. Not for us.

LILLY: Do you have the whole book in existence or do you let it flow out as you dictate?
GOLYGA: Both. At any moment, I can choose to go in a myriad directions with it—as long as I keep the various strands in hand and bring them back in to weave my web. Let's get to work and have some fun, okay?
LILLY: By the way, do I include the above as well or not?
GOLYGA: Include it. Better to have our relationship clear throughout. You are, after all, a conscious channel and as such can be a teacher of sorts in that area.
LILLY: "Of sorts"? Not that I am in any way ready to teach channelling, but what is "of sorts"?
GOLYGA: Indirectly. By way of our clear communications to each other about the process and its various naturally arising questions. Now let's get to work.

What we have here now is this: an abandoned child, male; a Golyga in the form of a seagull with a slightly irritated patch of skin under one wing; a Lillykins in the shape of—what shall we say? A mother turtle, how's that?

Lillykins has told us she will be busy for a while so Golyga can't take off again to check out the tower on planet Earth; he has to stay with the kid and look after him.

Okay, says Golyga, but we would still like to hear what you'll be so busy with.

Right, says Lillykins. I'll tell you. First of all, I have to go thither and yon, gathering information about all the creatures who have been shunned all over the world for their unusual natures.

What are unusual natures, given the sheer infinity of variations?

Depends on context, says Lillykins. So I thought, if I mix up the varieties inhabiting various contexts, people would have to concede that there are no "usual" or "unusual" natures. I say "people," but you do understand I mean all living creatures. The stone people alone think everything that flies is unusual, but thank goodness stone people are not given to making a fuss. Though if they stopped thinking like that, perhaps birds would stop shitting on them so much. Well, as I was saying: if I mix up the creatures of various contexts to such an extent that no one could claim they were more natural than anyone else, would not all the universe be better off?

If it works, yes, said Golyga. Where are you going to start this experiment?

Oh, said Lillykins. I've started already—on the planet Earth. In several places at once. In Canada, for example. A country already populated by human people from many different contexts, all mixed together.

And how is it going? asked Golyga, truly fascinated and wondering whether his tower question would get answered through Lillykins' activities on that planet.

How it's going, said Lillykins, is hard to say. At this point, I still have hope the experiment will work. I have positioned teachers here and there who are spreading the words of peaceful co-existence, respect for all, and so on, but they're having a hard time getting through the incredibly dense web of broadcasting media. For some reason, human people have chosen to occupy much of their time with the broadcasting and repeating of horror stories, bad news, and disasters from all over their planet.

And this is the planet you chose for your experiment?

It's a challenge, admitted Lillykins. But hey. It's the planet you headed for just recently, isn't it? The planet where you found this little boy here, sleeping all over my back. Take him off now and hold him for a bit while I get some things together for him before I go.

Golyga lifted the sleeping child into his wings, and Lillykins dug a warm hole in the sand on the beach.

There, she said. Lay him in there till he wakes up. And in the meantime, get to work and prepare some food, shelter, and some fun for the kid. He could use some fun, I'm sure. What's his name, by the way?

Golyga didn't know.

We'll call him Eagle Feather, said Lillykins.

Why Eagle Feather? Golyga wanted to know. What's wrong with Seagull Feather? After all, I rescued the kid as a seagull, not an eagle.

You haven't rescued him yet. So far, you've only brought him here. When he's truly rescued, he'll be ready to choose a name for himself. Meantime, why aim for seagull when you can aspire to eagle?

What kind of status-seeking is that? From the one who wants to teach that all of us are equal?

Equal, said Lillykins, but not the same. And my personal preference is eagle, soaring high above and not making an infernal racket all over every beach, fighting over bits of this and that.

Aha! You're a prejudiced, judgmental snob and you'll never be able to pull off your experiment. Golyga was righteous in his condemnation.

Yeah, right, said Lillykins. Like I can't choose my friends according to the noises they make eating, or the way they do or do not share their goodies, or the habits they have developed around the talent of flight.

Confusing, said Golyga. Have to think about it. First, have to get busy preparing stuff for the kid. Buzz off now.

So Lillykins did, and the story of her experiment will surface anon. Meantime, the child slept, Golyga chopped wood—having turned himself into a beaver for the purpose—and the island floated peacefully in the waters of the Universe.

* * *

And so we continue on our journey with Golyga, Lillykins, Hylie, and others. Such as the little boy called...?

LILLY: I can't remember his name. Did he even have one?
GOLYGA: He certainly did, and I am glad to say your inability to remember his name—or many other names—gives me the opportunity to prove to you that all this is truly coming from somewhere other than your own head.
LILLY: That doubt was laid to rest some time ago. What about that boy's name now?
GOLYGA: Hoppalong Cassidy.
LILLY: No way, I would have remembered that.
GOLYGA: All right, what can I tell you: that I can't remember his name either? That I've got it wrong?
LILLY: That you're stalling for time?
GOLYGA: Shame on you. You know quite well there is no time here. And that I could simply, should I indeed have forgotten, look over your own notes and come up with it.
LILLY: Are you playing with the computer? Capital letters and spacing and such?
GOLYGA: What do you think?
LILLY: I think it's no coincidence that when the computer suddenly goes into capital letters, as it has several times before, it seems to suggest emphasis.

GOLYGA: *Keep that in mind, my dear. And now, on with it.*
LILLY: *Do I include all the above?*
GOLYGA: *Yes. We'll check it over later, but likely yes. All right, now.*

Hylie, friend of Golyga and brother of Lillykins, was eagerly awaiting some news of a little fish he had loved for a long time. A little silvery goldfish with a talent for singing arias that Hylie particularly liked.

Hylie was awaiting this little fish on the banks of a wide river, of sluggish lazy waters, which shone in the light of the three suns in an iridescent green. On either bank of the river stood tall trees, their foliage like a pink cloud studded with blue blossoms. Whenever the blossoms fell into the river water, they turned a lovely shade of gold and rode on the surface for a long time. So there you have the visual background to our next scene—iridescent green waters, moving slowly, carrying little golden blossoms like slivers of the three suns. And Hylie, sitting on the riverbank, waiting for his friend the silver goldfish to come and sing for him.

Suddenly, a big wind blew up, whipping the river waters into a frenzy of swirling vortices that rose up into the sky and joined together to form a tornado. Astounded at the suddenness and the ferocity, Hylie worried about his little fish friend and jumped up to go and look for him. But where?

Then, from the branches of the nearest tree, Hylie heard, in the midst of a tornado-sized wind, a sweet voice singing the "Toreador Song" from *Carmen*. Hylie couldn't help it, he had to laugh, which upset his friend the silver goldfish so that he came plopping out of the tree, landing beside Hylie's feet.

What? What? Only big fat bipeds are supposed to sing that one. What?

No, no, Hylie assured his friend. Not at all. You sing it very well indeed. It's just a bit hard to imagine you fighting a bull, that's all.

Ah well, said the little fish. If that's all it is. A failure of your imagination. I can certainly live with that. Let's go.

Hylie and the silver goldfish set out, away from the river and the tornado-like funnel of wind swirling high above, and went looking for their favourite spot: a grove of trees with a wonderful patch of moss in the middle, covering some ancient rocks like a soft green blanket with little white star flowers all over it. Here, Hylie and the fish sat and talked philosophy. And soon came to the conclusion that what they really needed, just at that moment, was to have a little nap. So they curled up on the moss and slept, and each had a wonderful dream, and we'll be sure to tell you both of the dreams very soon.

Meantime, Lillykins was setting off for her latest endeavour; Golyga was chopping wood for the boy child named Rectangle...

LILLY: That was not his name, I'd have remembered that.
GOLYGA: Never mind, not now.

...and the island gently swayed in the waters of the lake.

GOLYA: That's it for today, dear Lilly. Go out into the sunshine and enjoy and don't let a failure of the imagination stop you from anything whatsoever! Okay?

* * *

And so today I must make my way through a dense emotional body to dictate my story. What the emotional storm is about is, of course, Lilly's secret, but I can tell her and you with confidence—and without betraying Lilly's confidence—that it is all a matter of self-love. Compassion and self-love are the very backbone of spiritual work, and most earthlings have a long way to go to increase their abilities in this area to their fullest potential. Where lack of self-love comes from is no secret: it's the outcome of a long process of recriminations—whether by parents, teachers, religious leaders of the stern and forbidding sort, or the general guilt-and-shame ethic that permeates the planet's human population. Well, Lilly and the rest of you, it's time to shed those fetters and set out and sail forth on a wave of pure joy. Joy untainted by "a price to pay" or the notion that it is somehow antithetical to being a good person. Do you really think the starving of the world will benefit from your lack of joy? They will benefit from your self-love and compassion and your capacity for joy in a most direct way, as well as a worldwide way. The latter because the rising vibration of joy and compassion and love benefits all humans, and the former—the more direct way—by your increasing ability to see opportunities for helping and spreading joy. A kind word to a street person, spontaneously offered, is not without weight, and a kind action anywhere spreads its wings and grows huge. Be assured that all this, Lilly dear, is part of our work and will be included in the adventure story both this way, directly, and more indirectly and entertainingly as well. Now, back to our story.

We are on the island again, floating in the lake and therefore in the universe, and we are rejoining Golyga—our hero—and the baby boy. Sleeping and dreaming of one day getting a name all his own.

LILLY: You are teasing me.
GOLYGA: Well, it did get a smile.

Now, Golyga, while chopping wood as a beaver, had a novel thought. What if he went and cut down not trees but a delightful tree-shaped cloud floating above? Would that benefit the child as much as a wood fire? Could he be wrapped and kept cozy in a tree-shaped cloud? Worth a try, Golyga said to himself, and reached up toward the cloud. Being a beaver, however, he couldn't reach far, and the cloud was rapidly changing its shape, becoming, even as he watched, more rounded, more bluish, and then it was gone. Dissolved, up in the sky.

Hm, thought Golyga. What if I could conjure tree-shaped clouds myself? Just stand here and whistle, and a cloud came floating up on the horizon in any shape I pleased? Think I'll try it.

First, though, Golyga changed himself into the shape of a large butterfly—beautifully blue and golden—then he found he couldn't whistle very well.

That does it, said Golyga to himself. Obviously, some sort of thinking ahead is necessary for this task of baby-minding, and I'd better get to it. The aim is to keep Baby warm and fed, the method is to whistle up clouds, so the best shape to be for this is…one of those long thingamajigs the humans in Australia use as a musical instrument. A something-maroon. Long long horns to blow into, and if you whistled as a horn like that, it's bound to be heard far and wide and bring clouds from all directions. Then I can shape them, and etc., etc.

25

Golyga changed himself into a long long horn and whistled. Immediately, a horde of clouds rushed in from all directions and went zipping and sliding into the horn, so that Golyga was blowing up like a balloon and in dreadful straits just from the pressure of ingested clouds.

GOLYGA: No, Lilly, it didn't feel like an attack of gas in any way, it felt like a swallowed tornado. Get used to thinking more expansively, please.
LILLY: Sorry. Personal experience has tended to be more of the gas attack than the swallowed tornado.
GOLYGA: Well, thank goodness we're not confined to your personal experiences.

Now, Golyga did not find the experience comfortable in any way and decided to expand rapidly to allow room for all the clouds inside him. But the more he expanded, the more room the clouds had to move about—and move about they did. Just as the entire tornado-like cloud formation was at its largest, there came Lillykins, swooping to the rescue. Though neither Golyga nor Lillykins would have referred to it as swooping to the rescue.

What are you up to? asked Lillykins. Where is the firewood for Baby, and the shelter and the food? Where, for that matter, *is* the baby? Here. Settle down, you clouds. Buzz off, I have to talk to Golyga.

The clouds buzzed off, Golyga resumed the shape of the long long horn but quickly added a goatlike shape underneath so he looked part antelope with one long horn, and Lillykins, fists on her hips, stood looking around for Baby. Frowning.

He was right here a few moments ago, said Golyga, pointing to the sandy hollow in the ground. Sleeping and dreaming. He can't have gone far, at his age. He must still be crawling, don't you think?

If he's a human baby, yes, said Lillykins. But we didn't stop to find out whether that's what he is, did we? He could be any kind of creature from anywhere, for all we know. And now he's gone. I can't believe you were so inattentive!

Golyga bristled, which made a strange sound up his horn, and then he defended himself: I was bringing in tree-shaped clouds for him and it got a bit out of hand, but he really cannot have gone more than a moment ago or two—or maybe an hour or two...

Golyga was never sure of the time dimension, and it often brought him trouble. For one thing, time dimensions differed depending on the context, and for another, that particular skill of reading time dimensions was taught in a course he had always managed to miss out on. Like Lilly missing the mathematics/logic course at university because it was given so early in the morning.

LILLY: No need to bring that up. Or, if you have to, include that I actually did very well in logic.

GOLYGA: So you did. And we'll be magnanimous and refrain from mentioning math at any level.

LILLY: Thank you. By the way, what shape is Lillykins in at this moment in your adventure story?

GOLYGA: Let's see. A great big spider comes to mind, but perhaps that's not so appropriate, since she already has her fists on her hips. Better make that a cute upright pig.

LILLY: Better yet, make it something else. What with Golyga being an antelope with a very long horn. Something more dignified, please.

GOLYGA: All right, a swan. No, a tall bulrush, or how about a willowy stand of Arbuckles?

LILLY: What in the world are Arbuckles?

GOLYGA: No idea. Just imagine what you will, as long as it's standing, willowy, dignified, and has its fists on its hips. Okay? Now let's get on with the last bit for today.

Golyga looked around for the baby as well, and even galloped a bit here and there on the island, but he couldn't see the baby boy anywhere either.

Perhaps, he said, we have to be looking underneath or up above or even altogether elsewhere.

We will, said Lillykins, but first we'll try calling. But…calling what? Or whom? He has no name, remember? On the other hand, there are no others on this island, so we can call out anything at all and he'll likely hear and respond. Try it, go ahead.

Calling out what? Golyga asked. For goodness' sake, I can't just make some random noise!

Really, said Lillykins. You could have fooled me. Okay, call out: Baby boy! Baby boy! Go ahead. Blow it out your horn!

Well, what choice did Golyga have?

Baby boy! he called out. Baby boy!

And within moments, the entire island was filled with baby boys. Crawling, bawling, toddling, and waddling baby boys, all coming toward Lillykins and Golyga, whose mouths were agape in astonishment.

Now you've done it, said Lillykins, when she regained the power of speech. Now you've really done it!

Golyga never did regain his own power of speech, at least not for quite a while, so we won't find out what he said until the next time we get together.

GOLYGA: Considering that you actually had a good laugh or two, Lilly, you might mention your enjoyment of today's episode.

LILLY: Oh, I'd be delighted. Thank you for the laughs and the fun. Very much.

GOYGA: You are most welcome. Now shine forth and we'll continue soonest.

✳ ✳ ✳

And so here we are, after a hiatus of several eons, back to work on our tale.

GOLYGA: Let's briefly recap so Lilly won't begin to doubt we remember what's going on. She doesn't, of course, but that's to be expected, given her occupations and preoccupations. I, on the other hand, have nothing else to do or think of, so I keep the last line in mind, unwavering in my focus, and can begin again any time.

LILLY: Sarcasm does not become a Being of Light.

GOLYGA: And why not? Sarcasm is akin to satire, is it not? Satire is an entirely respectable form of literature, which is what we are engaged in, I believe. Literature. A tale of adventure and high endeavours. So, now let's get back to it.

Hylie, to remind you, is at this time a turtle. No, wait. He's a cloud. Or was it a rabbit on snowshoes? Better leave Hylie to himself for now, until he can come up with a definite shape to suit our fancy.

Lillykins, then, and her mate and partner, Golyga. Those two are not going to be easy to pin down either, because their most engaging aspects tend to change and shift, and we certainly do not want any other of their aspects, do we? Or *do* we?

Could it be, for example, that Golyga's largely inflated sense of his abilities are going to come up now? Or that Lillykins' tiny but evolving sense of purpose in regard to her own self will be on the agenda?

You see, until recently, Lillykins' endeavours were all of the outward-bound missionary-type undertakings. Not religious conversion, mind you, but the bringing of help and sustenance to all around her. Now, suddenly, Lillykins is taking a good look at what her own solace might be, given that she wants no whooshing rescue and she has a baby boy to look after. She is finding herself in awe of all the amazing undertakings she was capable of without once looking to her own well-being. What? Dance on tightwires while in danger of her life? Certainly can't do that if you want to be alive to see another day. And with a baby on her hands... Well!

This is the thing, said Lillykins to Golyga. I have to sit down and do some thinking. Which is difficult enough without having a bawling baby around, so take him off somewhere until I'm done.

Where? Take him off where? asked Golyga. Aghast at the task but also thrilled to be actually engaged in concrete caretaking.

Let's face it, Golyga has not had much experience in baby care and he wants to add the skill to his amazing array of abilities.

Take him where?

Anywhere, said Lillykins. Anywhere safe, that is. And amusing, so he won't bawl. And while you're at it, find some food for him and make a few toys for his edification.

Golyga picked up the baby by his ear and was about to exit, when both Lillykins and Baby let out howls of outrage.

That isn't how you pick up a baby, yelled Lillykins. Put him down, put him down immediately.

Golyga dropped the baby, who luckily landed on some moss and remained unhurt in body. But his affronted dignity kept bawling. Lillykins picked up the baby and cradled him in her arms until he stopped that infernal howling, then she handed him to Golyga. Who now knew just exactly where to clasp the baby and how to hold his head and all that, being a quick study and absolutely hating the noises Baby and Lillykins had made at him.

Off went Golyga and Baby. Down sat Lillykins, to think. And here is what she thought:

I am going to have to become strong, resourceful, and terrifically organized if I want to have any life of my own, with this baby to take care of. So the first thing I need to do is train Golyga to undertake at least part of the work, and the second is to train the baby to become self-sufficient as fast as possible. How do you do that? Drop him into the lake to teach him to swim? Swim in the lake, carrying Baby on my back? What?

And then there are such skills as walking, talking, and arithmetic. And learning the language of the heart. And bringing joy to all around you. Oh my goodness, how does one do all that with one little baby bundle?

Lillykins' head, by now, was beginning to ache, unaccustomed as she was to practical considerations in her own life. She decided to go for a quick swim to clear her head and dove into the waters, turning into a swan as she hit the surface. And now, regally sailing on the lake, she was able to see clearly for the first time that, in fact, taking care of Baby was not going to be as difficult as she thought. After all, he could simply tag along on whatever mission she was currently engaging herself in and learn as they went. It was merely a matter of devising a carrying sack of some sort, and away they would go.

Now, where did the desire for her own developing self-living go?

LILLY: That's a terrible sentence.
GOLYGA: Yes, and it's your fault. You lost focus. Here we go again.

What happened to Lillykins' undertaking to make her own life central to her thoughts for a change?

LILLY: Don't you think this smacks of women's magazines?
GOLYGA: It could do, except there's a twist.

You see, Lillykins discovers that, in fact, her endeavours on behalf of others are the central purpose of her life. Not to the deterioration of her own life, of course, but to the joy and delight of giving and loving. So what do we have here now? Something feminists will lament? What if Lillykins' not inconsiderable energy and intelligence were engaged in causes of a feminist nature? Would that make it okay? Could it be that males and females in all times and fields do enjoy giving of themselves in love and helpful undertakings?

LILLY: Okay. Point taken. So now Lillykins continues in her ways, Baby on her back—or front—and...?

GOLYGA: And we pause for today because it's time to visit the travel agent and get yourself that ticket so you, Lilly dear, can set forth on your mission of mercy, visiting your mama in Europe.

LILLY: Before I go: I've just looked at the end of our previous session and there we left Golyga and Lillykins, mouths agape, as babies crawled toward them from everywhere on the island.

GOLYGA: Yes? That sounds interesting.

LILLY: But today's beginning doesn't connect up. Baby boy wasn't sleeping, he'd gone missing.

GOLYGA: And so now we have a terrible situation on our hands: logic has fled and we're condemned to gibberish. So declares Lilly, in her role as editor in chief.

LILLY: Don't you think the reader will want to be able to count on continuity in the tale? To know that he or she will find out what happened and what happens next?

GOLYGA: Yes, I think you're right. So let's quickly insert the following:

Golyga let out a mighty roar that scared all the babies into crawling backwards back into the bushes. Only the baby boy kept coming and, all exhausted, immediately fell into a deep sleep.

GOLYGA: How is that?

LILLY: Well, it connects up but it doesn't feel satisfactory somehow. Where did the babies come from and where did they go?

GOLYGA: That you'll find out another time, I assure you.

31

The mystery of the babies is far from over. You see, when all the babies crawled away, Golyga promised himself that he would, one day, find out where they came from and what was going on, anyway. So far, he hasn't had the time to pursue that particular curiosity, but there is still a long life ahead for him and for all of us who are reading this. Whether the babies will still be babies then, who knows…

* * *

GOLYGA: Yes, we are finally back at work. Have you noticed how the widening gaps in our sessions have come about by way of your earthly concerns, Lilly?
LILLY: Yes, I have.
GOLYGA: Then you also know those are inevitable, given that you are in body and on Earth. So please do not admonish yourself for these pauses. They are necessary and do not in any way alter the work or diminish its quality.
LILLY: Thank you for this reassurance.
GOLYGA: You are welcome. Now, on to the tale we're telling, all right?

Lillykins, as you will recall, is trying to think. She has decided that her life can actually go on pretty well as before, simply adding the baby on her back as would a loon on the lake. But she has yet to encounter actual life experiences under those conditions. Which we'll be bringing her way very shortly.

Golyga, meantime, is wandering about on the island, the baby slung over his shoulder in more or less acceptable fashion, as he looks for several things all at once: the babies he'd seen earlier, crawling and waddling around on the island, some food, shelter and toys for the baby boy's edification, and Hylie, who seemed to have vanished and who, Golyga was sure, was hanging about somewhere nearby, watching and tittering into his fist.

Well, Golyga was right, as he so often is, and Hylie was indeed watching and tittering. And also wondering how on earth Golyga was going to put up with the infant and his needs once said infant was awake and demanding. Hylie would never be willing to burden himself with such responsibilities, he was sure.

Suddenly, watching and tittering, Hylie saw an enormous boulder tumbling down the mountainside directly toward Golyga and Baby.

Hylie jumped out from his hiding place, ran as fast as he could, tackled Golyga and Baby, and pushed them out of the way.

Hey! yelled Golyga. What the—

And then Golyga saw and heard the boulder all at once, and realized his best friend had saved his life. The baby, awakened by the sudden push and jump, let out one big howl, then opened his eyes and looked around.

Hey, said Baby. Where are we? And when do I get some food? And why are we all three males and no female in sight? I've always found females more sympathetic to my needs and more helpful in general, so could we have some females around here, please? And anyway, where exactly are we?

Golyga and Hylie listened to Baby, hardly able to believe what was coming out of this tiny mouth: a big booming voice with a decidedly demanding tone.

Who are you? asked Golyga. And why are you in the body of a baby? And where in the world are you from?

Baby, still on Golyga's shoulder, bent forward to look into Golyga's face—upside down, mind you—and said: Wouldn't you like to know! And then he hopped off Golyga's shoulder and onto the ground.

Well, he continued. No reason to stick around here that I can see. Better get myself some company I can relate to as equals. Cheerio and toodeloo and don't tie yourselves into knots looking for me, I'll find you when I need you.

And off Baby went, marching like a miniature trooper on little bandy legs, around the boulder lying in his path and right out of sight.

Well, I never, said Hylie in his intellectual way. Well, I really never—

Hey! said Golyga. How am I going to explain this to Lillykins? She thinks I'm looking after this baby, feeding it and such. She'll think it's my fault he's gone missing again.

Why worry? said Hylie. Let's be off to do some adventuring, and by the time we get back, Lillykins will be busy with one of her missions and will have forgotten all about this baby.

You don't know Lillykins, said Golyga. Not that I claim any great knowledge myself, but I sure do know she won't be forgetting about any baby. Not Lillykins.

Well then, said Hylie. We'll have to stay away longer, that's all. Come on.

Oh, don't be such a typical male, said Golyga. Taking off at the sign of problems as if they'll solve themselves while you're gone. Try to put yourself into Lillykins' moccasins for a mile, will you? She is under the impression babies can't survive without the loving care of adults. Well, of older beings, anyway.

This baby sounded like it could take care of itself and a few others along with it, said Hylie.

Yes, but how to convince Lillykins of that? Listen, Hylie: you go ahead adventuring. I have to sit and think awhile, okay?

So Hylie took off, soaring through the sky like a well-shaved arrow, and was gone in a flash. Golyga, sitting down on the boulder, began to think.

We are going to leave Golyga there for a while because we have to check and see what Lillykins is up to, just climbing out of the lake onto land and now looking around for Golyga and Baby, to tell them her decision about her life with Baby.

Lillykins looked and looked but saw neither of them. What she did see was an enormous rat, staring at her from a hollow in the bottom of a tree.

Who are you staring at? said Lillykins. Don't you have anything better to do?

The rat blinked once, blinked again, and then said in a clear light voice that rang out like a bell: Yes, I have something better to do but you have to come and help me with it. I have to go rescue an entire population from the bubonic plague, but whenever I get near anyone, people scream and try to kill me.

They think you cause bubonic plague, said Lillykins. That's why.

What nonsense, said the rat. Typical, though. They always get things backwards, don't they? The rat shook its head and sighed. So, anyway, are you going to help me or what?

Depends what you have in mind, said Lillykins. Depends how long it would take. You see, I'm waiting for Golyga and Baby to show... I have no idea where they are or what they're up to.

The rat shook its head and sighed again. Always personal concerns first. Isn't that the way of you earthlings. Always personal concerns first, and the good of the community, let alone of the entire universe, trailing behind. No wonder everything's a mess.

Please, said Lillykins. No lectures from a rat, okay? Just tell me what needs to be done.

Water, said the rat. We need to clean the water. It's been getting polluted for years and years now, and suddenly, when the plague broke out, people started yelling and blaming all kinds of innocent beings instead of blaming themselves for polluting the planet's waters at such a criminal rate.

Okay, said Lillykins. We'll do it. We'll clean up the water. Where do we start?

Where does one always start if one wants results? In one's own backyard. Or water system, in this case. Unfortunately, there are just the two of us right now, so we have to use the methods of sabotage for some drastic education. Let's go.

Off they went, Lillykins and the rat, and soon we'll find out what sabotage they undertake.

Meantime, Golyga, tired of thinking, got up and started pounding the boulder with his feet, dancing and stomping and chanting in all directions. This is something Golyga was wont to do once in a while, and it always led to interesting results.

* * *

GOLYGA: *This segment is going to be not only short but specifically placed to fill some holes in the adventure series about Golyga, Lillykins, Baby boy, and Hylie. To wit: remember Lillykins standing in front of a great big buffalo?*
LILLY: *No.*
GOLYGA: *So which monstrous apparition was Lillykins standing in front of?*
LILLY: *Don't ask me to remember, please. You know my memory is notoriously bad.*
GOLYGA: *Well, let's nudge it, shall we?*
LILLY: *Oh, I remember one. There was the rat. But Lillykins went off with it to do sabotage and we never heard about it again.*
GOLYGA: *Then we had better remedy that immediately. Here we go:*

Lillykins and the rat went off together. The rat had sabotage in mind, in aid of preventing water pollution from decimating the local population, which would result in rats being blamed—as usual, Rat would say—for whatever plague had arrived.

As they went, Lillykins asked questions:

What exactly are you planning, for this sabotage of yours? I mean, I'm certainly not getting involved in anything that would hurt people.

How noble of you, replied the rat. How about other creatures on Earth? How about trees? Caterpillars? Rats?

Well, yes, of course, said Lillykins, ashamed she'd been so race-conscious. The human race being what it is, that's hardly surprising, but Lillykins would have expected a more all-encompassing view from herself. Goodness, she thought. Could it be that with taking on a human body I also take on certain characteristics of the human race? If so, I had better monitor myself carefully because I certainly don't want to be part of any chauvinism toward other living forms.

All right, said Lillykins out loud. I apologize for the formulation of my comment. I would not want to be involved in anything hurting any living creature or being whatever.

That's better, said the rat. Now, what we are about to do is going to hit at a human characteristic that, I am sure you will agree, is the cause of much disarray of the natural pro-life forces that abound. Greed. That's what I'm talking about. Which goes along with a total lack of respect. Using everything and everybody as a means to an end. That sort of thing. I know you are familiar with greed, have seen it many times, and can recognize its fallout everywhere. But how to scotch it is the question here. Not easy, because the material rewards of greed tend to blind its practitioners to its hazards—not only on the larger scale but also on the personal one. So, to bring home a full recognition of both, this is the sabotage I have planned—together with my brethren rats— and you will help us implement the plan. Okay?

Let's hear it, said Lillykins. I never buy a cat in a bag.

Oh, for heaven's sake, watch your analogies, would you? said the rat with an irritated shudder that ended in its pointed tail. Now listen: We will, you and I, make our way to the White House.

Which white house?

The one in the United States where the big honcho hangs out. With your talents for shape-shifting and what with me being a rat, we won't have any problems getting in there. Once inside, you pick me up and place me conspicuously in the most important room of that house—the president's bedroom.

Are you serious? That's the most important room in the White House?

Trust me, said the rat. We rats have sources of information nobody has ever dreamt of. So here I am, in the bedroom. The presidential pair come in, getting ready for bed. The president is barefoot. And that's when I run across the floor toward his naked feet. Screams, jumping, the First Lady comes running to catch the president, security hears the screams and comes pounding on the door. Shhh, says the president to his wife. We can't tell them what we saw here. Let's just say it was all a mistake.

So they do that. Then they sit down and discuss the rat. Me, meantime, I'm hiding somewhere, ready to come running out again if they don't reach the right conclusion. Which is, of course, about damage control. They can't actually admit to a rat in the White House, can they? I mean, if there's a rat in the White House, what place is safe from rats? And if they're everywhere, what shape is the country in? And if the US is rat-infested, what shape is the rest of the world in?

The First Lady, being both practical and civic-minded, comes up with a plan that takes care of water pollution in the US and, pretty soon, worldwide, and we all live happily ever after. And me, I get to be famous as the rat that saved the world. How's that, my dear?

Lillykins had to admit the plan was well thought out and would probably work. All right, she said. We have to make it snappy because I have to get back soon, to do more thinking about Baby or something. So, let's go.

And they did, and they did it, and it all worked out perfectly, except, of course, this is a tale of adventure about creatures who may or may not exist, so you, the reader, will have to be the judge of whether it all really took place—and the results are in evidence around you—or whether it was, perhaps, told just for fun and games.

LILLY: Thank you for this. It was fun, as always.
GOLYGA: You are welcome, my dear. And do place this segment right after the rat/ sabotage loose end in the manuscript.

Golyga as told to Lilly Barnes

LILLY: *Will do. So long, Beeswax and all.*

* * *

GOLYGA: *So, computer not working yet. We suggest that a session is nevertheless possible as long as we make it relatively short and you take little breaks during it. What say?*
LILLY: *I'm ready and eager.*
GOLYGA: *So we see. All right then, put on the heater, pee, and off we go.*

A number of issues plague humans to no avail, and nothing useful will come of being in constant turmoil with these issues. One of them is the insistent indication by many learned earthlings that we—you as well as ourselves—are all doomed because evil is in the ascendancy and will soon cause the demise of "civilized" life as we know it. Without going into any definitions of "civilized" at this moment, we suggest that a more useful scenario runs as follows: perceptions and perspectives are always changing. And the present changes, far from leading to destruction, are great cause for optimism. At this time, there is more, not less, awareness of all the negatives, and more, not less, activity on behalf of positive energy. True, multinational corporations are reaping huge profits while unemployment rises and starvation is a scourge on the face of the planet, but those facts have been with us since time immemorial. 'Twas always thus. What has changed, and for the better, is a general awareness, even by money grubbers, that it's a bad state of affairs and must be corrected.

We can feel Lilly dear balk at the "money grubbers" who have an awareness of being wrong and also at the "must be corrected." The fact that your own perception does not yet include solutions, and because your experience with money grubbers has been minimal, will not dissuade us from our statements.

More and more corporations are forced to consult even their own shareholders about acceptable practices, and this will continue until there is a shift even you will recognize. And solutions are indeed possible, and their nature will become evident.

So we say to you: concern yourselves not with lamenting or despair, with complaints large and small about the direction humanity is taking, but instead become aware and recite all the big and little changes that show movement toward positive energy. It will not only improve your own life and energy, it will also contribute to the flow of energy in positive directions.

This is not, Lilly dear, a way of playing head-in-the-sand ostrich, but of countering the enormous tendency for doom and gloom already firmly entrenched in the thinking, the media, the general perception and perspectives of present society. In fact, even those who are being discovered to have lived in the lap of Mother Earth and Nature immediately become the victims of concern: "They'll be ruined" (by contact with others) and thereby infected with the notion that things are bound to get worse for them.

And don't they? asks Lilly dear. Well, if you're going to tell people over and over they're about to be run over by a truck, do you suppose those people, trucks or not, will enjoy life much?

Lilly dear is smiling. Take a moment's break for your hand and we'll continue.

Now: Another bugaboo of humanity is the tendency to be blithely confident that humans are the crown of creation and have no superior. That all other creatures, all other things, everything created before or after them, is subservient, lowly, intended for use by humans. This attitude, which many have overcome but still is prevalent in relating to anything non-human, must change. Not only change in perception but in action as well. Once humans have recognized that all these non-human things are living Beings they will curtail their senseless destruction of nature, but it takes respect to be in a truly positive relationship to the rest of the world. Not only is a tree to be respected, but human-created artifacts as well. If respect is extended to the achievement of the littlest hairpin and the most dangerous bomb, you will have no careless use of either, nor a blind dismissal of them. So the gradual increase of respect, ever-widening in inclusivity, will inevitably become so saturated that, as a simple extension of the general attitude, no human will disrespect another.

Respect is at the base of many great achievements even now, but once it has taken hold and begun to sprout, the advances in all fields of endeavour will be astonishing, war will become unthinkable, and life will be a dwelling in joy and harmony.

Yes, an impossible dream at this time, Lilly dear, but nevertheless the direction to aim for. You will see, in your own daily life, the changes brought about by increased respect. For your own body, just as one example. For the food you eat, the sounds you hear, and the delightful invention of the VCR to entertain you of an evening alone. Respect even your entertainment, Lilly dear, instead of deriding yourself for not being "more productive" at the end of the day, because fallow fields recuperate faster than ever-producing ones.

To be brief about our two-pronged recommendations of the day: Shape-shift doom-and-gloom energy by noting all evidence of positive energy manifestations, and respect everything in your path, your thoughts, your body, your life, and all that you encounter.

* * *

GOLYGA: Well then, we are ready and excited to be back at work on our tale of adventure. And here it is, as told to the delightful Lilly, whose own life is—while not always a valley of joy—certainly an adventure worthy of the telling. However, we'll leave that to her own efforts, if she so chooses. We are concerned here with Golyga, our hero; Lillykins, his sometimes reluctant heroine; and Hylie. And then there's that baby, of course. Who may or may not be a human baby, but then, did we ever establish just what kind of beings we have in Golyga or Lillykins? We didn't, so I don't see why we ought to be suddenly concerned about the exact nature of the baby. Especially since he isn't even around just now—or is he?

Could it be, for just one example, that the blossom-covered bush slowly revolving around and around is really that baby boy of whom we spoke? Or even that the rolling pebble heading down a gentle slope for the waters of the lake is really that baby? Never mind. We're off to check in with another of our creatures altogether. We're about to visit Hylie.

Hylie, you will recall, is the brother of Lillykins, though they rarely spend time together. The reason for this is simple, though not obvious. Lillykins and Hylie are so similar in nature, so alike in thought and deed, that if they were to "hang out," they would soon bore each other to distraction. So:

Hylie was off somewhere on his own, as he often was when not with Golyga, and enjoying himself. He was gliding in tandem with a beaver through the waters of the lake and, as soon as the beaver came to his home, grandly dubbed his beaver lodge, Hylie stationed himself just outside and stood guard while the beaver tried to persuade his beaver daughter to come out and play with Hylie.

Come on, said the beaver. If you don't come out and play with him, I'll be saddled with this creature for goodness knows how long. Maybe he thinks he's a beaver? He does everything I do, right beside me, and he irritates the hell out of me. Come out and distract him, will you?

The beaver's daughter, however, had already met Hylie once or twice and had no intention of playing with him again. She would rather sit and gnaw on bark than play with Hylie, because Hylie had a disconcerting habit of imitating. Beaver, beaver's daughter, seagull, frog, kite or postman or small wooden log—Hylie would no sooner see something than imitate it, and while many creatures, such as logs for instance, had no objections, and while some creatures, such as frogs for instance, even thought imitation a form of flattery, beaver's daughter would have none of it. The chomping drove her nuts.

Meantime, Hylie was standing guard—or rather, standing there like the unfelled birch just beside him, looking up into its branches, and he was just beginning to arrange his limbs in a branchlike fashion and send forth hair like a crown of leaves, when lo! Golyga plopped out of the sky and landed right beside his feet.

Come with me, said Golyga. There's something I want you to do for me. Quick, quick, follow me.

Off flew Golyga, like an arrow, and off flew Hylie, like a second arrow, and both landed at almost the same moment on the shore of the lake where Lillykins sat thinking and the baby was nowhere to be seen.

He's gone again, said Golyga. I don't know how I'll tell Lillykins this and I want you here beside me when I do. Any suggestions?

Hylie didn't even have to think about it. Just tell her the baby is getting an education, he said. Lillykins is big on education. Though not necessarily academic education, you understand. But for a baby, she'd definitely recommend the learning of walking, talking, swimming, foraging, and digging.

Digging?

Well, for water, say. Or for clams. You know.

But where is this baby supposed to get such an education if not with us? She'll ask me where he is, you know.

Tell her he is with his people.

Oh, Hylie, said Golyga, getting short-tempered already. She knows I don't know who that baby's people are any more than she does. Or than you do, for that matter.

Not so fast, said Hylie. I happen to know exactly who his people are and I can take you to them, if you like.

Well, of course, said Golyga. Let's go. Quick, before Lillykins starts asking questions.

So, off the two of them flew again, like arrows, with Hylie in the lead this time, and soon they landed in a great gorse bush. A gorse bush, for those who don't know—is a rough-skinned, many-branched bush with prickles and thorns and not much to recommend it except size. This particular gorse bush was huge—the size of two or three houses— and by the time Golyga and Hylie extricated themselves from the thorns and branches, they were more than a little disgruntled.

Hylie looked around for the baby's people, saw them, and pointed. There, he said. There they are and the baby is with them, just like I said.

Sure enough, the baby boy was there, swinging from the branch of a tree, looking at them as if to say: What do you two want here, anyway? I thought I'd gotten away from you. And don't for a minute think I'm leaving here again until I'm good and ready!

And who could blame him? His people, who were gathered around him and obviously glad to see him again, were loons. Beautiful, regal, utterly calm and dignified, and looking not one bit like the baby boy, swinging from a branch. So how do we even know that these were his people? you might ask. How do we even know that?

Because the baby, even as they watched, dropped from the branch of the tree down to the ground, rolled down the gentle incline of the land right into the water, and turned into a loon.

Well now, said Golyga. I am so glad to have seen this, and thank you for bringing me here, Hylie. Now I can tell Lillykins what I saw and she won't berate me for negligence or laziness or ignorance… Hylie?

Hylie was gone. Into the water, into feathers and wings and beak and the pearls all over his back—a loon among loons and doing like loons do. Hylie was gliding on the water right beside the baby boy loon and having such a good time that Golyga simply waved goodbye and took off by himself. To the island, to tell Lillykins what he had just seen.

Unfortunately, when he returned to the spot where he had last seen Lillykins sitting and thinking, she was gone.

Golyga: And, as you might have anticipated by now, that's the end of the episode for today. More anon.

* * *

GOLYGA: Here is another loose-end tie-up. Or perhaps it's more an explanation of how things work where Golyga and Lillykins, Baby and Hylie hang out.

When Hylie brought Golyga to where Baby was cavorting "with his people the loons," Golyga asked no questions such as: But wait a minute—his mother was an Earth person and she committed suicide, so how can these loons be Baby's people?

No, Golyga wouldn't dream of asking such a question because he knew that everyone has more than one family. There is the birth family, of course, and everyone has one of those, though many people don't grow up with their birth families. So there is the family or faux family that is your growing-up family. Then the family of friends you choose and, if you're lucky, keep for a long time. And then the family of souls, among which you also have a place.

A family of souls consists of souls who reincarnate in various relationships over a number of lifetimes and, in each of them, work in relation to every other family member—not only on matters of relationship but also other aspects of learning they undertook to complete, or at least to work away at, in a given lifetime. It's much more difficult to recognize these family members than any others because it's altogether a matter of feel, and the feel can be uncomfortable as easily as it can be comforting, and it can be disorienting or frightening—all depending on what the relationship is meant to be a school for.

In the case of Baby, the loons brought him solace and comfort and complete and total acceptance of himself just as he was, so Baby quite often disappeared from all other locations and joined the gathering of his loon family. However, he also always returned to Golyga and Lillykins because much of his education was taking place through their participation, and Hylie, too, was an important member of his growing-up family.

GOLYGA: Now, have we tied up that loose end to your satisfaction, Lilly dear?
LILLY: Yes, you have. Thank you.

* * *

Yes, Lillykins had disappeared and Golyga had no idea where to begin to look for her. Not that he was in a great hurry. She is not a baby, after all, Golyga said to himself. She does know how to look after herself most of the time, and there's no need to rush about trying to find her right this minute.

So Golyga gave himself some time off to do whatever he felt like doing, and what he felt like doing was nothing. Walk on the shore of the lake, watch the clouds cross the sky, think of nothing, enjoy every breeze.

I should do this more often, Golyga thought. I really don't know why I don't. It isn't as though anything else is more important, except now and then when survival becomes a matter of urgency. The rest of the time I'd be perfectly content to continue being a lakeshore walker and cloud watcher, and don't anybody tell me that's a bad life. Or that there's anything wrong with that.

At about this time, Golyga noticed a sound he'd been hearing for a while. It was getting louder, more insistent, and soon it filled his entire attention with its low-rumbling grumbling monotone. Whatever can be making that sound? Golyga kept asking himself. It sounds familiar, but I can't for the life of me figure out just what it is and who is making it. Again, Golyga listened closely, and now he finally recognized it: it was the sound of his stomach, grumbling. It was hunger, low-rumbling its complaint. Golyga's stomach wanted food!

Well, for goodness' sake, said Golyga to his stomach. Stop your grumbling and complaining. I'll get you some food right away, okay, so just you quiet down now.

Golyga looked around for something he could eat. Nothing on the shore, nothing he could easily get out of the lake. He moved farther away from the water, into the bushes and trees, looking for something to eat, and pretty soon he saw some berries on a bush.

Here we go, said Golyga to his stomach. Berries. Healthy and delicious. I'll pick and eat, pick and eat until you're satisfied.

Which is exactly what Golyga did: pick and eat, pick and eat, but his stomach refused to be satisfied.

What is this? said his stomach. Nothing but berries? Am I supposed to be happy and healthy on nothing but berries?

Well, what else do you want? asked Golyga. I can try to get you something else, if you'll let me in on your predilections.

"Predilections," scoffed his stomach. Berries and predilections. How about a steak? A chop? A side of roast beef?

Golyga was amazed. His stomach had never before asked for anything of that sort—in fact, he couldn't remember ever touching the flesh of an animal with his tongue or teeth.

What's the matter with you? Golyga asked his stomach. What's this sudden carnivorous turn?

Why not? said the stomach. You gave me nothing at all for so long, I started thinking about all the various possibilities, and those are the ones that came up hard and strong. Meat. I want meat and I want plenty of it.

Golyga sighed, but he promised his stomach he would provide meat, and set off, trying to find some. Since there was nothing on the island that would supply steak or chop, Golyga hied himself over to the mainland and the nearest farm. A dairy farm, as it turned out, with dairy cows all over the place, and nobody minding them, so he could really just have slaughtered himself the meatiest-looking cow of them all and dragged it off somewhere. But that was hardly the thing to do when you have no idea about how to slaughter a cow and, anyway, there's all that skin and probably blood and such. No, Golyga decided he had better check on other possibilities. Perhaps the farmyard would be a helpful place for his undertaking.

Golyga arrived at the farmyard just as the farmer's wife was throwing stuff about for the chickens, and they were so noisy and smelly and hysterical, too, as soon as they sensed Golyga's approach that Golyga decided to keep going. And immediately saw what he could do to solve his problem: there, hanging in the doorway of the barn, was a freshly slaughtered calf. Dead, anyway. And already skinned. He would only have to cut a slice out of it and he'd have a steak or chop to satisfy his stomach.

Golyga looked around for a knife. There was none. So he changed himself into a fox, jumped at the calf, took hold of some flesh with his teeth, and started tearing off a nice long strip. Thinking: Excellent. This is working very well indeed. And then: screeching and hollering and a great deal of flurry and rushing about, and the next thing Golyga knew he'd better change ever so fast out of being a fox. Because the farmer and his wife were all over the place, with pitchfork and shotgun and voices and flailing about. So Golyga became the tiniest of ants, fell off onto the ground and scooted away. The only things the farmer and his wife were left with were two open mouths and a loud and lingering sound of grumbling.

I'm trying my best, Golyga said to his stomach. I really am. But it's not as easy as you think. I mean, I'm not used to being a carnivore and don't know their ways. Look, now that I'm an ant, wouldn't you be satisfied with something else?

Not for a minute, said his stomach. You happen to have become a meat-eating ant, the kind you find all over roadkill and such, so just you hurry up and get some meat somewhere, before I eat you from the inside out.

Golyga was antsing down a country road by this time, sniffing around and hoping for some roadkill, though when he stopped to think of it, that wasn't really what would make him happy to be eating again.

All right then, he said to his stomach, I promise to give you the very first thing to come along—on its own legs—that is meat. Whatever the source, you shall have it, and then you had better leave me alone for a while.

It's a deal, said his stomach, jumping and belching with every step. But no chickening out of it!

And right then Golyga saw an awesome sight coming down the country road and, let me tell you, even his stomach quailed at the vision. It was a great big buffalo, with great big horns, and it had no intention at all to become—or even to give over any part of itself to become—steak, chop, or hunk of roast.

GOLYGA: Shall we leave it here for today?
LILLY: I guess so, though I must say, it's always hard to leave it hanging from a cliff like this.
GOLYGA: Never mind. We can continue soon, now that your energy has returned to a better level. We certainly want to have several more sessions before your trip to Europe, do we not?
LILLY: We certainly do. Thank you for today, I enjoyed the tale.

* * *

GOLYGA: And so we resume our tale as Golyga sets out to seek his mate Lillykins, and we don't even wait to check whether it hooks up to the last segment.
LILLY: We don't? Why not? Is this a test of faith?
GOLYGA: Yes. Because if it were a test of memory, you'd have already failed it.
LILLY: My memory is good enough to niggle at me with doubts—wasn't Golyga in the midst of something else when we left him?
GOLYGA: Yes, he was. He was in the middle of thinking about flesh-eating and such concerns of the stomach as hunger brings about. He was not, however, in any way incapable of wondering what in the world happened to Lillykins, and even hunger would not erase his deep love and concern for that creature of many talents. So he is setting off to find her—okay with you?
LILLY: Oh, certainly.

Golyga set out, stomach grumbling, his eyes on the frightening sight before him. He circled around the danger in his path because he was in no mood or shape to engage it in combat or even to endeavour to flee the enormous, big-eared—wait for it, yes, this is a test of focus and of trust—the enormous, as I said, and big-eared, otherworldly, perplexed-looking, ambulatory but nearly stock still at this time, quietly breathing and eye-riveting and out-of-court-settling, astonishingly diverse and interestingly comatose assortment of flesh, bones, brain cells, rumbling sounds and high-piping ones, all emerging from the one body in front of Golyga that was in the shape of a kangaroo.

LILLY: A kangaroo? Really?

GOLYGA: Want to check it?

LILLY: If I do and find it's not a kangaroo at all, you'll only claim you intended to tweak my mistrust. So I won't check it.

GOLYGA: In that case, let me tell you: it wasn't a kangaroo. It was an aardvark.

LILLY: Now, I know it wasn't an aardvark, I'd have remembered that. In fact, I find it definitely odd that I haven't remembered what creature was standing in Golyga's path. Are you throwing up smokescreens inside my memory?

GOLYGA: Concentrate, dear Lilly. Just concentrate on listening. Let those who have a decent memory exercise it at this moment. If you want to exercise yours in order to improve it, that's another matter and to be dealt with at another time. Okay?

LILLY: Okay. Do let's get on with it.

GOLYGA: All right now All right now. Golyga went around the best-known-as-kingfisher in his path and immediately encountered Lilly's memory. Saying, No, no, no. That wasn't it either.

LILLY: Sorry. I'll shut up now, I really will.

All right then. Golyga circled around the X on the path and basically snuck off into the bush, heading out to find Lillykins. His stomach was loud enough to be heard for miles, so he had high hopes that Lillykins would hear him and find *him*, but just in case that didn't happen, Golyga now started calling and yodelling and even yelling as loud as he could. Surely somebody—if not Lillykins herself—would hear him and have news of his vanished mate.

The one who heard him turned out to be Hylie, and he came flying, loonlike, with strong wings and a lilting song, and landed beside Golyga's feet. Carrying a fish in his beak.

For you, said Hylie the loon. So your stomach can stop its growling. Not even the baby loons can sleep, with that enormous noise flying around. Eat the fish.

Oh no, said Golyga, mostly to himself. Flesh again. What do I do? The fish is dead, mind you, and I wasn't even the one who killed it, but nevertheless...

Golyga sighed, and Hylie watched him, confused.

What is your problem? said Hylie. You're hungry. There is food. Eat it.

Golyga picked up the fish. It seemed to him the fish was looking at him and was about to speak. Golyga waited. And sure enough, that dead fish opened its mouth, just a tiny bit, mind you, but opened it and spoke.

Go ahead, said the fish. Eat me. I'm dead already, anyway, so what the hell.

So Golyga ate the fish and, immediately, just as soon as he'd swallowed the last bit of tail, became violently ill. Upchucking every bit of fish he'd eaten.

Hey! said Golyga, as soon as it was possible to speak and long before it was pleasant to see him do so: you encouraged me to eat you and now look! You've made me sick!

Well, for heaven's sake, said the fish bits. Who ever heard of eating tail, bones, fins, and every bit in between! Use your noggin', as they say. Eat the edible parts. Although it seems I had better hasten to add: there aren't any of those left now. So go fish or something.

Golyga sighed. Hylie, who had turned away at the sight of Golyga bringing up fish bits all over the place, suggested he had better lie down somewhere and rest. Or at least brush his teeth. Which seemed like a good idea to Golyga's mouth, and so off the two of them went, to the lakeshore. And there, sitting on a rock, rocking the baby boy, sat Lillykins, singing a quaint little ditty and paying no attention at all to Golyga's presence, rumbling stomach, and dire-smelling breath.

Here, Hylie, said Lillykins. Take the baby for a bit. But do not put him down lest he disappear again, and do not give him to Golyga, who needs some babying himself obviously and had better stop gawking at me as though he hasn't seen me before.

Golyga was, in fact, gawking, because while he knew this was Lillykins, speaking to him, he certainly had never before seen her look quite like this. Lillykins was covered in fur, wearing a headdress made of feathers, and had long dangling earrings made of fish eyes suspended from her earlobes. And then, before Golyga had a chance to comment on her interesting getup, Lillykins opened the fur covering her body and pulled out a whole series of little dancing ingots.

Now Golyga really couldn't keep himself from asking: What in the world are little dancing ingots? Obviously something entirely different than statues or icons or any other such static and sometimes massive…

49

GOLYGA: Good for you, Lilly my dear. The longest pause you have as yet been able to maintain without filling it. Held receptive and still and waiting for the next word, which never came. Good for you, I say. And enough for today, too, because you do have a headache and we do not want to tax your energy to your detriment in any way. Thank you for this display of trust and also for your channelling ability, my dear. Looking forward to our next session, yours as ever, Golyga.
LILLY: Thank you, Golyga.

* * *

GOLYGA: Yes, we are ready to work and want to add a section to your already organized material—i.e., some loose-end tie-ups. First, there was the matter of dancing ingots.

Lillykins sat, befurred and befeathered, pulling dancing ingots out all in a row, and as Golyga watched with amazement, she cried out over and over again: See them dance, see them gyrate and pippilate and bow and scrape and call one another by the most ridiculous names!

Golyga watched and saw that everything Lillykins described was true. Still, it was no help at all in understanding the nature or category of creature they were watching here.

Who or what are these dancing ingots? asked Golyga. Surely they must have a name, a function, at least a mission in life?

Oh, but they do, they do, said Lillykins. They, much like ourselves, delight in every breath they take—see how they breathe? see how they delight?—and they, much like ourselves, are at times forgetting altogether to delight in breath and life and go about sour of mien and utterly devoid of dancing.

So if you want to occupy yourself, Golyga, with trying to figure out what or who they are rather than watching them delight in dancing, then you go right ahead. As for me, I am going to watch them until they disappear, as they surely will, never to be seen again, and I'll enjoy every second they're here to the best of my ability. Got it?

Golyga sighed. Yes, he got it. And Lillykins was not only hoisting him with his own petard, whatever that meant, but she was actually hovering just above ground, so delighted was she, and here he was sitting heavy as a lump, thinking.

Begone, categorization and divisive musings of any kind, he said to his mind. Begone until further notice. I mean to enjoy watching these dancing ingots as Lillykins is doing and don't want interference from you in any way.

And so both of them, Lillykins and Golyga, watched with ever-growing delight as the ingots danced and gambolled and caterwauled and seemed altogether to be without a worry in the universe.

Lucky little ingots, eh, what?

And Golyga and Lillykins were so utterly charmed and filled with appreciation for their lively delightful presence that they sat back and sighed, thanking their lucky stars they hadn't been too busy turning up their noses at strange little dancing ingots to enjoy every moment of their sojourn with them.

* * *

GOLYGA: A short segment today, just to keep our hand in, so to speak. It's going to be all about the baby.

All right then. The baby boy, who we have met time and time again, is awake and wondering why nobody has yet bothered to talk to him directly. Why all the talk about his food, his name, his shelter, his whereabouts, etc., but not a word addressed to him?

Is this the way people deal with babies? he asked himself. Thinking babies can comprehend nothing, communicate nothing but basic physical needs? What is it with these people. Don't they know babies are born with immense knowledge that, as they grow up and get educated in the ways of humans, gets overlaid by layer after layer of misinformation, not to speak of the disinformation by way of mass media and the intellectual bunch? Ah, how sad that all the knowledge built right in us gets wasted and ignored and lost, so that only after a lifetime of evolving do some few humans achieve what babies already know at birth. That we are divine, all of us humans—and yes, the baby boy is indeed human—and that we are but a moment's awakening away from full awareness of this fact. How sad, also, that those humans who have an inkling and have had experiences to bring them close to the knowledge of the divine tend to wrap it up, embellish it, and treat it like a fragile vessel that must be protected from all others by way of rules and rituals and all manner of absurd activities, whether mental or physical, when, in fact, the divine cannot be broken or crushed like a fragile vessel at all but is the sturdiest part about us. Absolutely indestructible. You cannot, with the greatest effort in the world, do away with the divine in each of us, you can only fail to uncover it, fail to embrace it, fail to enjoy it.

But do you think that humans will ask their babies about the divine? Considering they have most recently been pure potential and are therefore still closest to the purely divine state? No, not they. They change diapers with great regularity and look to all those other needs they recognize, but never once do they say: Hey, Baby, let's hear about your recent journey from pure potential to this state of affairs we're in. Let's hear about where we come from, how we come to be here, wherever that is, and what it's all about!

Ha!

Koochykoochykoo is what they say instead. And wiggle wiggle waggle nose, let me tickle your little toes. That sort of thing. I tell you, it's enough to make one despair of the human race, the way it wastes its resources, whether of knowledge or any other kind.

Of course, size has a lot to do with it. Ever notice how much more reverence people show an elephant than, say, a mosquito? Or even, given the mosquito's fondness for sucking blood, something as innocent but small as an ant? If babies were born huge, that's my point, you bet people would up and ask it all kinds of questions. But being small and needing help in getting around on this planet for quite a while makes people think googlegoo is enough communication for any baby. Oh lordy, how bored I sometimes am with the results of this attitude. How I wish I had a dolphin to talk with, or any other intelligent being, like a dandelion. Well—let's just hope I either grow up very fast and very large, or somebody looks closely enough into my eyes to see my immense desire to communicate before I forget all about everything in the sheer effort of growing bigger fast.

Let's hope, and let's try to steer this story in that direction, all right? *Is* anybody listening?

GOLYGA: *That's it for today, dear Lilly. Until next time, bon voyage and be good to yourself.*

LILLY: *Thank you, Golyga. And thank you for being in touch.*

GOLYGA: *You are most welcome. We do love you humans, you know. You are a great source of delight, laughter, and learning for us. So long for now.*

LILLY: *Bye for now.*

* * *

GOLYGA: *Hello, greetings and salutations!*

LILLY: *Hello, Golyga. It's been a long time.*

GOLYGA: *No fault of mine. And yes, I know: no fault of yours either. Some living you had to do, in the Earth world of mothers in Austria, aunts in Belgium, and so on. Doing your heart duty as Earth daughter of earthlings. And doing it, I might add, very well indeed. Missing me a little, I hope?*

LILLY: *Missing you a great deal.*

GOLYGA: *Well, here we are, ready to resume our work and also to have some of that fun you missed most of all. Yes?*

LILLY: *Yes. Exactly.*

GOLYGA: *All right then.*

We left our characters all over the place but still pursuing their essentially puzzling endeavours. What was it Golyga wanted, exactly, when he followed his mate Lillykins hither and yon and even engaged in shape-shifting to be in communication with her? And what was that baby all about, crawling one moment, pontificating the next? Not to speak of that elusive brother of Lillykins' who seems to have little more to do than pop off adventuring, pop in to be a foil here and there, pop off again without further ado or serious purpose. Well, let's try to address these questions anon but not right now. Right now, there's something going on that you'll want to know about immediately, lest the whole story get into a muddle and you not even around to worry about it.

All right then.

Lillykins has just said to Golyga: Where in the world is that baby now? Can you not be left alone with it for a moment without either losing the little thing or else doing something outrageously inappropriate with it?

Golyga had no answer ready, so he simply stood there, looking a little foolish and resenting it. After all, *he* was no baby and shouldn't have to hold still for such ridiculous accusations. (Why babies should have to hold still for them is something earthlings will have to answer; it is not within our scope here to sort that out.)

Golyga raised his head, hoping for some retort to come flying toward him out of the blue, and immediately noticed that, instead, "the blue" was flying toward him. A blue something that gradually took on the shape of a cloud, darker in colour than the sky and moving rapidly while growing larger.

Since there was nothing menacing about this cloud, Golyga merely watched it without warning Lillykins. When the cloud suddenly swooped down and enveloped them, Lillykins was taken by surprise and let out a high-pitched squeak that did nothing to keep Golyga from jumping up and down and laughing, as the cloud tickled, danced, and hopped all around them. Lillykins, on the other hand, tried to fathom the nature of this cloud with her mind and so missed the fun of moving with it altogether.

Hold it! said Lillykins.

What or who are you and what is all this dancing, hopping, and tickling that I, for one, did not ask for nor had a notion to enjoy at this particular time.

Come on, said Golyga. What's wrong with a little spontaneous hopping and dancing? Why do you always have to know first what or who and what it's for and about? A lovely blue cloud, inviting us to join its play, that's what it's about.

I didn't hear any invitation, said Lillykins. I didn't even hear a "by your leave." What if I'm not in the mood to dance and hop around just now? What if I have more important things to do right now and would rather hop and dance later?

But the blue cloud might be gone later, said Golyga. You can't order a blue cloud to appear the way you order a pizza, you know. Maybe this is the very last time you'll ever have a chance to hop and dance with this blue cloud. How can you resist the opportunity?

Lillykins did hear the logic in what Golyga said and she started to think about it. Unfortunately, while she was thinking about it, the blue cloud dispersed and disappeared. Leaving Golyga all tickled and warm and still chuckling, and Lillykins all serious and thoughtful and, now, sighing with disappointment.

Oh, for heaven's sake, said Lillykins. I was just going to start dancing, too. I suppose now I'll be regretting a lost opportunity for the rest of my life.

Or, said Golyga, you could keep an eye open for any opportunity that presents itself, in whatever shape, at whatever time, and make sure you don't miss another one.

Lillykins snorted. How can one possibly recognize every opportunity as it presents itself? It might come in a completely different form next time. Instead of being a blue cloud, it might be the footprint of a rabbit, or the hair of a wizened old wizard, or the helium-filled balloon of a weather station—who knows, and how can one possibly recognize it then?

Listen, said Golyga. I can tell you exactly how to recognize it. But you have to spend a bit of time practising. Here's how: opportunities, whatever shape they come in, have a special feel to them. Yes, yes, I know that's vague, but it's true. Opportunities have a special feel and the feel is recognizable, once you have experienced it. So I suggest we go looking for an opportunity for you, and then, once you've had the feeling, you need only stay open to recognizing it again.

Okay, said Lillykins. Let's do it. Let's go look for an opportunity for me. But not an opportunity to be tickled and to hop around and dance. Let's make it an opportunity for something more weighty and important and useful than that.

Golyga let out a long, loud groan and slowly sank to the ground, as though a heavy weight were pushing him down.

There you go, said Lillykins angrily, two fists on her hips. Always making fun. Don't you ever feel the need to contribute something useful and important to life as we know it?

Golyga wiggled on the ground where he lay, but didn't answer Lillykins. Then he wiggled again, and this time he suddenly turned into an earthworm of huge proportions.

Excuse me, he said to Lillykins. I have some work to do, immediately. I have to dig some holes into this ground right here, because I can sense a lack of aeration, which can lead to serious damage for a myriad of organisms, so if you'll just leave me to my very important work and contribution here, I'll be joining you sometime in the future. So long for now, though. And as for recognizing the feel of opportunities, I guess you'll have to learn that yourself, since I'm too busy with this weighty task at hand to waste energy on frivolity. Best wishes and so long.

Lillykins was thoroughly annoyed at Golyga but she couldn't very well object to his endeavour on any grounds whatsoever, so she moseyed off and left him to it.

Golyga watched her disappear from view and then he sat up—a rather delightful sight, he thought to himself, a huge earthworm sitting up, and had himself a good, long yawn. So much for today, he thought. So much for the current installment. The next one had better get this story into some forward-moving gear and start answering some of those questions or, at least, locating that baby. Meantime, good luck to Lillykins. I can use a break from serious endeavours—I'm going off to look for that blue cloud.

LILLY: Thank you, Golyga, I enjoyed that.
GOLYGA: You are welcome. See you soon.

* * *

GOLYGA: Yes, and so it goes with our little tale: one day this and another day that, but always more to be told about the great Golyga, his mate Lillykins, the brother and friend whose name escapes Lilly once again, but that's all right because we remember it clearly. The brother of Lillykins and Golyga's friend, named—no, not wretched of the earth, or wrack and ruin, or… Better get on with it and stop testing Lilly's ability to receive whatever comes in without judgment or editing.
LILLY: Okay, on with it then.

We were recounting our list of characters for this tale. We were pausing over the name of Lillykins' brother and Golyga's friend, giving Lilly a chance to dredge the name from her memory. It failed to come. So if it now comes up, can we be sure it isn't Lilly dredging her unconscious that produces this tale but rather a consciousness coming through hers from another dimension? Can we assume that, once and for all, the imagination of our channel, Lilly, is not involved here, in the telling of our tale?

No, we cannot. Because it is Lilly's imagination that allows us to enter and play. Our own invention is useless unless the channel through which we enter your dimension has a well-developed imagination and a willingness to suspend the rigid "laws of reality" that earthlings are so fond of adhering to. Don't ask me why, because I myself see no advantage in such adherence, but then I am not in body and cannot perhaps see the benefits that ensue from such belief systems as clearly as you can.

However, all the strict so-called reality rules aside, the imagination doth play in wondrous ways even among earthlings, and I was fortunate to encounter the imagination of Lilly—by way of her guide and mentor and soulmate whose name she still hasn't got quite right, but never mind. Names just aren't her strong suit, I guess—and so, having encountered this lovely, playful imagination of hers, I am enjoying the encounter and the delightful resultant endeavour on which we have embarked: the telling of a tale. There you have it: in case you were wondering how this works. Lilly's wide-open imagination and ability to channel are the vehicles for my driving intelligence and master teaching by way of playful adventures.

I can hear Lilly thinking "…not to forget your modesty."

Goodness, what advantage is there in modesty? False modesty, at that. Isn't it more fun to crow and wave a flag about the wonderful capacities we all have? Isn't it far more honest and incrementally joy-increasing to crow from the rooftops: Look at me having fun and getting great joy out of life by way of my talents and gifts and the sharing thereof?

Obviously, a rhetorical question. I am firmly convinced that the modesty—false, usually—and the reluctance to take joy in one's talents is a culturally induced straitjacket that squeezes the life force out of endeavours and makes them into steep, plodding paths up a sunless mountainside when it would be just as easy to go dancing across mountain meadows, yodelling one's joyful message to the echoes all around.

GOLYGA: So. What was that you were saying about "modesty"?

LILLY: Not a word. Ever again. Though I might mention "boasting," I suppose.

GOLYGA: Ah, yes. Boasting. Do you mean by that the expressed intention of all you mean to do in future with your new-found gifts and talents? A kind of throwing forward of the imagination to the accomplishments you intend? Or do you mean a verbal hammering at others to make them feel your advantage over them? It's a rather amorphous term, this "boasting." There are tall tales, you know, that are nothing but boasting and elicit the most wonderful chuckles and delighted smiles. Can you be meaning that sort of "boasting"?

LILLY: Of course not. I mean, for one example, the temptation I experience to tell somebody about, let's say, the message I received from your realm for a friend yesterday and how, when I gave her the message, she was powerfully struck by how appropriate and helpful it was. Somehow, I feel the weight of that doesn't really come home to me unless I talk about it to somebody. But that's boasting. See what I mean?

GOLYGA: Yes, I most certainly do see what you mean. We have to sort out two separate notions here. One is that you, Lilly, don't experience as directly as you might and therefore resort to laying the experience out in words to experience it more fully. Thereby robbing some experiences of their full impact rather than the other way around.

LILLY: Yes, I understand. You are right. I am trying to change that.

GOLYGA: And you are well on your way, too. The other aspect, the actual "boasting" one, as you see it, has nothing to do with this example. It's a sharing and, if done with the appropriate person, is not a bad thing at all. It's a sharing of the joy of what you are able to do for people. Does that not ring true?

LILLY: Yes, it does. You are right. And, I must tell you, I love getting and giving messages that are so helpful.

GOLYGA: All right then. And I love sharing with you and other earthlings the joy of a boundless imagination playing, dancing, boasting—as in tall tales—and bringing with it, all unsuspected, some wisdom here and there. Get it?

LILLY: Got it. Yes. Thank you.

GOLYGA: Here we go, moving on.

There was once a brother and friend whose name escaped the teller of the tale for just long enough to remember many other things, and then the name popped up: Dionysius.

LILLY: That wasn't it.

GOLYGA: How do you know? You don't remember what it was.

LILLY: I know that wasn't it.

GOLYGA: How about Andromedus?

LILLY: That's not it either.

GOLYGA: All right then, we'll just have to leave it blank for today.

LILLY: Are you saying you can't remember it either?

GOLYGA: Certainly not. But to make it a test of my superhuman abilities is beneath both of us, don't you think?

LILLY: Yes. It is.

GOLYGA: All right then, we'll say "so long" for today and continue the tale itself during our next session. Welcome back to work, Lilly. It's a pleasure, as usual.

LILLY: Thank you, Golyga. I'm glad to be working with you again.

* * *

GOLYGA: Here we are, still no closer to the question of Lillykins' brother's name. On the other hand, no longer, I suspect, quite as determined to make that a test of my skills or memory or authenticity as a source of this writing. So, on with the story.

Once upon a time, there was a Great Blue Heron called Abigail. Abigail was a wonderfully beautiful Bird of mammoth proportions, ever ready to fling herself into the sky for the sheer joy of flying about in it, but rather shy of being seen. Odd, wouldn't you say? Beautiful and obviously talented though Abigail was, she was shy and would come out to fling and fly only when no one else was about to witness her doings. However, one fine day—and it was a fine one: blue skies, sunny and mild, breezes and blossoms all around—as Abigail was peeking forth out of her nesting area among the flotsam some call dead branches and others see as wind-worn and water-shaped works of art, she saw, to her utter amazement, a little human baby, crawling along at the water's edge, calling out: Where are you, Lillykins? I could use some food and something sweet to drink and I'm all tired out and wet and...

Abigail approached the baby, slowly and cautiously, and the baby, looking up Abigail's enormously long thin legs, grew quiet. The two of them watched each other for several moments. Then Abigail opened her wings wide, wide, and the baby crawled under them, and Abigail enfolded the baby in warmth and safety and began a low humming/drumming in her chest, which immediately sent the baby into a deep sleep.

There they sat, Abigail and the enfolded baby, enjoying their closeness and deep heartbeat communing, and neither said a word. No need to. And yet…and yet…as soon as the baby woke up, there it was, poking its head out from among the feathers and starting to call out again: Lillykins, where are you, Lillykins? I got lost and I can't see you anywhere. I need you, Lillykins.

Abigail was curious. What do you need this Lillykins for? she asked. What's wrong with my warmth and care? I can even take you for high flights into the sky and teach you to fish and…

The baby listened and nodded, but every time there was a pause in Abigail's utterances, the baby called out again: Lillykins, where are you, Lillykins?

Oh, for heaven's sakes, said Abigail. If you're going to make such a racket all the time you're not with Lillykins, I'd better help you find her pronto. Now, what does she look like, this Lillykins?

The baby looked up at Abigail, its mouth open so it looked more like a fledgling heron than a human baby.

I don't know, the baby said. I never really looked. I can tell you what Lillykins smells like, and feels like, and sounds like, but what she looks like…well, I just don't know.

Then you'd better come with me, said Abigail. We'll go looking for her together, and when we find her, you can recognize her somehow and let me know. Get on my back and hold on.

The baby crawled up on Abigail's back. Holding on would not be easy without ruffling a few feathers but that couldn't be helped.

Just don't pull them out, said Abigail. Lie down flat, too, so you won't stick up and make flying harder for me. Ready?

Abigail moved her mighty wings once, twice, and then up she flew with mighty strokes of the air, up, up, and soon they were soaring high above the water. The baby was amazed to see right through the water into the deep, as though it had acquired heron eyes, and delighted in seeing fish and sea creatures of every kind. Then they were flying over a mountain range where the baby could see every river within miles, and then they were right above the island, which the baby recognized and on which he saw a familiar-looking shape.

Go down, go down, Baby yelled right in Abigail's ear. Land right there, see? I think maybe that's Lillykins!

But when they landed, the shape turned out to be not Lillykins but Golyga, Lillykins' mate. And he was very very glad to see the baby because he'd been looking for it high and low and everywhere else and was supposed to be giving it food and shelter and such, which he now could finally accomplish.

As soon as the baby completed introductions, Abigail, shy as ever, flew away again. The baby called after her: Thank you, thank you. Come and visit me sometime. And Abigail waved her long legs as if to say: Maybe, we'll see, I'll have to get back to you on that and let you know if it's possible.

And then she was gone.

Well! said Golyga. Where have you been? I've been worried about you and so has Lillykins. What have you been doing?

The baby thought about that for a moment and said: I've been around and about. Doing this and that. Might as well save the tale until Lillykins is back and you can both hear me tell it. Where is Lillykins, by the way?

Golyga shrugged his shoulders. Can't actually tell you that, he said. She'll be back, though. She and I have plans and such, so I know she'll return sooner or later. Meantime, let's get you fed and so on.

Golyga lifted the baby up off the ground and to his shoulder, holding it just the way he'd been taught, and finding himself enjoying the feeling of a baby against his chest. Maybe we'll walk around a bit first, he said, starting out across the sand. Walking and just sort of humming in his chest where the baby's heart was drumming away.

Oh sure, said the baby. Walking me around. Or flying me around. Or even letting me sleep all warm and cozy among your feathers. You all have lots of nice ideas for me and you all do nice things and I do appreciate every one of them, but how about asking me what I really really want right now? What I really really need right now? How about that? Anybody thought that might be a good idea? Asking *me*? What *I* want?

Golyga was startled. He'd never heard such a thing: a baby demanding so forthrightly and emphatically to be asked what it wanted. Goodness, what was the world coming to? Was this what the new generation brought with it into the world from the start? This kind of certainty of its rights to be heard and to have itself looked after according to its needs and wants? Was that the right way to look after a baby?

Since Golyga wasn't sure, he thought he'd just ask what it was the baby wanted.

Well, for one thing, I want to see Lillykins soon. But right now, above everything else, I need some food. Not walking or sleeping or flying, but food to eat and something sweet to drink. Get it?

Oh yes, said Golyga. Definitely. You're very clear, so I'd best set out and find some food for you. Did you want to come with me or wait here? Golyga thought he'd better ask before he got told to ask.

I'll wait right here, said the baby. Just in case Lillykins comes back. But don't take too long with the food. Don't get sidetracked somewhere and forget about it, okay?

Promise, said Golyga. I'll be back with something edible as soon as I find it. Meantime...well, do whatever you need to do, I guess. See you soon.

Off went Golyga.

The baby settled into the groove in the sand that looked most comfortable and even felt familiar because it had snuggled into it once before. And there it waited for developments, hoping for food, for Lillykins, hoping to see Abigail again someday, but having no idea what all would be happening before it even got out of its snuggly sand nest again.

LILLY: Is that it for today?
GOLYGA: Yes, it is. We have to leave you energy for Christmas preparations and for further developments with your internal baby. I do hope you recognize the message of today's instalment.
LILLY: I do, thank you. Will anyone else find it interesting to read this segment?
GOLYGA: Yes, because the strands will all lead somewhere, tie in, and then lead elsewhere to become part of the whole adventure.

LILLY: *Great. Thank you, Golyga. See you soon.*
GOLYGA: *Hope so. Meantime, enjoy the season.*

* * *

Next, the loose end of Abigail.

That lovely heron of large proportions and heart who took care of Baby for a while and was puzzled by his need for Lillykins, despite her own excellent and appreciated care of him.

Lillykins, you see, is the mother of Baby's heart.

All his many other needs well taken care of, including love from Abigail, Baby would still yearn for the mother of his heart. Whether that is a real biological mother or not matters less than whether soul love is involved.

So whoever you are reading this, and whoever your biological mother is or was, and whatever the relationship you have with her, look again: is she the mother of your heart? Or does someone else occupy that position? For the mother of your heart exists for everyone and, once recognized, will give you love and solace for the rest of your life. And beyond, of course, but that's another story.

* * *

Once upon a time, when Golyga was wandering about in search of food for Baby, he ran into a grasshopper full of self-importance. Golyga tried to avoid greeting and talking to the grasshopper because no one is more boring than a self-important grasshopper, but unfortunately the grasshopper had spotted Golyga and wasn't going to let him go by without accosting him.

Excuse me, said the grasshopper. Aren't you the great and mighty Golyga, known far and wide as a teacher and educator of babies?

Golyga stopped, amazed at this grasshopper's wisdom and perspicuity.

Why yes, said Golyga. I am he.

Well then, said the grasshopper. Perhaps you can help me with a profound problem I am experiencing at this time with my offspring. To wit: the damned little twerp won't do anything I say and has taken it

63

into his head to become a mouse instead of growing up as a grasshopper. I ask you!

You ask me what? said Golyga, trying hard not to laugh at the picture of a grasshopper/mouse teenager, sulking and refusing to listen to this father of his who seemed no longer so wise at all.

I ask you: what am I to do to straighten out the crazy notions of my teenaged son?

Why do anything? said Golyga. Why not wait and see whether he really does turn into a mouse? Time enough then to make a fuss. I rather doubt he'll have the temerity for the long haul—few people do—to grow against the grain. If he does, come and see me then.

The grasshopper went off, thinking that Golyga just might be right and his son would most likely give up all notions of becoming a mouse once he, grasshopper father, stopped making a fuss about it. As it happened, however, that particular son was one of the few creatures strong enough and smart enough and daring enough to persist in his unusual quest: he intended to become a mouse, he went about planning to become a mouse, and, in the end, he became a mouse. So, of course, the grasshopper father came roaring around to seek out Golyga and blame him for the catastrophe.

Whoa, said Golyga. If you recall, it was your son who intended this in the first place. Well, he's a mouse now, good for him for making it, and what exactly is your complaint?

The grasshopper father sputtered and stuttered something about how grasshoppers are meant to be grasshoppers, not mice, and what was to be done now?

Well, is your son happy as a mouse? asked Golyga.

That has nothing to do with anything, said the grasshopper. Imagine, when the entire family gets together, grasshoppers all, and smack in the middle there sits my son the mouse. It's not to be borne, I tell you.

Hm, said Golyga. You could always introduce him as your son the Mighty Mouse. Or you could say, He's no mouse of mine. Or you could introduce him as your son and leave others to form their opinions about what a mouse in a grasshopper family might mean. Or you could get busy with your own life and leave your son to lead his.

Don't be so silly, said the grasshopper. I am the father and it's my responsibility to see to it that my son is a credit to the family. No mouse could ever be a credit to a grasshopper family.

Just then a great big cat came bouncing along, patting with its paws at a grasshopper, to make it jump, and fully intending to eat the little creature, or at least to lick it to death.

Stop that! yelled the grasshopper at the cat. That's my aunt Myrna you're pawing. Leave her alone!

But the cat, of course, heard none of that. The cat was intent on what it was about and never even thought that a grasshopper might have something to say to a cat.

Just as Aunt Myrna was about to expire from sheer fright, not to speak of the rough licks she was getting, the cat became distracted. She turned her head and watched as a mouse came running along from behind a bush, ran across her path, the cheeky little thing, and disappeared around the corner. In a flash, the cat was after the mouse, completely forgetting Aunt Myrna. The grasshopper went to his aunt and tried to soothe her nerves. Myrna, however, would have none of that.

Who, she asked, was that brave mouse, drawing the cat's attention to itself at the risk of its life just to save mine, an old grasshopper?

Who do you think? said grasshopper father. That was my son!

Well, well, said Golyga. I believe my work is done here, and he went off, resuming his search for food for Baby. The grasshoppers ignored his going, didn't even see him chuckle on his way. Golyga, however, vowed that he would not interfere with any choices Baby would want to make for his future. Grasshopper, mouse, or any other goal in life, Baby was going to be free to choose and to put his life energy into his own choice.

Just then, Golyga ran into a bush full of berries. He sat down to pick some so he could bring them to Baby for his next meal. But he had neither pocket nor bag nor any container in which to carry the berries. What ho! he thought to himself. and turned himself into a kangaroo mom with pouch but no baby kangaroo in it. Thus equipped, Golyga filled the pouch with berries, then set off to return to Baby.

Baby was delighted by the colour of the berries and by the smell, but as for eating them, no way. Baby yelled and whined and simply would not eat even one berry until Golyga was fed up and ready to do some yelling himself. Just then he remembered grasshopper/father and, instead of yelling at baby, he asked: What is it you would like to eat? What do you want?

Baby thought about it. I don't really know, he said. I just know that I don't want any berries.

Golyga sighed. All right then, he said. You stay here and I'll be back with some other food for you, and let's hope you like that one.

Don't be silly, said Baby. That's a waste of time and effort. Just take me with you and then I'll tell you on the spot what's a yes and what's a no-no.

So Golyga hoisted Baby onto his shoulders, and off the two of them went.

* * *

GOLYGA: So, we are back at work and enjoying the very thought of it, I noticed.
LILLY: Yes, I was looking forward to it.
GOLYGA: In that case, let's get right to it.

Lillykins is sitting and thinking again. She does a great deal of this, have you noticed? Some of the thinking is productive and brings delight and other good things. Some of it is a circle game humans seem to be fond of: thinking circles around subjects or several subjects without ever getting out of the circles into productive lanes. Like a circular maze in which no exit is discovered until somebody else points it out. Anyway:

Lillykins is thinking, and we are beginning to wonder which of these think-ways she is undertaking, when suddenly she jumps to her feet and shouts: Eureka! I've got it! The way to take care of this baby is to bring it with us everywhere so it begins to learn about all of life in every which way. The only question is this: which of us, Golyga or I, had better carry this baby? Which of us is going to be seeing more life of the educational kind?

Just then Golyga turned up, carrying the baby on his shoulders, singing a little ditty about sheep and black wool and a maiden come a-gathering.

That settles that, says Lillykins. Better give me the baby so it can encounter life as it is, not some nursery-song version.

What makes you think nursery rhymes and ditties are less about life as it is than your so-called real life?

Lillykins simply snorted the way she tended to do and held out her arms. The baby, however, refused to come to her.

No way, said the baby. I like it up here. It's high enough to see quite far, and I won't be earnestly reproached every time something frivolous and fun happens. I'm staying put right here.

Oh great, said Lillykins. Now you've converted this baby to your frivolous ways and no hope that it will become an earnest and useful member of society.

Which society? asked Golyga. Have you any notion just how many so-called societies there are to choose from? I certainly belong to one and you don't hear any member of my society complaining that there is too much fun in life.

Lillykins had to stop, in all fairness, and consider Golyga's claim. And she found it to be true and was greatly intrigued.

Are you telling me that to be earnest and useful is but an attitude and has no actual value attached, over and above your frivolous way of living?

Exactly, says Golyga. I get as much done as you. Just as soon as I set my mind to anything I please to accomplish, I do so, and none of your Sturm und Drang and other earnest concepts improves your output or accomplishments over mine. So where are you? Certainly not where a baby would choose to be, given it can be having fun while going about the learning life.

All right, said Lillykins. I'll give you two a good six months to prove your way is better than mine. Then, if it turns out not to be, Baby will adopt my way for the next ten months.

What kind of arithmetic is that?

Just kidding, says Lillykins. Just conceding that, in my way, six months may well seem as long as ten. In other words, I am willing to see you on this. Go for it. Of course, I'll have to stick fairly close to you and Baby to assess the results and the various means and methods. Agreed?

Well! Golyga could wish for nothing better than to have Lillykins around for a change, and so he agreed most readily indeed.

Now then, said Lillykins. Where are we off to first?

To a dance, said Golyga.

Hooray, shouted the baby. I love sitting up high while you dance me around.

Not so fast, said Golyga. Not so fast. You'll be doing your own dancing, my child.

Nothing like learning to get off your knees and stop crawling than the desire to get on your feet and dance!

Do you mean to tell me, this baby will be expected to dance before it can even stand, let alone walk?

Exactly, said Golyga. Don't you think walking will be more eagerly achieved if the goal is dancing? Come on! Off we go!

And so off they went, Lillykins and Golyga, with Baby sitting on Golyga's shoulders: taking great leaps as though wearing those seven-league boots of story fame, and sometimes even flying for short punts. Pretty soon all three were singing at the top of their lungs, lustily bellowing and tiraleeraling as they went.

And so, before long, they arrived in a clearing in the forest where a hundred Beings of Light were assembled, sitting in a circle and waiting.

LILLY: Waiting for what?
GOLYGA: Well may you ask. And well may you hope to find out soon because today's session had better end here.
LILLY: What a perfect cliffhanger!
GOLYGA: I know. And on top of that, it leaves you feeling good, doesn't it?
LILLY: Yes, it does. See you soon then.
GOLYGA: Very soon. Yes.

* * *

Once, when all three—Golyga, Lillykins, and Baby—were amazed to see the Beings of Light and didn't quite know what to make of them or what they were making of the three themselves, there was a long pause during which no one said anything, and a beautiful peace descended on all. Slowly, sounds began to drift into the silence, and they were the sounds of birds, singing, and of water, lapping, and of the breeze in the trees, gently caressing the leaves and even inviting a few of them to dance. It was, in a word, wonderful. Until, suddenly, a loud, shrill sound came upon them all where they lay, suspended in peace and tranquility, and with one great rift of the silence, this sound took over. Everybody looked for the source of the sound, but no one could see anything that might have caused it. They looked and looked, and finally it was Baby who figured it out: It's not anything we can see! he said. It's not even something we can hear very often. What's making that sound is "regret." You know, when you regret something you did or didn't do, said or didn't say, decided or decided against. If you let those hang around with each other for a while, those regrets will eventually start grating out just the sound we hear now.

Everybody looked at Baby in astonishment. Here they all were, one hundred Beings of Light, a Golyga who certainly laid claim to having some wisdom, and Lillykins, who often thought she knew rather a lot, and yet it was Baby who had come up with this profound insight into the nature of the noise. Because noise it was, they all had to concede that.

Well, said Baby sulkily, very pouty and baby-like, right after all that wisdom poured forth and astonished everybody. I don't see, he said, why I can't be the one who knows more once in a while. Don't they have a saying about the mouth of babies?

Yes, yes, they do, said Golyga, and Lillykins put a soothing hand on Baby's head.

You are quite right, she said. We know that saying well and use it all the time: out of the mouth of babes, we say. It's just that we don't often pay attention to what it means, which is that the truth and wisdom and insight might well come out of their mouth and we ought to listen to babies and children as much as we listen to old folks—neither of which we do very much.

Good, said Baby. I'm glad to have reminded you. Now, can I go play with that caterpillar over there?

And off he went, leaving the rest of them smiling and happy— because the mystery had been cleared up and the sound had stopped. That sound of accumulated regrets that had so disturbed their peace.

And now, said Golyga, it behooves us to ask you, Beings of Light, for advice regarding the prevention of that shrill sound of accumulated regrets. How to prevent it from gathering force, from coming about in the first place, and how to dispel it and bring forth peaceful silence once it has erupted.

The Beings of Light all turned to Golyga in great surprise. Goodness, said one. Don't you know?

Well… said Golyga. I'm not sure… It's not something I suffer from: accumulation of regrets. I seem to remember something along the lines of forgiving yourself for not being perfect and making mistakes?

And Lillykins jumped in, eager to contribute: Making reparation where possible.

And, of course, said Golyga, staying alert to not going there anymore. Not making the same mistake again. Not doing or saying or deciding those things that will fill you with regrets and shrill, loud sounds.

All right then, said the Beings of Light. No need for us around here, we can see that. Between the three of you, you have it all quite figured out and in hand.

And in a flash, all one hundred Beings of Light disappeared. Just like that.

Lillykins and Golyga were rather miffed, both of them. It seems you have to be stupid or stuck in a rut to get Beings of Light to feel needed and have them stick around. It seems you have to be in trouble or asking for help, or…

Suddenly, there was the sound of laughter. Loud and jolly and joyous and delighted and a hundred other ways of laughter came over them from where Baby and the hundred Beings of Light were playing together.

Golyga and Lillykins watched for a moment, looked at each other in amazement, and then, with glee, and quick as a wink, they were over there, joining in the fun and laughter.

This, whispered one Being of Light to the two of them, is the very best way of making sure you never have a regret nestling inside you, preparing to make shrill loud sounds. Laughter and joy are absolutely the very best insurance against such a thing happening. So, enjoy!

And they all did.

And so can you!

* * *

GOLYGA: Now to work. Loose ending one: regarding the one hundred Beings of Light.

As the three of them watched, the one hundred Beings of Light rose to encircle them, to bathe them in their Light, and to give them the following advice: Never ever go barefoot through a jungle.

LILLY: Amusing but sounds a bit like an easy way out of a loose end.
GOLYGA: So you say, but you have been in a position close to barefoot, in the rainforest of Costa Rica, and did you not hear, standing there in the thick of it, about snakes whose venom can kill within half an hour?
LILLY: True, but how relevant is that to "our three" and why bring on one hundred Beings of Light to tell it?
GOLYGA: This is our story, Lilly dear, and we can do with it as we like, right?
LILLY: Oh yes. You certainly don't need me to prod you to maintain the high standards you yourself have set.
GOLYGA: Heavy ammunition! Definitely from the editor who, as you will recall, is supposed to be off in a corner and not at all engaged in this undertaking. Not while we're at it, anyway.
LILLY: I apologize. This is your book and I bow to your decisions.
GOLYGA: All sarcasm aside…
LILLY: Well, more teasing than sarcasm, I would say.
GOLYGA: All right then, all teasing aside…

The one hundred Beings of Light went on to say a couple more things to our three intrepid adventurers. Such as: If you do find yourself in the jungle with no shoes on, *fly!* Shape-shift into any creature with wings and fly! You do remember to whom they are talking, do you not? To those masters of shape-shifting—Golyga, Lillykins, and Baby. And then the one hundred Beings of Light broke into giggles and, dancing all around the three arrivals, sang this ditty:
Lilly dear notwithstanding,
Take to the air and fly,

Spread your wings and flap them hard,
Rise and kiss the sky.

And so that is what they did, all three of them. They wished themselves wings, they flapped and flew, and before the eye could blink, they reached the horizon and were gone.

LILLY: Is that the end of that loose end?
GOLYGA: Yes. However, there is an addendum already in existence to be tagged on. It had to do with the ability to be firmly planted in this world, on this earth, while at the same time being fully aware of one's spiritual nature. All right?
LILLY: Thank you, yes.

* * *

GOLYGA: Yes, we are here and ready to work. First, we want to congratulate you on some new developments in your growth. You have reached a new stage, in fact, wherein you are always aware when disconnecting from your self and uneasy about it. In the past, you went for stretches of time not aware that you were disconnected from your own core and then had to scramble back through emotional turmoil to reach your self again. Recently, you have become conscious of the discomfort of such disconnecting almost immediately and have returned yourself to connection without the emotional turmoil. Yes, some restlessness and some not-so-comfortable moments ensued, but nothing like the emotional storms of the past. True?
LILLY: True. Thank you for putting my recent restlessness in such positive terms.
GOLYGA: Because these are true terms, they will help you in future to recognize any return of such occasions. However, you will also be more aware in any given situation of the danger of disconnecting and will develop a comfort never before experienced in the state of dual consciousness. In other words, even with your son Daniel, you will be able to stay connected with your own self while being sensitive and caring and giving about the Other. In the past it has always been an either/or situation for you, and because you have been more comfortable in the state of selflessness, you have not developed the dual consciousness. But selflessness is far from the usual interpretation of the state. It's a fear, an abandonment, a leaving behind of the self for complex reasons, always with negative results. The self is not the same thing as the ego. The self is your core being and is absolutely necessary if you are to develop into a fully human, fully incarnated, fully evolved being. So: dual consciousness. To be strengthened and to be enjoyed.

And now, to our next instalment…

Once upon a time, Lillykins was imagining herself in the throes of love. She experimented with the feeling as though it were a beach ball—tossing it up and down, turning it this way and that, letting it roll, catching it, and sometimes even deflating it entirely, only to blow it up again. Lillykins had undertaken this endeavour to try and understand what it was that discombobulated humans so at the beginnings of their male/female relationships. Or, for that matter, their gay relationships, as Lilly points out. Lillykins, you see, was determined to understand humans better than ever because she had the distinct impression that she would be able to help humans get out of their various self-destructive ruts and emerge into a life of joy and love. Such was Lillykins' ambition, and you can't blame her, can you?

Well, Golyga did. He blamed her for being a do-gooder, for taking too much time away from just being, having fun, hanging out with him and Baby, and generally didn't like her preoccupation with the concerns of humans.

Why not take some time off? he asked Lillykins one morning. Let's go for a swim, for a run through the woods, for a berry-picking expedition to an island. Those, too, are earth activities. Why be constantly concerned with the human creatures on that planet? It seems to me they are less worthy of your interest and efforts than many other beings on Earth.

Lillykins thought seriously about this, and she had to agree. Snakes, for example, were far more rewarding as a subject of study, and monkeys were a lot more fun. However, it also seemed to her that the very complexity of humans gave her talents more scope and that the effects of humans on the planet were really the concern here. When she told Golyga her thoughts, he had to agree, and so they came to a compromise: Lillykins would spend a certain amount of time and effort on bettering humans in any way she could, and Golyga would help her. After which efforts, both would take off in the pursuit of pleasure and delight. And so it went for a while and went well, too. Lillykins was able to teach at least three people how better to employ their energies than by getting stressed out in jobs they hated, she was able to convert five companies to the use of recyclable packaging, and she changed the educational system of one entire town to concentrate on the creative capacities of children. Golyga helped and meanwhile was grateful for the small mercies of her attention. At the end of this period of endeavour, they sat down and evaluated their results.

It seems to me, said Golyga, there must be a far more efficient and far-reaching way of working with these humans. Some huge influx of understanding would help. Could we not devise something that would open many eyes at once?

Lillykins agreed. Yes, she said. It does seem that my way would take forever and this planet doesn't have forever, if it and humans are to survive. What do you suggest?

A joy cloud, said Golyga. We need to generate a joy cloud, cover the planet with it until the vapours of the cloud seep into every part of it, infect all creatures on the planet with joy, and then see who goes to war or builds weapons or robs widows blind.

Lillykins was skeptical. How do you produce a joy cloud? she wanted to know. Especially one that big.

Not necessary, said Golyga. You and I need only produce a joy cloud big enough for a few ants to get under. Or a hummingbird to sit on. Or a tree to get tangled up in. As soon as any creature comes into contact with a joy cloud, the joy infects it, the cloud grows, and the entire process repeats itself until the cloud covers a planet the size of Earth in no time. Get it?

Got it, said Lillykins. And I sure would enjoy that more than going through the ups and downs of being in love in order to study one of those human habits I find so puzzling. Let's get started right away!

Golyga was all for it. Joy was his thing, and he was always ready to go ride it. Next thing you know, Golyga and Lillykins were off and flying, one as a bumblebee and the other as a snowflake. The snowflake soon became too hot to sustain its shape, so it became a butterfly. Bumblebee and butterfly made their way to a flower garden and there they bumbled and buttered away to their hearts' content. Pretty soon, a little cloud of joy began to form around them, spreading a delicate aroma. This aroma invited other creatures to gather around and enjoy, and thus the cloud began to grow, and grow, and grow until it was the size of Cincinnati. It continued on until it covered all the Earth and infected all the planet's creatures, as Golyga had predicted. And there it was: a planet inhabited by joyful creatures. No strife, no nastiness of any kind, everything running smoothly and getting better every day.

What do you say to that? Impossible? How do you know? Have you tried generating joy clouds lately? Have you gathered with others for the purpose of generating joy? Are you even able to sustain joy for more than a moment? Be assured, all of you, the generating of joy is a huge and effective means of altering everything it touches, of spreading itself easily and over vast areas of life—your own and everyone else's—and it is by far the best remedy for the ills of the planet and its inhabitants.

We are not speaking of vacuous smiles and holier-than-thou wafting about. We are not talking about a determined effort to have fun. We are not even talking about the joys that come with tasks well accomplished, growth appreciated, goals attained. No, we are talking about a Feeling. A state of being that cannot be forced but only invited. That can be generated but never brought about as a means to an end. It is a tool, yes, but that is not its main-self. Its main-self is a state of grace, of dwelling in the highest energy and light, of generating it for others by the experiencing of it. Try it, you might like it.

LILLY: But isn't the state of being human necessarily one of "clouds come and clouds go"? So that a constant state of joy is impossible for humans?

GOLYGA: Smarty-pants Lilly thinks she has outfoxed us.

LILLY: Come on, I'm confused.

GOLYGA: Or relying on our superior formulation of the perceived dilemma. Here it is: the state of being human includes emotional ups and downs, learning curves, spiralling evolution, and so on. However, the state of joy of which we speak is independent of these ups and downs. We are back to dual consciousness—the subject introduced at the beginning of this session that you, Lilly dear, thought was personal but is in fact a very universal experience. Dual consciousness: of both the ups and downs, the spiral of growth, etc., as well as of the state of grace, of joy, of love and connection with the benevolent universe and with Spirit.

LILLY: I understand. Any pointers on how to practise this dual consciousness?

GOLYGA: Of course. It's what we are here to do: help everyone interested in attaining it. And the pointer is simple: remind yourself to experience the dual consciousness in every situation you're in, every time you become aware of discomfort, of joy, of being shaken up in any way, of every single experience in the day. The opportunities to experience dual consciousness are myriad because every experience on Earth includes duality: the material or physical, and spirit. The individual and the all-encompassing One. The lofty and the mundane, as you were once wont to put it. Above all, remember: you can ask for help at any time with this ongoing practice and you will improve in great leaps and bounds for every little effort you put in. After a while, it will become a habitual state, and then the cloud of joy will have gained another steadily supplying generator.

LILLY: I thank you for this. I can already feel the benefits in a personal way.

GOLYGA: Yes, my dear, you are close to being able to maintain dual consciousness a great deal of the time, and that was the congratulations at the beginning of our session today.

We are now going to close, leaving Golyga and Lillykins just where they are, ready to generate their cloud of joy and not anticipating what obstacles and results lie in their future.

LILLY: Great cliffhanger ending. Thank you.

GOLYGA: You are welcome, my dear. All the best until very soon.

* * *

And so we continue our tale.

On this day, Lillykins and Golyga, being happily together for the first time in a while, were singing and taking jolly little dance steps as they went, with the baby aloft and enjoying the view.

Pretty soon, they came to a deep, wide river that Lillykins thought they ought to cross. But where? There were no bridges in sight, no ferry boat or even canoe available, and the tree branches on the riverside were useless for Tarzaning across the water. What to do?

Well, for goodness' sake, said Baby. You both know how to shape-shift, don't you? How about a swan, Golyga? If you were a swan, I could sit on your back and ride across, and we'd look terrific, don't you think? Or how about a winged horse? That's always a nice image. And Lillykins could be a fish or a leaping deer— No, wait a minute. That's a nice image, a leaping deer, but not the best way to get across a river. Never mind, Lillykins could come up with something useful as well as elegant, I'm sure she could.

I have a better idea, said Lillykins, just a bit annoyed at not being central to Baby's scheme. Why don't you, oh Baby boy, shape-shift and take us both across? We know you can do it. Go for it.

All right, said baby, and turned himself into a crocodile.

Oh, for heaven's sake, said Lillykins. Now we both have to dangle our legs in the water and get wet and probably end up muddy as well. Oh well, I guess I asked for it. Go ahead. We're ready.

Off they swam, Baby as a huge long crocodile, Lillykins and Golyga riding on his back. And pretty soon they were on the other side.

Now you see the value of life-as-school, said Golyga, putting on his most wise and learned expression. You have walked in the shoes of a crocodile and will never again be able to despise or be mean to one of those creatures.

Walked in crocodile shoes? said Baby. Is that what you call it? I'm more inclined to say: swam in a crocodile's skin.

Nitpicking, said Golyga. You know exactly what I mean. Now tell us what you have learned, being a crocodile.

Well, said Baby. I've learned that the two of you are heavy, riding on my back, but that I could nevertheless make it across the river, to the other side.

Excellent, said Golyga. Burdens, in other words, do not need to sink you. They can make you strong, self-reliant, and, if you don't watch out, overconfident.

What do you mean by that? demanded Lillykins, who was still brushing mud and river weeds off herself. What do you mean by overconfident?

Well, if Baby here had tried swimming the length of the river with us on his back, for example, just because he was able to cross it, he'd have come a cropper, as they say. Gauge your strength, is all I say. Don't get ridiculous about the burdens you shoulder.

I agree, said Lillykins. A very good lesson in life indeed. You may turn out to be right about Baby's schooling, Golyga. What next? Where are we off to, on this side of the river?

I thought, said Golyga, we might look for your brother. One of his favourite spots is right beyond that hillock you see to the right. Among the trees and bushes on top of the hillock is a soft pillow of moss, and

77

your brother likes to go there for a little doze and dreaming now and then.

Great, let's go check, said Lillykins.

Meantime, Baby had turned himself back into a baby boy, and so Golyga hoisted him up again onto his shoulders. The three set off in a good mood and continued that way until they ran across a huge caterpillar on their path.

Careful, said Lillykins. Don't step on it.

As if I would, said Golyga. When have I ever been a caterpillar squasher?

I just thought you might not have seen it, said Lillykins. Don't be so sensitive.

While the two of them were idly passing the time with such chatter, the caterpillar reared up and blew fierce flames in their direction.

Some caterpillar, said Golyga. More like a hairy dragon, I'd say.

Well, whatever, said Lillykins. We have no quarrel with dragons, hairy or otherwise, so I'm sure he'll let us pass without troubling us.

What makes you think it's a he? asked Golyga. I'm not pleased by how you've jumped to that conclusion. Fierceness is not an exclusively male characteristic, and you know it.

Oh, I do, said Lillykins, a bit peeved at having resorted to that old cliché. Perhaps I meant that he is likely to be a he because of the beauty of his fierceness. The flames shooting forth in such shapes and colours and the elegant curve of his back as he rears…

Golyga looked at Lillykins and both of them just had to laugh. And Baby, though not quite sure why, also laughed out loud. Until the caterpillar stopped rearing and breathing fire and looked perplexed.

What's going on? he asked. Can't you tell I mean to frighten you?

Oh, we can, we can, Lillykins assured the caterpillar. And you are doing quite a good job of it, too. It's just that we are three intrepid travellers who are not easily frightened or intimidated, and we have so many talents and powers between us that few aggressive tactics would succeed against us.

LILLY: I'm sorry, Golyga. I have a terrible stomachache, real cramps, just now, so I have to go lie down. We can conclude this later if you like, or another time.

GOLYGA: Indeed we can. Go lie down. Until soon, my dear.

* * *

LILLY: I'm better. Shall we go on?
GOLYGA: Very briefly then, because you're not better enough.

We'll just say that Golyga told Lillykins she had a lot to learn about retreating from a position of untenable nonsense, and that Baby had better not be listening too closely to what had just been said lest he learn such sophistry instead of the life lessons Golyga had in mind for him.

Lillykins didn't say anything. She was busy examining the perplexed expression of the caterpillar and was quite sure there was something familiar about it. In fact, she was beginning to suspect that this caterpillar was actually her brother.

GOLYGA: Whether she was right or not, we'll find out in our next session. All right?
LILLY: All right. Thank you, Golyga. Until very soon then.

* * *

GOLYGA: Yes, I am here and you are well-enough connected. Never fear that I can't get through as long as you intend it and are able to keep your mind at bay. Okay?
LILLY: Thank you, yes.
GOLYGA: All right then, we go on.

Lillykins is wondering whether the rearing caterpillar/dragon is her brother Hailu.

LILLY: That wasn't his name, was it?
GOLYGA: No. Just testing your memory.
LILLY: What is it then? I'm not getting anything.
GOLYGA: Then let's just call him Hailu for now, shall we?

So Lillykins said to the caterpillar/dragon, who was still rearing and throwing about tongues of flame: Are you Hailu?

Oh, for heaven's sake, said her brother. Must you always recognize me and spoil my fun?

Well, if your fun consists of being a caterpillar spewing flames, you're not losing too much, are you?

Stop it, you two, said Golyga. Sibling bickering is not the most pleasant exchange to listen to. And Baby could be better served by an educational discourse on the hair of caterpillars or the effect of flames on all things than by these mini-tantrums you two are so fond of.

Oh, don't be so puffed, said Lillykins. A brother is the only one you can get shirty with and not have major emotional upheavals as a result.

In that case, what do you call our little brouhahas? Because we are certainly not brother and sister, are we?

I call them, said Lillykins, contretemps. I find it a useful term because I'm not entirely sure what it means except that it's not severe or deleterious.

Baby had been listening to all these words barrelling past his ears and he was getting tired of understanding only one third of them.

Baa baa black sheep, said Baby. When the bough breaks. Have you any flowers in your garden all contrary?

What happened to Baby? asked Hailu. Why is he talking such gibberish?

Perhaps he has picked up our habits already, said Golyga. Let's give him something better to occupy his mind, shall we? Let's see him experience at first hand the feel of fire.

What are you thinking? shouted Lillykins. Are you out of your mind? Do you intend to burn Baby?

Golyga and Hailu looked at Lillykins as though she was the one gone berserk.

What a thought, said Golyga. Whatever gave you that idea?

But you said...you said... Lillykins tried to remember Golyga's precise words. But since she'd gotten even her brother's name wrong, it wasn't likely she'd remember his precise words, was it?

There was "hand" in it, and "experience fire," and didn't that mean burn, baby, burn?

Okay, said Lillykins. Tell me what exactly you had in mind.

Will do, said Golyga. And then he took the baby's hand and held it right inside his mouth.

All of it—that's how small the hand was and how big Golyga's mouth was at that moment.

Baby wiggled his fingers in Golyga's mouth and tickled his tonsils.

Stop that, gurgled Golyga. No fooling around, please. I have a precise lesson to teach and you have to hold still for it.

Golyga bent down toward the flames shooting from caterpillar/dragon Hailu's mouth. He opened his mouth, brought it even closer to the flames, and inhaled.

Ooooh, hot, said Baby. Very hot.

Exactly, said Golyga. And if not wet at the same time, burning.

Unfortunately, because Baby's hand was still in his mouth, the words came out garbled and Baby understood him to say: Take out your hand and put it into the flame. So Baby did that and screeched.

And Lillykins jumped and pushed Golyga out of the way of the flames. And Hailu turned himself into a brook. And Golyga popped Baby off his shoulders and into the brook.

And Baby turned himself into a trout.

And Lillykins sat on the shore of the brook and wept.

And Golyga sat down beside her and mumbled and mumbled and felt awful.

And Hailu jumped up and down, up and down, giving the trout the ride of its life.

And Baby giggled, in a troutlike way, and bubbled and flipped and enjoyed himself tremendously.

Until Golyga and Lillykins stopped everything and watched and started smiling. And so everything and everybody was fine again.

Now, said Hailu the brook. Let's just recapture what exactly you learned here, Baby.

Flames are hot. They burn you. Water puts out the burning. I will never again go near flames. Golyga made a mistake and Lillykins will give him a hard time over it.

Wrong, said Lillykins. Nobody can know everything in advance. The best you can do is to prepare, be alert, and then flow with it. A lesson you might like to pay attention to as well, baby boy.

I will, I will, said Baby. Though I'll probably need to do that lesson more than once. I mean, it's not like the lesson of flames, is it?

A bit more advanced, said Golyga, that's true. But you're a smart little tyke. You'll learn it fast enough.

Good, said Baby. For now, I'm having too good a time, swimming and flipping, to engage in any more pedagogy. I'm gone, babies. Catch you later!

And away he flipped and swam, before Lillykins or Golyga could say another word.

And Hailu?

I'll be back when you get my name right! he called, and flowed along, rolling up the waters behind him as he went.

And that is where we are going to leave them all today.

LILLY: I notice that your instalments are always relevant to current situations in my life and learning. Thank you very much, Golyga. And thank you for wrapping the lessons in such entertaining garb.
GOLYGA: You are welcome. Until soon, Lillykins. Oh, pardon me—Lilly, I mean.
LILLY: I am so tempted to look up Lillykins' brother's name.
GOLYGA: Go for it.
LILLY: All right…it's "Hylie." What a surprise!

* * *

And now we're getting on with another instalment so we can finally determine the answers to a number of questions that have arisen about this work.

First, though this is an adventure story, we are pleased to tell you at this time that it is also an educational tome, well-disguised though that aspect is.

Second, we are going to pull together all the strands eventually to give our readers the satisfying feeling of a universe in harmony, with all questions answered and all loose ends neatly tied. Unrealistic though such an ending is, it seems to respond to a hunger in the human psyche and we see no reason not to satisfy this hunger. Obviously, no one can construe this tale as anything but fantasy, so there is no danger that humans will suddenly begin to expect neat endings in life, or even all questions answered and all loose ends tied.

Third, both Lillykins and Golyga will reappear at some future date in other tales to be told and they will want to have a starting platform that is not merely a collection of tangled, chaotic planks. They will want to start with a strong basis underfoot from which to take off and begin their new series of adventures.

LILLY: You are not, I hope, suggesting the present series of adventures is drawing to a close?
GOLYGA: Not indeed. Merely clarifying some premises as we go along. Lest you, dear Lilly, become impatient with the meandering nature of this tale-unfolding.
LILLY: I wouldn't. I am, even as I take this down, admiring your elegance of language and your precision.
GOLYGA: Thank you. Flattery always welcome. Now.

To ensure that all our characters will be equally engaged in exciting ongoing endeavours, we will concentrate on Hailu for today. Hailu, who but recently was a brook, rolled himself up in the wake of the baby/trout, then set off on his own. He was going to find himself a lovely young friend because he was getting jealous of his sister's marvellous relationship with her mate Golyga.

Yes, marvellous relationship. You heard right. What would you call it when there is mutual respect, enjoyment of each other's being, and, above all, a connection so strong and everlasting that neither ever even contemplates not having the other as partner and mate and friend and lover. What would you call that?

A rhetorical question, yes.

So Hailu took off, hoping for something at least similar and certainly exciting, and the first being he encountered, on a hillside covered with buttercups, was a butterfly. A lovely red-and-green-and-yellow-and-black-and-white butterfly. A veritable eruption of colours in a light light-being of beauty and joy.

Hello, said Hailu, taking on the shape and form of a rather jaunty-looking grasshopper. You're a fine-looking beauty to behold. Could I convince you to hang out for a bit, maybe sip some dew together, enjoy some music? I could play for you... Hailu sat up on his hind legs and began imitating a violinist, à la some cartoons he'd seen.

The butterfly looked at him briefly and laughed and laughed as she flew about here and there in a circle all around Hailu the grasshopper. Hailu was getting dizzy, trying to keep his eyes on her, so he lay down on his back and breathed deeply and calmly, intending to sit up again and try another approach with the lovely butterfly.

But when he sat up, she was gone.

Hailu sighed and, in a melancholy sort of way, played a little tune on his hind legs. Then he took off again, until he saw, way up on top of the hill, a lovely white mountain goat with a long silky beard. A nanny goat, he said to himself. In other words, a female, and very regal and beautiful she is, too.

Up popped Hailu, up the hillside, taking on the form of a mountain goat as he went. Unfortunately, he forgot the hooves, so his feet were rather sore when he reached the top, and he had immediately to find a brook and insert his chafed and hurting little feet.

Ouch, ouch, ouch, said Hailu. Wish I hadn't been so quick to see and chase. In fact, maybe "seeing and chasing" isn't the way to go with this kind of thing. Maybe seeing and chasing gets you nothing but sore feet and other unpleasant consequences. Maybe I ought to ask Golyga and Lillykins exactly how they found each other in this vast and complicated universe. I mean, did they just bump into each other somewhere and both knew they were each other's mate? Could there be a secret to recognizing one another I don't know but ought to learn? Do I have to be in an altogether different frame of mind than this urge to mate? What, what, what?

Hailu shook his head. Why didn't he ask all these questions of Golyga when he was around? His sister Lillykins would not be the person to ask because she was too likely to give him a lecture on the subject just because he was the younger. Golyga, on the other hand, was likely to make an amusing adventure tale out of the life lesson or maybe even introduce him to a likely somebody...but where *was* Golyga?

Hailu remembered a method of calling for Golyga revealed to him by Golyga himself on the occasion of a rather nasty fall Hailu had

had—chasing a young deer, as it happens—and this method went as follows:

Make a fire on top of a hill, surround it with rocks, and let the smoke rise for two seconds at a time, covering the flames with a blanket or poncho or whatever was handy for five seconds in between.

You mean smoke signals, right? Hailu had asked Golyga, and Golyga had said: Yes, of course, but isn't there much more interest and dramatic tension if you say "two seconds smoke and then…" etc., etc.?

Hailu had complained to himself, at the time, that Golyga was rather too fond of being a teacher, making every little thing an occasion for teaching, and whatever made Golyga think that Hailu was trying to become a writer who cared about dramatic tension and such, but anyway, now that he needed to remember the method, there it sat, right in the front part of his mind, and Hailu had to say to himself: I guess dramatic tension makes you remember better, too, so anyway, here I go.

Hailu made the fire, blew the smoke signals up into the sky, and waited for Golyga to appear. Waited and waited for quite a while because Golyga was by now engaged in a much more urgent undertaking than that of teaching Hailu how to find a mate. Golyga was, in fact, engaged in a matter of life and death, and you'll hear about that before too long, I'm sure.

LILLY: I hope so.
GOLYGA: It's not entirely up to me, as you know.
LILLY: True. So I'll say: I hope so and certainly intend to make it possible very soon. Thank you for this, Golyga.

* * *

GOLYA: We have loose ends to tie up and we have also to give you further instructions for organizing material. On the other hand, we could just indulge ourselves and do a new episode to add to the main part of the book. What say you?
LILLY: I'm ready for anything.
GOLYGA: Good. We think it best to give you a bit of a lift by way of an episode to enjoy, so here we go…

Golyga was on the run. He'd had no contact with anyone for ages because he couldn't bear to be seen in the shape he was in. If you remember, a chafing feather under his arm/wing was, long ago, an irritation to our dear Golyga. Now it has recurred and worsened to become a disastrous patch of mayhem. Yes, we are not exaggerating. The patch of skin under his arm was taking on a terrible strength and power of its own, demanding this and that, causing Golyga to fly hither and yon to act on its demands. How, you say, can a patch of skin grow so imperious and obnoxious? Well, think about it: if Golyga's entire self was capable of being anything he pleased in the way of form—in other words, if he could shape-shift himself into anything he wanted, then any part of himself could do likewise. His arm might decide to become a worm while the other arm might decide on an aardvark and seek to reach the worm arm forthwith. Yes, yes, such developments are entirely possible if you let your skills and powers run away with you and don't keep a common focus and intention going at all times.

Right now, Golyga had neither focus nor intention except one: not to be seen arguing with the patch of skin under his arm, no matter what. So he ran and hid and generally made himself miserable as can be. Until, one day, he ran into a great blue blob—the very same one Lillykins had encountered—and the blob, humming and throbbing with the pulse of life and love, simply engulfed poor, silly Golyga and kept him right in the middle of itself until Golyga stopped moving about and muttering and resigned himself to remaining in the middle of a blue blob and getting gradually suffused with a warmth and light and chuckle that relaxed him right to his very nerve cells.

That's better, said the blue blob and floated off, leaving behind a Golyga who was shaking his head, grinning, and holding one hand over the mutinous patch of skin under his arm.

When he had watched the blue blob disappear over the horizon, Golyga turned to the patch and told it to listen and listen well: Henceforth, patch of skin, you will behave, act, and live as part of the whole of my body—whether it be human-like, birdlike, or any other shape. You will attempt no mutinous behaviour because you will be immediately treated with ointments and unguents and band-aids and such, until you will be able neither to see nor breathe and will wish to have kept your rebellion well under wraps. You, patch of skin, will see yourself as part of this body, interacting with it for its highest good and being treated, in return, as part of its entirety and deserving of every respect and all the little goodies provided. Now, is that clear?

The patch of skin grumbled. It had rather enjoyed being autonomous and imperious and driving the entire Golyga body hither and yon. But it did have to concede that being smothered and bandaged was not its cup of tea, and so it muttered or growled its agreement.

Phew, thought Golyga. What would I have done if the patch had not agreed? I hate having stuff stuck on me. Well, let's see now what we can make of this tale so it can be useful as a teaching tool. Can we say that focus and intention are necessary for good health, happiness, the use of one's skills and powers, for any activity that includes a hammer and nails, and so on? Yes, we could say that but it would be rather redundant. Therefore let us say that focus and intention are the very building blocks of the material universe. As thought, with its energy, is sent by focused intention, so it has a target into which its energy goes. Dispersed energy of unfocused thought, or ambivalent intention, both result in mishmash—a bit of this, a bit of that, nothing to write home about. But use that same thought-energy with focused intention, and you will be astounded at the results.

Golyga knew all that, of course, hence his speech to the patch of skin about straying and dispersing the energy focus of the whole. Hence his head-shaking when the blue blob had restored him to knowledge of his focus, for his entirety—the joy of life. And his grin at his own foolishness for hiding and running about instead of sitting down and talking to his patch of skin.

You might have been more kind about it, said the patch—being privy to all Golyga's thoughts. You might have threatened less and been more inviting.

Sure, said Golyga. But would you have listened? I remember well that I tried reasoning with you at the beginning of the rash, but you stubbornly determined to go your own way in this.

Well, said the patch of skin. You didn't exactly pay a great deal of attention to the irritation either. You kept thinking other things more important than just a patch of skin, remember?

Golyga had to admit that was true. There had been the advent of the baby, and then—goodness, one thing after another; he had to admit to being less than focused…

No, no, wait a minute, said Golyga. You'll have me living by a rigid schedule and agenda next. Life happens. This and that go on, whether you plan it or not. So yes, there were some more important things than a patch of irritated skin and that's the way it was.

The patch became huffy in tone. If we're not worth even a few moments of time here and there, even a nugget of attention—

Oh, stuff it, said Golyga. Stop whining and blathering. Let's just say I might have struck a better balance between roaring about in life and ignoring you or, on the other hand, making a schedule for inspecting every little patch of skin and each tooth and toe and— Well, you know what I mean. Balance. All right. I suppose you'll want to take credit for reminding me of this necessary element for living a good life?

The patch of skin sighed, satisfied. Finally, it seemed to say, he's got it. By Jove, he's got it. And in a flash, the scarlet of its rash faded, the bumps undulated for a moment and then smoothed out, and the itch and discomfort disappeared.

Golyga sighed, too, and relaxed and stroked his patch of skin in gratitude.

And what about the feather, you say? The feather he picked up in Viberion that had caused the problem in the first place and had been a message to or from a certain king? Are we to forget altogether about this feather?

Well, yes, we might as well, because Golyga certainly had. In all the ongoing commotion of life, he had long ago forgotten all about that feather—as well as a number of other things—and right now is no time to remind him of it. Right now, he is busy making sure he remembers all he was reminded of today: that three ingredients of the good life are intention, focus, and balance.

LILLY: I take it you are suggesting I should stop berating the parts of my body not functioning at optimum capacity?
GOLYGA: You can take it. You can also look at it this way: when any part of your physical being is not "in the fold," it is lacking in the support and life force it needs.

Consciously make the connection by way of blood vessels and arteries, by way of nerves and messages and loving vibrations. You can bring in healing energies from anywhere and everywhere and you can also focus and direct them to the areas where they are most needed. If you can't exercise, keep energies moving by other means: baths, massages, the energy waves of continuum, mentally exercising and moving— you can go and do your beloved skiing, mentally. Or swim in the lake. We are not suggesting this as a substitute for the real thing when that is possible, but only for times when actual physical exercise is not in the cards. So yes, altogether this section was in part for your benefit and in part for the reader's, and isn't that how we have always worked?

LILLY: Yes, and so you have helped me enormously and I appreciate it.

GOLYGA: You're welcome, my dear. Now go lie down and let us do our adjustments. See you soon, yes?

* * *

GOLYGA: And so we return to the endeavour at hand and hope that Lilly's headache is the last for a while. Clouds of dust will be transformed into the billowing of thousands of wings as they sail in the skies above San Miguel de Allende, leaving Lilly in paroxysms of joy as she sits on her rooftop, ogling their display. And now on with our tale.

Lillykins was ogling a very different sort of sight altogether as she sat on the riverbank and contemplated her immediate plans. She was devastated by the responsibility she had taken on with the education of Baby and not at all sure she was up to it. Not that she had any intention of letting Golyga know about this uncertainty. It was Lillykins' firm conviction that men had better be told about half of what she knew and felt, in terms suitable for a child of few years, little experience, and no tolerance for the frustrations of life. Golyga, however, had a way of making her spill the beans, as they say, and so Lillykins sat there and, quite frankly, did her best to come up with a plan so subversive and outrageous that she herself had some scruples about it. However, before she had even finished formulating this outrageous plan, along came another creature to divert her attention. This one was an oblong, undulating, and resolutely meowing catterpicker.

LILLY: Is that correct?
GOLYGA: Yes, it is. A catterpicker is not familiar to you, I know, but it is, nevertheless, a creature Lillykins is encountering even as we speak.

The catterpicker then sat down right beside Lillykins and said to her: You have been thinking, I see.

How do you know that? asked Lillykins, looking down at the little catterpicker.

You're a strange colour I only see on those who have been heavily engaged in thinking. Do you not believe you had better stop it and get on with some living? You might do yourself harm if you go on like this.

But thinking isn't bad for you, surely? It's an important activity and leads to clear action and lucid living. Is that not so, you cute little catterpicker?

The catterpicker looked up at Lillykins, and she thought he had a rather contemptuous expression on his little snout. Perhaps she ought not to be thinking him cute, after all.

Let me tell you this, said the catterpicker. There was a time when I, too, engaged in the activity of thinking and eventually became that ghastly colour you are now sporting on your countenance. However, one fine day I realized that all the thinking I'd been doing had brought me not one whit closer to living life with enjoyment, and I decided forthwith to give up thinking and begin having a good time.

But that's totally irresponsible of you, said Lillykins. How can you justify a thoughtless life in the face of all the ills and wrongs that need to be righted. Not to speak of your own learning curve.

Ha! said the catterpicker. You have no idea what all I've learned since I stopped thinking. I tell you, the amount to be learned by living in the NOW and bringing about the best possible attention on whatever the NOW has to offer—that is all the learning anybody ever needs to move forward on the path of wisdom, and at a great rate. As for the ills and wrongs of the world, why, let everyone do as I do and there will be none.

What are you talking about? Let everybody be irresponsibly and thoughtlessly undulating through life and all will be well? You're nuts.

Hahahaha, laughed the catterpicker. This is delicious. You are calling me nuts? You are sitting here turning grey in the face; even the blood in your veins is sluggish with all the stop and go your thoughts are causing it, and you are telling me, the one who is in robust and delicious health, mood, and undulatingness, that *I* am nuts? Show me one thing your thinking has improved and I'll consider your words seriously. Until then, just let me happily undulate in the NOW and you go on getting grey in the face and we'll see who spreads more joy and compassion in the world, okay?

Lillykins didn't know what to say to that.

An unexamined life is... she started, and then lost her train of thought. In fact, the train of thought had left the station and taken off for parts unknown, and Lillykins was left behind, sitting beside the happily undulating catterpicker, and there wasn't a thought left in her head. For a second or less, she began to panic. Then she couldn't come up with a good reason for that, having no thoughts available to her, and so she let the panic dissolve and go. And sat there, quietly, unthinkingly, noting with astonishment that her body was beginning to undulate.

What a delightful feeling this is, said Lillykins to the catterpicker. I had no idea that undulating was so deliciously pleasurable. Why, I may just sit here for the rest of my life and undulate.

There you go making plans again, said the catterpicker. You're quite incorrigible, aren't you? Never mind. Try it on a regular basis and after a while you'll get the knack of undulating thoughtlessly and happily and giving no one at all a hard time. Good luck to you and yours, said the catterpicker, and disappeared. Zip. Just like that.

Lillykins looked around but saw no catterpicker anywhere. However, her own undulating was continuing, and so she didn't give it one single thought and went right on being deliciously in the NOW.

We are going to leave her there for now and see her again at our next session. Obviously, Lillykins is nowhere near mastering the technique of undulating in the NOW, so we will have more story to tell, but why disturb her when she is actually getting some practice in the delight of living thoughtlessly.

GOLYGA: *What do you think about that, Lilly?*

LILLY: Obviously, I am often of Lillykins' mind. To abdicate all responsibility is to live a selfish life.

GOLYGA: Let your first goal be to harm no one and you'll see how lofty an achievement undulating in the NOW actually is. But we'll talk of this again, dear Lilly. Meantime, a little undulating may well do your headaches some good. So long, my dear. Enjoy.

LILLY: Thank you. And yes, I'll practise some undulating.

GOLYA: As long as you don't get too serious and determined to get it right. Instead, let the moment flow through you, and as it does…enjoy! So long!

* * *

GOLYGA: Not so soon, after all. Well, things happen. Life happens. San Miguel de Allende and a 6,400-foot elevation happens. And here we are again, as though no time at all has passed and we have not crossed a continent or changed climate or been otherwise transported in any way. As is certainly true of me, Golyga. I have been busy devising the most marvellous plan for you, my dear Lilly, so you'll be able to be in touch more often and enjoy our endeavour on a regular basis. I have provided a sunny apartment with a grand view, both conducive to staying on course rather than escaping dark walls and gallivanting with company instead of advancing your work as planned.

LILLY: Thank you. I know the new apartment will help me to a productive time.

GOLYGA: And in the meantime, here we are nevertheless, in touch and ready for another instalment of our adventure story, yes?

LILLY: Yes. I am looking forward to it.

GOLYGA: We'll make it a short one today because you do have to rest and bring about increased health after this bout of the cold—both in and outside your body. So here we go.

Lillykins was about to become a very different shape, thinking idly of lizards in the sun or blue birds in flight, when she realized the task at hand would best be served by adherence to a human form. And the task at hand was to make some decisions about Baby's education, as you remember, and to allow Golyga to take the lead while keeping a clear and critical eye on everything afoot.

So Lillykins kept her human form, but lest she get bored with this long sojourn in a human body, she decorated it with long tresses of silvery hair and a great smile and a hanging chin, down to her waist.

What, you don't think that an attractive feature? Well, you obviously don't know the advantages of a chin hanging to the waist. For example, you can always use it for storage of various favourite foods, you can bring it into play with the elements to determine what to wear by just sticking it out the window, if any, and you can also attract other long-chinned beings like pelicans and duck-billed platypuses. Which is what happened almost immediately. A duck-billed platypus caught sight of Lillykins and her chin and her long silvery tresses and flew close enough to communicate with her.

Hello, said he, ogling Lillykins and her wondrous chin. You are a most attractive sort of being, but what exactly are you?

Now, Lillykins had a great aversion to explaining herself, thinking it much too lengthy a subject for casual chatter with strangers. So she said, in a friendly but firm tone of voice: I am your future.

The duck-billed platypus was nonplussed. Whatever do you mean? he asked. I have no future. I have the present and I have this wonderful bill that juts chinlike in front of me, and that is all I have. The future is somewhere out there, floating around and possibly heading my way, but I don't *have* it, do I?

Lillykins was impressed. A wise duck-billed platypus was something new in her experience—in fact, any platypus was, so she decided to take him seriously enough to explain one thing about herself.

I am, she said, a creature given to much thought about the future. Well, perhaps not as much as some are given to it, but I do tend to zip into its nebulous realm rather frequently instead of, as you point out, being where I already am, which is in the present.

Fascinating, said the duck-billed platypus. And what do you do there, in the nebulous and problematic (because fluid) future, when you zip into it?

I suppose I project onto it what I know about the present and remember from the past.

In other words, said the platypus, you restrict it out of your limited knowledge of possibilities, leaving it less munificent than it might be.

That's rather well put, said Lillykins. And you are right. My goodness, who would have guessed that giving myself a long chin would bring about this profound change in my thinking. I will endeavour henceforth not to zip into the future but to enjoy with all my might what I do have, which is the present. And thank you, dear stranger, for your wisdom and insight.

No hay problema, said the duck-billed platypus. But now I do have to be going because my present stomach is grumbling about present emptiness, and as that is an uncomfortable state, I feel moved to change it. I do hope to see you and your lovely chin again. Adios and hasta luego!

The duck-billed platypus took off, skimming along as though sliding through the air, and Lillykins remained behind and thought about his words. Then she noticed that her own stomach was making roiling sounds and motions and she decided to dine on something delectable. Perhaps a bit of seaweed, if such were available, or a rather small but sweet-tasting fish by the name of Howard.

We shall leave Lillykins here, and when we resume our story, we won't even bother to say "bon appetite" because we'll be concerned with some entirely different developments of the story that will drive all thoughts of food right out of our minds.

And so we say "until soon" and end our instalment for the day.

LILLY: Thank you, Golyga. Both enjoyable and enlightening, as always.
GOLYGA: You are welcome, my dear. Appreciation always appreciated. Remember that and give yourself some of it—just the fact that you are able to be a conduit under such very different conditions and with ease, too, should send you off to buy yourself a little appreciation gift. From us to you. Okay?
LILLY: Thank you, I will. Until soon then.
GOLYGA: Yes, until soon, my dear.

* * *

GOLYGA: And so we go on—different country, different apartment, different year of your life, Lilly dear, and we go on, spinning our tale. Ready?
LILLY: Yes, I am.

Lillykins, as you remember, had just decided to do nothing precipitous in relation to anything ever again. It was her intention to learn from the ways of the platypus, to remain firmly ensconced in the NOW and be not a whit dismayed by any developments that might or might not occur in the future. And so she sat, on the riverbank, and began to breathe most deliciously, with nothing on her mind but the sweet breath going in and out of her body, the sweet sound of water as it moved past her, sitting there on the riverbank, and the even sweeter sound of birds in the air. Much like the birds you are hearing, Lilly dear, from the rooftops of San Miguel de Allende.

The difference was that Lillykins could not sustain all that sweetness for long. So used was she to Sturm und Drang and other absurdities of Western thought that she soon began to feel guilty. Guilty about not being engaged in some form of work, some form of difficulty, some form of devising plans, some endeavour that would prove to her she was a worthwhile creature on this planet or any other and would be acceptable to all those who expect achievement as proof of worthwhileness. As a result, Lillykins soon got up, dove into the waters of the river to wash away her sloth and insolent time of non-endeavour, and came up…with a mouthful of mud.

This, she said to herself, is what comes of doing anything without proper planning and anticipating all possibilities and angles and taking precautions.

Not at all, said a voice from the deep. This is what comes from leaving the state of grace and being, and diving into the murky mud of guilt, strain, and ridiculous endeavours to be other than fully alive.

Who are you? asked Lillykins, looking around and seeing no one who might have spoken those words.

Never mind who, said the voice. Listen to what I am saying to you.

I'm not listening to any invisible beings, said Lillykins. How do I know you even exist?

How many voices of non-existent beings have you heard in your life? asked the voice, and Lillykins had to concede that she had never actually heard the voice of a non-existent being.

On the other hand, she said, I've not heard voices of invisible beings before either.

That's what you think, said the voice. Try to recall the times in your life when you were at crossroads and the voices in your head proliferated. Wasn't there always at least one voice that surprised you and tried to teach you something new and quite without precedent in your thinking?

Lillykins tried to recall crossroads in her life. There was the time she went off by herself to a distant planet and found that neither walking nor swimming nor even flying could bring her from one point to another. Stumped about how to move forward, she had asked for advice of the powers that be and heard a voice tell her to stop moving. That she was, in fact, in a place where movement occurred on the inside, not out in space, and she was at that very moment moving very rapidly indeed.

Lillykins was so surprised that she stopped all motion in space and looked into herself. She found that everything inside of her was in motion. Not only her blood and her breath but the very cells of her body and all the components therein—all were rapidly and gracefully and delightfully moving in a dance of life. Lillykins was astounded and captivated for quite some time. Then she recalled her mind to the task she thought she had at hand—a task she could no longer remember, alas—and left that planet of interior movement.

Well, you are right, said Lillykins to the invisible voice. And so I intend to accept your existence without further proof. But could you at least give me some idea of the kind of creature you are? I'd appreciate it.

Of course, said the voice. I am a creature of the deep. I am a dweller in the mud. Whenever I have to get a message through to such creatures as you, that is. The rest of the time I am a dweller in Light and there I am known as the right honourable Golyga.

Oh, for heaven's sake, said Lillykins. Golyga is not invisible. I have seen him any number of times in all kinds of shapes and guises, and there is no need, if it really is you, Golyga, to be so mysterious, suddenly, and so utterly without scruples as to lie to me about your nature.

By now Lillykins had confused herself altogether. If this was Golyga, why didn't he show himself in some form or other? If it wasn't, why claim he was?

The voice said: Aha! Now you are confused and that is excellent. Because it is out of confusion that new learning emerges. Certainties tend to be mind-closers, but confusion is a state of fluid and open-ended thought processes that allow the new to enter. Good on you, said the voice.

As for who I really am, why, I do believe I'll let you in on that secret during our next session.

LILLY: You really are a master of the cliffhanger.
GOLYGA: Thank you, my dear. And you are getting to be a master of channelling my little tale. Hardly a balk at any turn of events in the tale, and no objections at all to their sometimes unfathomable direction.
LILLY: I am enjoying the surprises, actually.
GOLYGA: Good. See you soon then.
LILLY: Yes, and thank you.

* * *

There was no longer any doubt in Golyga's mind that the advent of the baby was a good thing. Having accrued much pleasure in this creature's company, he was willing to admit that he was totally delighted and utterly smitten with the little tyke. However, Lillykins' propensity to worry about him and his education gave him both pause and dyspepsia—he had to do something to get her off that worry kick and onto the pleasurable aspects of the experience. And how to do that eluded him at this moment.

What exactly was there to worry about, was the question he had to ask her, but Lillykins wasn't holding still for questions. She was off and flying somewhere or other, trying to assuage her worries by getting away from them. Not something humans are wont to do, of course. They never take off for a holiday, leaving worries behind, and then come back and find them waiting—and bigger than ever. No, Lillykins hoped that Golyga would take care of some of her worries, or at least reduce their size. Not something Golyga was able to do, these being her worries and, he thought, totally unnecessary as well. So he sat and worried about it all for a while and then jumped up, yanked the baby out of his musings, and took off, intending to find Lillykins and give her a piece of his now very disturbed mind.

Hey! yelled Baby, so rudely dislodged from his own concerns. Why are you yanking me about like this? I was busy studying the language of rocks. I've already learned that some rocks whisper and others roar, and I was about to get the first lesson in rocks' warning signs, which would be useful to anyone near them when they are about to split, burst, roll, or get very slippery underfoot. Now you've interrupted, and who knows when they'll be in the mood again to teach me.

Sorry, said Golyga. I really am sorry. I herewith promise not to interrupt any more lessons you are learning but to wait patiently and maybe learn along with you rather than disturb the flow of your education.

Okay then, grumbled Baby. Leave me here and tell Lillykins to please not interrupt me either, with her constant designs for my education. I'm really too busy getting my education to be bothered like that.

Golyga promised he would tell Lillykins, but really, he couldn't leave Baby all alone, not yet—so they would both simply stay put and wait for Lillykins to return.

And that is what they did, amiably and happily learning as they waited, and then playing some amazingly silly games they both enjoyed, and then falling asleep together in the shade of a big moss-covered rock who sang them a lovely lullaby for hours and hours—rock time being rather more generous than most other creatures'.

LILLY: Is that it?
GOLYGA: Yes.

It is a reiteration of something said, but we feel it needs saying over and over in the context of present beliefs about children's education. Think about all the equipment, all the theories, the many words spilled over the subject of education, which is really so very simple a matter of following a child's interests and answering questions. Yes, that takes personal interest and a completely different ratio of child and teacher. On the other hand, education is not confined to classrooms and official teachers, is it? If a rock can be a teacher, and an ant, then why worry so much about universal provisions of computers? If somebody studying ants with deep attention can discover the cure for epilepsy, say, why spend millions on semi-educating a thousand scientists? Why make all these universal rules when everything on this Earth has as its prime characteristic that it is unique, one of a kind, diverse, wonderfully other, and all one at the same time?

These questions are meant to stimulate your mind, to allow some air into ruts of thinking, to encourage the exploration of new ideas or the rediscovery of old discarded ones. There is such bountiful rich fodder for the mind, if you but free it of useless worry and old ruts. There is sheer unmitigated excitement for anyone willing to spring forth out of those ruts and begin the journey of discovery—of, i.e., true education.

GOLYGA: That's it for now, Lilly dear. We want to leave you with this amount that you will be able to place rather easily, we think, and will continue next time we get together.

* * *

GOLYGA: And so we resume our tale, once again in Toronto. You, that is.
LILLY: And you?
GOLYGA: Wouldn't you like to know?
LILLY: Yes, I would. Very much.
GOLYGA: Want to join me?
LILLY: Depends on where you are and what I would have to undergo to get there.
GOLYGA: Aha! Prevarications and precautions and conditions. How human.
LILLY: I don't claim to be anything else.
GOLYGA: How about a human willing to fling herself onto the bosom of the universe in complete trust and surrender?
LILLY: Not there yet, as you well know. Though I can now sense that it isn't beyond the realm of the possible that I will be there someday.
GOLYGA: Make it soon, will you. We'd have a great time, if you did.
LILLY: You're the one who can see all time—does it look to you that I'll make it in this lifetime?
GOLYGA: That would be telling! No, my dear, I am not in the business of prediction, and you know it. I am in the business of teaching and entertaining, so let's get on with that, shall we?
LILLY: Right.

Golyga of the Tale is no longer as malleable, in this episode, as we have come to know him. Golyga is, in fact, rather incensed and would like it known he has no intention of getting himself tied into knots about anything to do with Baby's education, ever again. Golyga, you see, has decided that Baby ought to learn as he goes along, growing up, by way of whatever experiences come his way. And that planning and devising educational experiences for Baby is not only a waste of time but counterproductive.

As who says? Lillykins wants to know. And whatever do you mean by all this fiddle fuddle? Have you merely turned lazy and so want to abdicate your responsibility as an educator?

No, said Golyga. I want merely to state that true education is a matter of living consciously and that many attempts at learning are hampered by shutting down some faculties at the expense of other faculties. Not a complicated concept. All you need to do is to look at schoolchildren sitting at their desks or even on the floor, among cushions and books, in order to see that they have to shut down a large number of faculties to be able to sit there and concentrate on but a few.

What are you suggesting—a sort of noble savage–style education in the wild? Where are you going to find the wild these days?

Not at all, said Golyga. Let me demonstrate:

Baby wanders off on his own. Before either of us reaches him to retrieve and prevent him from further exploration, he has learned: how the stuff under his feet responds when he steps on it, how he responds when he falls on it, how the sounds around him tell him what's going on, what the sensations of his senses tell him about the world, and whether or not he wishes to continue in the direction he has taken. Now, isn't that a whole lot more than he would have learned in the same time while sitting at a desk, reading or doing arithmetic?

And when, asked Lillykins, do you suggest that Baby learn reading and arithmetic? Or are you saying those skills are not important?

You know me better than that, said Golyga. And you can figure out for yourself that Baby will be motivated, sooner or later, to learn both reading and arithmetic in a quick and thorough fashion. Whether by way of signs or marbles or the thirst of the imagination to experience more than his body can sustain in any given hour.

Well, said Lillykins. I don't object to giving your method a try, Golyga, but I am warning you: if any harm comes to Baby, be prepared for eternal accusations!

Oh, good lord, said Golyga. As though no harm ever came to a child in school or in school-related activities. What about falling on his face in the paved-over schoolyard? What about getting pushed into a river on the way to or from school? What about—

All right, all right, said Lillykins. But I still have an objection: our baby here might benefit from your kind of educational method, but many children on Earth are left to just such an education and they never learn to read and write and are stuck in menial jobs all their life. What about that?

Ah yes, said Golyga. The Universal Education question. Let me tell you, Lillykin, I am not a believer in universal anything. I tell you frankly, I am a believer in the unique and appropriate. As to the children of India, say, or of Mexico, at work by age four and for the rest of their lives, it's not a matter of lacking education that has them hawking and begging on the streets. It's a lack of humanity's ability to love.

How so? The parents might well love them every bit as much as we love Baby.

True. I was not speaking of parents in particular. I was speaking of humanity. Let humanity be motivated by love—whether in the matter of children and their education, or anything else—and you won't see anyone on the street begging, nor any children at work before their time.

Oh, Golyga, said Lillykins. You've just taken flight into the biggest generalization of them all. Didn't you just say you believe in the unique and appropriate?

Well, you tell me when love is not appropriate, and tell me also whether love is not unique in every single case of it that you know of. As unique as the humans involved in feeling it.

Lillykins sighed. Once again, Golyga had won a discussion's main points, and she'd lost, somewhere along the line, track of her own arguments. Nevertheless, she was not willing to give up all notion of formal education.

Oh, neither am I, said Golyga. I wish only to ensure that Baby have a good start on living and on learning through living before he gets behind a desk. And that humans stop trying to apply general and universal rules where only the unique and appropriate will actually do the job well.

Okay, said Lillykins. Okay. Now can we leave this behind and try to get more entertaining again by the next instalment?

Most certainly, said Golyga. In fact, I apologize profoundly for being so serious and preachy today. I blame it on Lilly, of course.

LILLY: Hey, wait a minute. Why me?

GOLYGA: Because your channelling definitely had a feel of "should" attached today.

LILLY: Well, it seemed to me high time to resume our work together.

GOLYGA: Phooey and yuck. A most unfortunate thought form, that. In future, please await the urging of joy and "want to" and the movement toward delight, before you get in touch for a next session.

LILLY: Okay. Sorry if I dragged you in in the wrong frame of mind.

GOLYGA: Heavy, heavy! Lighten up, my dear. Do you really think anybody "drags" me in?

LILLY: I guess not. Okay then, I promise to wait until an urging toward joy brings us together again.

GOLYGA: Good on you. See you then. And in the meantime, have a great old time for yourself!

LILLY: Thank you, Golyga.

* * *

Golyga, the mighty intellect and talent, was shaking his head at the absurdity of his situation. Here he was, in charge of a baby's education and certainly capable of the task, and yet here was Lillykins, claiming he was less than perfect as the teacher and loco parentis for said baby. How to assuage his bruised sensibility?

Gloomy and glum—a rarity in Sunshine Golyga—he looked out over the waters, up at the sky, and then let out a great whoop of a laugh. A hoot of joy. A galloping, caterwauling, rollicking yodel with echoes attached.

The reason for all that ruckus?

Golyga had remembered the old saying "the proof is in the pudding." All he had to do was produce a perfect mature adult in place of Baby or out of him, so to speak—and voilà!—proof of pudding.

At this point, however, Golyga had to stop and ask himself how he would do that, exactly, and then he was back at the beginning again and now no better off. Or was he? The rollicking joy and confidence he had felt and yodelled but for a moment found their way to a place where rollicking joy and confidence dwelt side by side, or perhaps one kitty corner from the other, and there Golyga's addition wafted in, blew about a bit, and then the whole lot of joy and confidence suddenly expanded tenfold, took a little running start, and lifted up into the ether, there to gather together all other yodels of joy and confidence, until the mass was a planet-sized kingdom of delight, with not a bit of anxiety anywhere, and it was in this kingdom that many wonderful beings and thoughts and creations came to be, to grow, to dwell in harmony, peace, and joy, and anytime anyone has the wish and sets the intention, they can go visit there, to enjoy, to learn, to dwell in the peace of it, to dance with the joy of it, and so on.

Golyga knew the place well, having helped to create it. He was always happy to go there, and now, suddenly, Golyga knew exactly what to do about Baby's education and upbringing. He swept Baby up and flew off to the Kingdom of Peace, Joy, and Confidence, showing Baby how to get there and how he could go there any time he wanted to.

That, said Golyga to Baby, is the most important part in growing up: to have a place of peace and joy where you can learn confidence.

Fantastic, said Baby. I like it here. Especially those wonderful motorbikes I see. I think I'll go ride one!

Golyga was dumfounded. Of all the possibilities available to Baby, why would he pick something dangerous and inappropriate for his size and strength?

Baby was watching Golyga for his reaction. When Golyga didn't jump and yell or even shake his head, Baby shrugged.

Maybe, he said, I'll do that another time. Maybe I'll slide down the rainbow instead.

And off he went, sliding and splashing off the end of the rainbow into a silvery pond where big lily pads scooped him out and tossed him onto land.

The joyous ruckus Baby made was added to the general joy of the kingdom, making it grow and grow, and Golyga sat back and relaxed so completely, he fell fast asleep.

GOLYGA: *And that's where we'll leave the two of them for now. All right?*

LILLY: All right, yes. Thank you. Good to be working with you.
GOLYGA: You have not forgotten how, which is good to know, yes?
LILLY: Yes. I guess I was a bit nervous that I might have "lost it."
GOLYGA: Never fear—we are here to stay.

* * *

GOLYGA: We will devise our session today to be rather shorter than the last. We will also insist that you be joyous and deliriously happy, and therefore we propose an instalment of Lillykins, Golyga, Baby, and Hylu. What do you say?
LILLY: I'm delighted, of course.
GOLYGA: All right then.

One fine day, Hylu was sitting on his Thinking Rock, as he liked to call it, attempting to devise a plan for himself. He was not usually a great planner and always found it tedious to engage in such mental shenanigans, but on this occasion he decided a plan was necessary. He wanted to teach both Lillykins and Golyga a lesson about their treatment of Baby. Because, in Hylu's opinion, they were going about Baby's education all wrong and would end by screwing up the little fella more than somewhat. But how to engage in lesson-giving without getting their backs up? Both Lillykins and Golyga thought of themselves as knowledgeable and of Hylu as less than responsible, so teaching them anything was going to be tricky and had to be planned carefully and meticulously.

Hylu sat and thought and, finally, jumped up with a large, loud "Hurrah" and was sure he had found the plan that would see him to his goal. Off he went in search of Lillykins, Golyga, and Baby. Unfortunately, not one of the three was at that moment in a form easily recognizable because they were engaged in an experiment in shape-shifting. Lillykins was being a seagull, flying circles above the rock, which was Golyga, and Baby was a grasshopper, enjoying his time off from the serious endeavour of growing up as the offspring of Lillykins and Goylga.

Offspring? you ask. Well, in a manner of speaking, so let's let it go for now.

Hylu, hard on the lookout for the three, saw nothing resembling his expectations, so he sat down on the nearest rock to await inspiration.

Instead, his bum began to itch. He jumped up and scratched and found he'd almost stepped on a grasshopper. While he was apologizing to the little hopper, a seagull pooped on his head.

What in the world is going on here? asked Hylu. Can't a person sit quietly awaiting the fulfillment of his plan? Is there no peace while living in expectation of an endeavour? Why am I being bothered and bewildered?

Right at that moment, the seagull landed on the rock, the grasshopper jumped on its back, and Hylu suddenly understood that he had found Lillykins, Baby, and, yes, here was Golyga, rearing up into an unlikely position for any rock Hylu had ever seen.

All right, said Hylu. You've had your fun. Now let's get serious.

The shock of this pronouncement made each of the three pop out of their shape and into the more frequently used of human bodies.

Serious? said Lillykins. Did we hear you say "get serious"?

Yes, said Hylu. I have something to say to you and it's serious. Sit down and listen and don't interrupt me.

The three sat down and listened. But because the intent of being serious was so difficult for Hylu, he lost his concentration and focus and was suddenly at a loss. What was he going to say again? What was the plan? What exactly did he have in mind, with this plan? Hylu could remember none of it and he was becoming rather embarrassed, sitting there with three listeners and nothing to tell.

Well now, he said. I do believe I have something useful to impart and I certainly intend to impart it just as soon as I remember what it was... Hm...

Baby, meantime, was getting impatient, as babies do, and started crawling off and away. On his path he found an ant to study, a leaf-cutting ant that acted like a beast of burden—except when you looked for a while, you discovered it was part of a long line of ants, carrying, marching along, and—Baby was willing to bet—singing a working song he probably couldn't hear.

Can you hear the song these ants are singing? Baby asked the world in general, and it was Hylu who said: No, but that doesn't mean you couldn't if you tried.

I can't hear it, said Baby.

You mean not yet, said Hylu.

That's right, said Baby. Guess I'll sit here for a while to listen.

And there you have it, said Hylu to Golyga and Lillykins. That's what I came to tell you.

Golyga and Lillykins looked at each other. Hylu, they seemed to agree, was getting more than a little strange, especially with regards to Baby.

No, no, said Hylu. I know exactly what I'm saying. You are always trying to shove information down Baby's throat. But the best way for him to learn is to have a chance to explore, ask questions, get some guidance or pointers on how to proceed, and be left in peace to pursue his interest until it wanes.

Golyga and Lillykins looked at each other again, and this time they agreed, silently but fervently, that Hylu was getting not only more strange when it came to Baby, but altogether too wise for their comfort.

Have you been…thinking? asked Golyga. He didn't like to make such an accusation lightly, but it sure looked like that's what Hylu had been up to.

Well, yes, admitted Hylu. But not for very long.

And did you make a plan? asked Lillykins incredulously.

Well, yes, admitted her brother again. But it didn't actually work. Baby himself demonstrated the way he learns best, you see, so the plan was neither necessary nor useful after that.

The education of babies, said Golyga, is hardly your field of expertise, I would say, but truth to tell, dear Hylu, you have hit upon the best and most delightful way of executing the undertaking that I have encountered, and henceforth I intend to follow your directives to the letter.

Hylu stared at Golyga, open-mouthed. Golyga assumed it was because of his praise and unaccustomed humility, but Hylu started shaking his head.

You're missing the point, he said to Golyga. Follow Baby's lead, not mine. Be aware of Baby's interests, of the length and degree of it, and supply what knowledge and guidance he asks for.

Yes, yes, said Golyga. Exactly. What I meant, of course.

Lillykins, who had been unusually quiet throughout this exchange, spoke up.

Hylu, she said. You have become the brother I have always hoped for. Coming to the rescue when I get too intent on a goal to note the alternatives, supplying a perspective hitherto unsuspected, and generally being a wise, supportive counsellor.

Well, as long as that is clear then, said Hylu, so long for now. And off he took, changing himself into a flying rhinoceros and rolling about the sky in so hilarious a manner that the three watching from below were convulsed in laughter and abandoned all attempts at being serious for some time to come.

GOLYGA: That's all for today. As always, a pleasure working with you, Lilly dear. Until soon.

LILLY: Thank you very much. Until soon, I hope.

* * *

GOLYGA: Yes, we are here, we are ready to work, and we are glad you can join us on this auspicious day.

LILLY: Auspicious?

GOLYGA: Yes, of course. Can you think of a more appropriate and therefore auspicious day for the Golyga stories than April Fools' Day? Fun and games? Laughter and delight?

LILLY: You have a rather lofty view of April Fools' Day. It's generally more pranks and deceits, albeit amusing ones.

GOLYGA: Close enough. Let's have some fun, shall we?

LILLY: Always ready for fun.

All right then. We have left the three of them, Golyga, Lillykins, and Baby, delighting in the sight of Hylu as flying rhinoceros, and while that makes for an enjoyable visual tableau, we do have to get them all going and doing and moving on, don't we? Otherwise, we might imagine them forever sitting together, enjoying the sight of a flying rhino, accomplishing nothing useful, productive, or laudable ever again. Ah, yes. That bugaboo of "shoulds" and "really must dos" soon raised its head—in Lillykins' head, anyway—so she decided to call the others to attention about matters at hand.

For instance, she said, we really ought to do something about the tendency on the planet Earth, among its peoples, to be "best, first, greatest," and so on. It's a competitive attitude that many if not most people believe necessary for survival and certainly for flourishing in any field of endeavour. Never considering the very real and proven advantages of co-operation and group endeavour. Even when there is a group endeavour, there seems also to be the belief that a leader or boss is necessary or else the entire undertaking will fail. Lest this go on and on, with more and more deleterious effect on all those poor striving folks who are not the best, first, or greatest, let the three of us, said Lillykins, be an example to the peoples of Earth in the matter of co-operation, the ability to move forward happily and confidently together, one for all and all for one, and be the shining examples of—

Whoa, said Baby. I don't want to do any such thing right now. I want to learn how to fly like a rhino.

Lillykins looked at Golyga, who was about to burst with laughter but had no intention of trying to get Lillykins out of this one.

Lillykins couldn't decide whether to explain to Baby that rhinos don't generally fly—not the real ones, that is—not the ones that haven't been shape-shifted to... Oh, this was all difficult as can be, not to mention that nothing would come of Baby's learning to fly like a rhino except his own pleasure and the fun of watching him, but how could she even try to persuade him to do what she thought was a worthwhile endeavour when, as he might well put it, she wasn't the boss of everybody.

Lillykins let out a big sigh. Golyga managed to breathe out rather more gently than guffawing, and Baby, distracted by a butterfly, was wondering how it might combine the flight of a rhino with that of a butterfly. He was sure that would be a big first in the history of flying achievements.

And so we leave our three, rather as we did before but with considerably more of that forward motion in evidence that is welcome in any good storyline.

GOLYGA: All right?

LILLY: All right, thank you. Any more for today?

GOLYGA: No, that's it. But we'll be together again tomorrow so we can do more on this or any other segment.

LILLY: Fine, then. See you tomorrow.

* * *

GOLYGA: And here we are, overlooking the rooftops and church spires of San Miguel, the birds, washerwomen with laundry, and the unseen but heard children of a kindergarten below. And we are happy to say this environment is proving, after all, to be conducive to work, channelling, and healthy living. Good on you, Lilly, and good on us. Because I am sure you do not imagine that we had no hand in your sojourn in San Miguel?

LILLY: No, I do not imagine such a thing. Though for quite a while I was asking myself how I could have imagined I'd be all right, alone and so far from home, with all my old traumatic stuff triggered in many ways.

GOLYGA: Ah yes, the courage to be flinging yourself into the universe, and into the lap of Mother Earth, and onto the bosom of yours truly and his confreres. Now that you can see the results and their beneficial effects, would you say the future looks brighter for it?

LILLY: I would, though I'm still feeling the aftermath of fear and pain too much to be making plans for further flinging. But I'm also quite sure I'll be making such plans in the future.

GOLYGA: Alright then. Let's get on with the next instalment of our adventure story. This one will have Golyga as the main protagonist. After all, he is a key character and we can't leave him waiting in the wings forever.

Golyga, carrying the baby high on his shoulders, walked along, musing on the frequent times the baby seemed to be demanding this and that of him, Golyga, the once and always free spirit, now burdened by responsibilities and baby-related plans to be carried out in careful, considered fashion. What a world, Golyga was thinking. When you think how full it is of parents and their offspring and their many tasks and doings that relate to bringing up children. It's no wonder so many people are utterly exhausted by the very thought of children. It's no wonder so many children are obstreperous by nature, to assert their freedom of imagination. If parents were to be the only mirrors of how

109

to live, children would probably just as soon not grow up. However, children have the advantage of believing themselves not only invincible but also far smarter and more abundantly endowed with life talents than their parents and thus they are encouraged to try living more brightly, more adventuresomely, and more lusciously than their parents.

Thus thought Golyga, as he walked along the riverbank, Baby high on his shoulders and in his left hand the necessary bag with necessities for said baby. Now, however, thinking was going to be over for a while because Baby was about to let out a wild squall and continue with such vigour that Golyga would immediately set him down on the ground and examine what might be wrong. But before any of this happens, here is the first sight to greet our eyes:

A huge boulder, rolling down the hillside toward the river, heading straight for the path on which Golyga and Baby were meandering. Baby saw the boulder first. Golyga heard the baby's cry and set it down. Boulder came rolling closer at enormous speed and with enormous force. Baby flung itself up into the sky to avoid boulder. Golyga watched Baby open-mouthed, reached up to hang on to Baby, jumped as high as he could to grab Baby's legs, and as he jumped, the boulder rolled through underneath him, and both Golyga and Baby were saved. Hallelujah.

What in the world! Where did this boulder come from? Why right now? How did Baby see it first and how did it fling itself so high, being but a baby at this time? And no, this is not our cliff-hanging end of session. These are questions we are about to answer, believe it or not.

Whenever a boulder feels the need to move, it moves. Whether the move is a subtle one, discernible by no one but the boulder, or an avalanche-triggering roll down the mountainside, the boulder moves when so inclined. Human grown-ups do not give credence to such an ability and therefore it was only natural that Baby saw boulder first. And had the foresight to jump. As for how Baby could manage such a high and mighty flinging of himself into the sky, why again: there was no belief limiting the baby and therefore nothing stood in his way. If you but recall all the teaching that has been drilled into you to bring you the perceptions of what is and is not possible, you will begin to have some notion about the nature of belief. Do away with but one little corner of one belief, and you change the entire paradigm of what is possible in the world. You'll find, for example, that babies can not only swim, as has been proven even "scientifically," but they can also read minds, fly, and chew without teeth.

Golyga was not without his own limitations by way of beliefs, but he certainly didn't wonder at Baby's ability to fling himself into the air. He did imagine it was unnecessary for Baby to set up such a howling and caterwauling afterwards, but then perhaps babies enjoy that sort of thing, and who was he to stop anyone enjoying himself?

Golyga sat down beside Baby and waited for the noises to stop. The noises, meantime, brought Lillykins running from wherever she'd been hanging out and she immediately demanded to know what was wrong and why Golyga was doing nothing about it.

Nothing's wrong, said Golyga. Baby is having an "aftermath." You know, when after an experience the entire thing begins to boggle the mind and you have to make noises to settle it down again?

Ah yes, said Lillykins. I know that one well. Perhaps even babies are astonished at themselves and their abilities when left to experience without limiting beliefs on every side.

Golyga was stunned by Lillykins' equanimity and was about to ask her wherefrom this new-found attitude when, to their surprise, Baby spoke up, loud and clear.

This is all very well, said Baby. The two of you are learning away, at my expense, and I am left to draw conclusions that, by right, should be presented to me all codified and fit into hourly sessions at a desk. What is this?

You're too young for school, said Lillykins, shocked. You're even too young to be talking like this. Kindly have some respect for your elders and get yourself into the right frame of reference here, for a baby your age.

Golyga looked at Lillykins and laughed. Long and hard. The surprising shift in attitude hadn't lasted long and he was glad to see Lillykins was still shifting her perceptions from one to another perspective and so he could hope to be surprised and delighted in the future by her unpredictable thoughts and behaviour. As for his part, he could anticipate the pleasure of being more evolved and knowledgeable for a while yet. Except he would not reveal such thoughts to Lillykins.

Because now Lillykins was taking off her shift or whatever it was she was wearing on her lovely body, and she was diving into the river for a swim.

Wait right here, said Golyga to Baby. I'll be back. And Golyga dove into the water after Lillykins.

Ha! said Baby. Fine how-de-do. I'm not waiting around here. And in dove Baby, after them, and next thing all three knew, they were sitting on the boulder in the middle of the river, listening to the wonderful tale the boulder had to tell. Which is, of course, today's boulder-hanger ending.

LILLY: Lovely tale. Thank you, Golyga.
GOLYGA: You are welcome. Always glad to see you smiling. Until soon!

* * *

GOLYGA: So, you are thinking this is easy, this writing by channelling as opposed to your own laborious efforts while writing your novel. But is easy good? Are you not feeling the least bit guilty that no struggle is entailed and no decisions to agonize over?
LILLY: Not when I'll be doing the struggling and agonizing later, when working on the novel.
GOLYGA: Ah, as long as there is enough agonizing in your life, you can allow yourself these sessions of easy, enjoyable, delightful outings into the imagination of yours truly, Golyga Himself. Is that right?
LILLY: Yes.
GOLYGA: And what if all writing was to become as easy as this? Would you feel cheated? Afraid it couldn't be any good? Guilty that the ease brought you no suffering when all about you—?
LILLY: I'm not sure but I wouldn't mind trying a life of ease and joy, even in the writing of the novel. Frankly, I believe that as long as I'm writing about things that trigger old traumatic stuff, ease and joy aren't likely to be popping up all over that writing.
GOLYGA: You are right, at that. However, you are also clearing the traumatic stuff, as you call it, and so in future you might well find yourself writing with joy, and delight in your own imagination.
LILLY: That sounds wonderful.
GOLYGA: All right then, for now we'll remember to inject regular doses of joy and delight wherever and whenever possible to counterbalance the agonizing writing

sessions and we'll even throw the occasional laugh into those sessions. After all, you chose a character capable of ironic laughter at himself and with a penchant for exaggeration, which should lead to the occasional chuckle as well.

LILLY: Thank you for reminding me, Golyga.

GOLYGA: You are most welcome, Lilly. Now let's get on with our tale, shall we?

Golyga the Adventurous, as he was known in certain circles—especially among the frogs and dragonflies of the riverside—was swimming vigorously around the boulder, splashing Lillykins and the baby with great glee and bringing the sounds of laughter and snorting into the sun-filled air. It was a time for play, and the entire universe was in agreement with this mood. The dragonflies aforementioned were cavorting as well and the frogs were positively sonorous with their bellow cheeks and their bellow voices.

Suddenly, out of the sparkling air, a shape descended, circled once around the boulder, high overhead, then flew off and away.

What was that? Lillykins wanted to know. Do you think he'll come back? Was he dangerous?

She felt it was her responsibility to worry, if there was anything at all to worry about, and a mysterious flying shape that circled and disappeared certainly seemed worrisome.

Why don't we forget about it unless it returns and then we'll have a good look before we start worrying about it.

Golyga had a very different perception of what was worth worrying about—a fact that had often before led to arguments and even fights. Verbal, of course, since neither Lillykins nor Golyga were given to physical violence. Not so Baby. Baby started jumping up and down on the boulder, yelling and screaming that he wanted to see that mysterious flying shape and wanted to see it now, immediately, or else he'd hold his breath till he turned blue and keeled over, and then what would Golyga and Lillykins do?

Lillykins was dumfounded. Golyga said: I don't really know what I would do, so why don't you go ahead and try it and we'll see what I do?

Baby didn't like the sound of that at all. He looked at Lillykins, who was smiling at Golyga in an affectionate, admiring way, and then he decided to lie down and kick his legs and scream some more. Golyga and Lillykins watched. Baby kicked once, twice, three times, and then stopped because the boulder was hard and his heels hurt. And just then, the flying shape returned, circled once more around the boulder, and dropped like a shoe right on top of Baby. Who was so surprised, he couldn't even catch his breath. In the meantime, the shape turned into Hylu, brother of Lillykins, though he certainly didn't spell his name like that.

LILLY: Sorry. How did he spell it?
GOLYGA: Ah, nice long pause without running interference, dear Lilly. How Hylu spelled his name isn't actually important. What is important is the following: Hylu had taken on the form of a dragonfly and there was an abundance of insects around that he found delicious in that state and so it was extremely difficult to hold a conversation with him. Though Lillykins did, of course, try.

Hylu, said Lillykins. Where have you been, what have you been doing, and why are you a dragonfly at this time?

Why not, said Hylu the dragonfly, and he dashed off after a delicious morsel. Then he returned, humming under his breath with pleasure and sat on Baby's stomach once more. Baby was delighted.

Hylu, said Baby. Can I be a dragonfly, too, and eat delicious morsels and fly about everywhere?

Oh, being a dragonfly isn't all delicious morsels and flying on beautiful wings, said Hylu. Being a dragonfly is also to be reviled, feared, caught and pinned, and sometimes fried and eaten.

Gosh, said Baby. I didn't know that. Guess I'd better think about this for a bit.

Then Baby turned over on his belly, the better to think, and if Hylu hadn't been quick about it, he would have been one squashed dragonfly. But he quickly took off into the air and circled once more around the boulder, then called down that he'd be back shortly and took off.

With Hylu gone again and Baby busy thinking, Golyga and Lillykins had a few moments to themselves. They decided to use those moments the way lovers do, canoodling and holding hands and rubbing noses and other parts of themselves against each other, never thinking they presented a rather hilarious picture because at this particular time, Lillykins was in the body of a Russian princess—don't ask me why—and Golyga was in the shape of a long-nosed Tiddlywinks. In case you've never seen a long-nosed Tiddlywinks, they are shaped like flying saucers, except for the long nose and the flowing hair and beard.

Well, rubbing and holding and canoodling as they were, Lillykins and Golyga paid no attention to the picture they presented, and wasn't that a good idea, since nobody was watching, anyway. The dragonflies and frogs, you see, were all busy, trying to catch a glimpse of something that was making enormously loud sounds. Which, however, only the dragonflies and frogs could hear.

Hylu, being a dragonfly, heard the sounds, returned to the boulder as fast as he could, and roused his family. Quick, he yelled. Let's get out of here while we can! Get on my back, hurry up!

Baby, Golyga, and Lillykins, too, hopped on Hylu's dragonfly back, and off he flew, away from those loud and frightening sounds. What they were, we'll find out sooner or later. Meantime, try not to ask yourself too many questions about the dragonfly capable of carrying three such creatures on his back. And try not to be confounded by the notion of Golyga as a flying saucer–shaped Tiddlywinks with flowing hair and beard and a very long nose. Think of these phenomena as the products of a lightly flying imagination with the purpose of entertaining, and you'll be far from the truth but probably satisfied.

LILLY: And what would be closer to the truth?
GOLYGA: That nothing is impossible, that everything is to be wondered at with amazement and glee, and that a saucer-shaped Golyga with flowing hair and beard and a very long nose is no more astounding or entertaining than the shape of a dragonfly. Think about it. And dragonflies are real, as you would say, and abundant, and a wonderful sight to behold. True?
LILLY: Very true.
GOLYGA: So nature is wondrous and astounding and a source of never-ending amazement and joy. And you can, any time you choose, get some of that joy and amazement into your life. How about that?
LILLY: Thank you for reminding me, Golyga.

GOLYGA: You are welcome, my dear. I'll see you soon.

* * *

GOLYGA: We have come to tell you that good news is on the way and our work together will now progress rapidly and successfully to its first-instalment conclusion. In other words, this book we are now working on will soon be ready for publication and find its niche very smoothly. We, meanwhile, will be undertaking the next book together, if you wish (I wish), and while you are also engaged in your own writing projects, you can combine the creative flow of both to good advantage. We are not so separate in our access to the creative flow and not at all separate in your ability to catch the energy of creative undertakings and run with it. So, the good news is our firm commitment to working together and also the promise that results will be smoothly forthcoming—not only for our book but also your novel. After all, your preoccupation with that has to come to an end in order to free up energy for future output. Not that you have been unduly preoccupied, my dear, only that you are still attached to the novel in an energy-draining way. For example, you give yourself messages of doubt about your business ability, even about the quality of the writing, and you believe the difficulties-scenario painted by other writers. Natural enough, we suppose, but not necessary. Trust that it's all on the way and do the little things we suggest to help us get it there. Okay?
LILLY: Okay. Yes. Thank you.
GOLYGA: Now: to work on our book.

We have been following the adventures of Golyga, Lillykins, Baby, and Hailu for some time and we have become quite attached to them and their moseying about their lives. However, all good things must come to an interruption now and then, and we have one of those here and now. We have the urge to do something entirely different: address the reader directly on the advantages of doing the few exercises and tasks listed below. Most people will not undertake them out of sheer laziness and the desire to remain in their relative comfort zone of spiritual development. Seeking ever elsewhere for the answers when these are actually within and can be so easily revealed if only the layers of habitual thinking were removed. However, removing those is hard work, and there we are again: laziness. It's amazing to watch humans run around like rats in a cage, huffing and puffing in their myriad endeavours to better their lot—whether in the material sense or emotionally or even spiritually—and at the same time, treading water and not moving one inch from their position. At the basis of this is the desire not to rock their own boat, not to make changes that will be serious alterations in lifestyle, in perceiving the universe, in all the big and little aspects of life—social, work-related, family roles, and community perceptions, too. We are talking about the courage to become a different person, live in a different context, with an entirely different orientation toward life. Now who is going to undertake such a mammoth change without being pushed and coerced? Very few.

However: those few of you who will do the work suggested in this book, here, now, and in the future, will see their lives change, not overnight, but little by little, in incremental steps, leaps, flights. And each step will bring about, as its own tail, so to speak, delight, joy, excitement, and the desire to move to the next stage of the journey. For all of life is a journey. The difference with this one is that it is undertaken in full consciousness of direction and outcome, and full awareness of every little change along the way. Until, before long, you find yourself committed to the joy of forward motion, of learning, of trusting in the new paradigm: if you but participate and make it so, the universe is benevolent and will cradle you in its loving arms.

If you find that a bit much to swallow, ask Lilly dear. Who came from the deepest mistrust and fear of the forces, a universe ever ready to hit her in the head if she raised it, jealous gods with the evil eye ever ready to put a curse on what bit of luck or joy might find its way into her life. A background in which people expected the worst and got it—violent revolutions, wars, fear of neighbours who might denounce, fears of bombs, starvation, and the evil motives of all humans. And look at her now. Taking off for New Mexico, throwing herself upon the bosom of the friendly forces that abound—in nature, in humans, in us. Floating on clouds, zipping around the mountains as though everything in the world were full of joy if you but call on it. Well, it is. And the work we suggest in this book will open the way for you to tap its source and receive its bounty.

And there you have it: a rah-rah kind of session today, encouraging you, the reader, to go for it, to ready yourself for an amazing influx of joy in your life, to bring you closer to the threshold. Stepping over it is up to you.

* * *

GOLYGA: Yes, my dear, we are here and ready to work, and good for you that you aren't letting a few glitches stop you—whether energy-related or computer-related. This surely is a sticky keyboard—better do something about it soon. Meanwhile, here is an instalment for the book…

Once upon a time, a young waif was sitting on the doorstep of a mansion, hoping to be allowed inside to do whatever work was available in exchange for food and lodgings. Her hopes were no higher than survival and for good reason: until now her life had been a series of mishaps and horrible incidents that put her survival in question over and over. Survival, in other words, was as good as it got, in her experience.

The waif—we shall call her Bibi—was indeed taken on in the mansion and soon she was working and singing from daybreak until the hour she finally sank into sleep, long after everyone else had been in bed for hours. Bibi was singing and cheerful throughout those long hours of work because she had tasted such deprivation in her earlier life that simply knowing there would be food to eat and a warm enough place to sleep in kept her spirits content with her lot in life.

However. As you can imagine—being human as Bibi was, too— this state of affairs didn't last forever. After Bibi had been well fed and warm enough for a few years, she began looking around and noticed that others who lived in the mansion were having a much easier life than she. Not only were they fed, too, and warm enough, they also worked fewer hours, did easier work, and had hours to themselves to do with as they liked. Soon, Bibi began to wonder how these others achieved their favoured state and she began to ask questions of them, such as: who are you? Her aim was to find out whether they were favoured above her because of their birth or their talents or some other reason she might find useful in becoming more like them.

GOLYGA: Thank you for going ahead with that word, Lilly dear, though we could feel you balking at it.

Well, the first thing she found out was that not one of the others came from the same background; each had different talents and achievements, and every one of them had nothing but complaints about their life. Too much work, too little free time, too little pay. Pay? Bibi asked herself. What in the world is "pay"? And on and on they complained.

Bibi stopped asking them questions. It was just too depressing to hear them go on and on about their lot. But she did ask about "pay" and when it was explained to her, she went straight to the boss and asked to have some pay, too.

But what in the world would you do with it? asked the boss. You have no time off, no time for going shopping or a holiday resort. What in the world would you do with pay?

That, said Bibi, is my concern. I want pay for my work just as the others get for theirs. And while we're at it, I want some time off, too.

The boss looked at her, Bibi the waif whom he'd taken in when she was starving and shivering on his doorstep, and he said to her: You are an ungrateful wretch. Leave my house and don't come back.

Bibi was frightened. Where would she go? What would she do now? What in the world had she done?

Right after which, she also said to herself: Maybe this is the best thing that has ever happened to me—I now can go out into the world to see what I can see, and when I need food, I'll be bound to find some work somewhere I can do and be paid for.

And off she went—not a penny in her pocket, but the confidence of years of hard work in her heart.

The very first day she encountered a rather dour-looking old lady who asked Bibi to help her cross from her wheelchair to the front door of her house. Bibi did so, then opened the door for the old lady and settled her into an armchair by the window. Then she brought in the wheelchair and asked the old lady whether she needed anything else before she, Bibi, went off in search of a job.

Oh, said the old lady. If it's a job you're looking for and you don't mind hard work, you've got one. Bibi was glad. She was even overjoyed at the offer. But this time she knew enough to ask a few questions before she started working: What time off? What amount the pay? And how was she to know whether or not she was doing her job well?

As soon as all those questions were answered, Bibi set to work. She worked happily singing, and the dour old lady was soon cheerful herself. And whenever she let Bibi know how she was doing at her job, she would say: You're doing wonderfully well, Bibi; the only thing still missing is the guarantee that you will stay with me until the day I die.

The old lady, it turned out, was mortally afraid of being put into a home, and she wanted to be looked after by Bibi until the end.

Can't give guarantees, said Bibi. In this life, one never knows. So let's enjoy today together and see what tomorrow brings!

And so the two women lived and sang together and got along for many many years. Then, one morning, the old lady wouldn't wake up. She had died, a smile on her face, and Bibi, sorry to see the old lady go, was nevertheless glad she had died so peacefully, in her sleep.

Bibi packed her few belongings and headed out of the house, ready to find yet another job. However, before she had gone more than a few steps, an old man came along and asked her whether she knew a Mrs. So-and-So. Mentioning the old lady by name.

Oh dear, thought Bibi. What should I do? Nothing for it, I guess, but to tell him the truth.

She died during the night, said Bibi. She's still upstairs, if you'd like to see her.

The old man went up and sat with the old lady for a while. Then he came to talk to Bibi, who had waited for him.

You, said the old man, must have been the one responsible for that smile on her face. You, he said, were leaving without taking anything, without making demands or asking for thanks. You are going to be blessed with all you wish for for the rest of your life.

And the old man disappeared.

Bibi pondered what the old man had said as she walked along and asked herself: What do I really wish for in my life? Hm, I've had the benefit of a good job now, with a good employer, and the benefit of hardship in my life, to teach me contentment. What is it I wish for after all this?

Bibi sat on a tree stump and pondered and thought and meditated on the question: What did she wish for in her life?

Finally, she jumped up. I know! I know! she exclaimed. I know exactly what I wish for: I wish for clarity. Clarity of purpose, of mind, of heart, and clarity in all my comings and goings for the rest of my life.

Good luck, she heard. A deep voice chuckled and said it again: Good luck! I suppose, the voice said, you have as good a chance as any human to achieve clarity, so good luck to you and all the best.

Whoosh, heard Bibi in the trees above, and she saw a white vapour rapidly disappear toward the horizon.

Well then, Bibi said out loud. In that case I wish for one more thing: good luck! And off she went, down the path toward a sun-filled meadow strewn with wild flowers. And there we shall leave Bibi to the rest of her life.

LILLY: That's it for today?

GOLYGA: Yes, my dear. Read it over later. And meanwhile, thank you for taking it all down without editing, though you are not yet convinced that this episode is "up to snuff."

LILLY: It just seems a little off the path of the teaching—clarity and luck—but then, I have not read it over and that generally brings "Aha."

GOLYGA: True. And then you'll also see the connections to the rest of the material. So, a good day to you, my dear. Until soon: good luck!

* * *

GOLYGA: And here we are again, a looming entity, hovering and deriding whenever not permitted access in order to continue our epic endeavour. Does that ring true, Lilly dear?

LILLY: Not at all. When there is "should," it's mine. I know that. It's complicated by the large share of "want tos" also involved. But I am learning to let go of agenda when the energy isn't there.

GOLYGA: Good on you. We had to point out that we are never ever hovering or impatient, lest you forget. We also observe your desire to work versus your present lack of energy to do as much as you would like. So let's agree that your other work has to take precedence for a while and that our work be ongoing but perhaps once a week, for this next stretch.

LILLY: All right, unless my energy improves enough to do everything I have to do and still have enough for two sessions a week.

GOLYGA: Just keep track of your "have-tos," alright? Our ongoing work is made easier and delightful by your undertaking to do the exercises yourself. We are throwing lots of information and knowledge at you, all in a short time, so you can be forgiven for ignoring all or part of it. However, since you are practising and participating even as you help us to write this book, Lilly dear, we suggest you extract the exercises and practices on separate sheets of paper that you can easily consult as reminders. For example, the energy/light work regarding "natural disasters," and the upcoming exercise and everything in between, which altogether takes no time to make part of your daily life but that will need reminders while you are developing the habit of mind and action in regards to them.

LILLY: I'll do that: a sheet with your practice summaries.
GOLYGA: *Good. Here is today's exercise:*

There are ways of bringing about desired consequences in your lives that have to do with the brightness of spirit, and the attitude of normalcy in the midst of crazy mores, which can be yours with a simple change in your daily undertakings. See your every action clearly in regard to motive and hoped-for outcome, and bring your attention to bear on the steps needed to facilitate that outcome. Then, allow us to take over and do what we can to shape and shift the events around you to bring you the desired outcome.

We have your best interests at heart, and there are times when your desired outcome is, in fact, not for your long-range or highest good, and in that case we'll make that as clear as we can. How fast you understand our signs and communications depends on you. Say you desire a new car—yes, that same old mundane goal, Lilly dear. However, if neither what you have to do to get it nor the degree of joy you'll have through attaining it would be worth the end result, we would let enough obstacles remain in the way of attaining this car so that, if you are paying attention, you would see it's not a good goal to aim for at this time.

LILLY: That sounds like: if there are obstacles, give up.
GOLYGA: Yes, it sounds like that. But…there is a decidedly different feel to a goal worth attaining that has to bring the best for you in the end but includes some hard

work or dedication or the development of new skills or attitudes. A goal that will be counterproductive for your development or demand too much of you compared to the end result's degree of satisfaction—those goals and obstacles have a different feel. The fact of our involvement in working toward a goal makes for the difference in feel. In other words, if we're doing our best to further a goal, there is the feel of a supported goal and little signs all along the way that tell you we're working on it. Just have to be aware of them. On the other hand, if we are not assisting and supporting a goal, the obstacles feel bigger, the thinking and action in relation to the goal are infused with a kind of futility feel. You might resist acknowledging that feel and want to hang on to your goal despite it—just become familiar with the difference, first of all. Later, you'll learn to see the unsupported goal with eyes that discern the larger picture and you'll be able to let go more easily.

So: examine your goals not only for the ongoing difficulties on the way, but for the feel. Support? Or a cold hanging-out-there feel?

If it feels supported, give yourself the minor goals of steps on the way. After each step, let go for a bit, let us do our thing until it's time for the next step. You'll be able to feel or observe events that tell you it's time for the next step.

If you're after a goal that feels unsupported but you're not willing to let go, observe your own positive qualities of determination until/unless it becomes a willful anti-productive hanging on and rigidity of plan.

In either case, you will be more clear and sail more smoothly with your endeavours and undertakings and desires.

Summary: examine goals and their feel—supported or not?

Supported goals: take one step at a time toward it, letting go in between to allow us to do our part for you.

Unsupported goal: let go or observe yourself and learn.

For both, keep alert to the signs and signals on the path.

LILLY: *Question: what's the difference between "gut feeling" about a goal and "supportive feel" with you as the source?*

GOLYGA: *There is none. Support is support, and if you feel it, you've got it. What you call gut feelings is the combination of your own deeper knowledge and ours. Sometimes we can communicate by way of "gut feeling," but often people aren't paying attention to it, or if they are, they're not acting on it, and in those cases we try to communicate in other ways as well. Gut feelings don't lie and neither does the heart. We would be happy and satisfied if you apprehend and act on the knowledge you get by way of gut feelings and heart. Okay?*

LILLY: Yes, thank you.
GOLYGA: So now we'll close for this day. Until soon, with much love and affection and support for you, Lilly dear, your Mentor and Companion in this Endeavour, Beeswax.

* * *

Lillykins and Golyga notwithstanding, we have other fish to fry today. We have herring on our mind. We even have trout and gefillte fish on our minds. It all came about because we decided that, the weather being so lovely this summer, we would go on a fishing expedition to bring back trout and whatever else the lake would present to us. Thus, one fine very early morning we set out in our canoes.

LILLY: Who is "we," please?

We thought you'd never ask. "We," in this case, is yours truly, Beeswax, grown curious about the doings of humans on the planet Earth, and especially this activity called fishing. You see, it had always seemed to us that if you want something in your life, you invite it in. You open yourself to receiving that which you believe you want, then sit back and allow the universe to bring it to you. If nothing happens, you invite again and then take a step or two in the direction of your desired goal. Then you sit back again, to expect it to come to fruition. However, fishing, according to the way Beeswax saw humans undertaking this activity, involved a complex set of activities, an expensive mass of equipment, and much time as well. So he wanted to try out in what way this might be superior as a method of acquiring one's desired goal, which, he assumed, was the bagging or hooking or netting of fish.

Well, off he set, in the company of several other curious and adventurous beings from other places, and here they were, all sitting in a boat, in the shadow of an island, fishing away. Nothing was happening, but they'd been told it takes time and experience, so they were patient. Beeswax, after a time, relaxed his hold on the fishing rod and sank into a pleasant doze, listening to the waves lap against the canoe, the distant birds, breezes in the treetops, and other delights. Pretty soon,

124

he fell asleep altogether, and goodness knows what he heard while in the arms of slumber.

Suddenly, a huge shock accosted the canoe and its passengers. A bump, a grind, a crunching, a howl, a vast sucking of air, a loud crash and bang. What in the world...? Beeswax had woken up and was startled to find he was alone in the boat and had drifted right across the lake, ramming into a dock. Really hard.

What was going on here? Where were his companions? Where were the fish? The peace, the tranquility, the... Beeswax looked all around and saw no one—not a sign of his companions nor of any fish. The dock and the entire shoreline he could see were deserted and he seemed to be all alone on this vast lake. Fishing wasn't one bit as he had imagined it, and he wondered again why people engaged in it when they could so easily simply invite fish into their lives.

Well! Right in front of his nose, Beeswax suddenly saw a great big fish jumping out of the waters of the lake and onto the dock.

Finally, said the fish. You keep asking questions but then you don't hold still to listen to the answers. Now sit there and just listen, will you?

Beeswax was astounded at being given an order—wasn't at all used to it—and said to the fish: Here, you. You think I'm going to sit here and listen to you when all my companions have disappeared and the canoe may well be damaged and, and...

The fish waited for Beeswax to finish, then shook his head from side to side—which, in a fish, is a ridiculous sight, there being no neck to speak of, and more and more of the body getting involved in the motion, so that pretty soon the fish—a big one, remember—was up on his tail, weaving like a drunken sailor.

Listen, I said, said the fish. Here are the answers to your questions: Your companions are fine, they're having a picnic on an island. They neglected to tie up the boat properly, with you sleeping in it, so the boat floated off and crashed into this dock. Most of the time, fishing as a human activity has nothing to do with getting fish. It has everything to do with engaging in struggle, in drama, and being triumphant. That's fishermen I'm talking about. Not those who simply like going out in the boat and sit there, surrounded by water and peace, and attach this desire to the act of fishing so they can be seen to have a "reasonable" goal. No, fishing is but one of those "engagement" things. Where humans engage in setting up a conflict they then proceed to conquer. You see?

Beeswax saw but didn't fully understand. Why is it, he asked, that humans prefer conflict to the peaceful achievement of their desire? Prefer dramatic engagement, winning and losing and such, to the peaceful process of co-existing with all of creation?

Ah, said the fish. There you are asking the big question. We have all endeavoured to find out the answer to that one for millennia. It's something in the big left toe, we think. Something that drives them to such irrational behaviour and brings them so much discomfort and Sturm und Drang and so on. It seems that without it, they feel there is no progress being made and so they keep regaining the feeling of progress by engaging in conflict, and their left big toe must be the seat of all this need to "engage," because why else would they suck on it while still babies except to activate something inside of it that sets them on a conflict course?

Beeswax and the big fish looked at each other and burst out laughing.

For one thing, hooted Beeswax, surely not all human babies suck on their left big toes?

Yes they do, said the fish. You don't always catch them at it, but they do. It's been documented over and over by various observers we stationed around in order to get to the bottom of this human puzzle. So that's it. The left big toe.

Beeswax wasn't ready to argue that conclusion, knowing little about left toes or fishing or anything else in this absurd experience, so he simply said: Well, if humans ever want to change and achieve their goals without struggle and conflict, let me know. I'll tell them how it's done:

Be clear what you wish for and state it clearly, take a step in the direction of achieving your goal, sit back and let the universe bring it to you. Repeat until the goal has been achieved.

LILLY: Don't we already have a section dealing with goals and how to to achieve them?

GOLYGA: Yes, we do. And believe me, it's one humans need to hear more than once. It's one of the great obstacles to peace in the world, having all humans assume that struggle and conflict are necessary components of human life and without them no progress is possible. It's so important a misapprehension of reality that we might well do yet another segment on the subject. Meantime, become as a baby, sucking your left big toe, and see what it does.

LILLY: What makes you think I can get my left big toe into my mouth?

GOLYGA: Well, if you can't, use a straw.

LILLY: Very funny. I take it that's it for today?

* * *

GOLYGA: Yes, hello, and welcome! We are glad to see your health improving again and that you are eager to work. Here is the latest instalment for our book...

Once upon a time there was a young lad who was eager to work on a project that had interested him since childhood. He had trained for it, anticipated its rewards, even promised himself he would never never rest until he had achieved the work he intended to finish. Then, to his surprise and horror, the entire project fell through, made obsolete by new technological developments, and his life work was gone. His dreams, his aspirations, his passionate engagement in the project were all over in one fell swoop.

Still a young man, he recovered from the reeling and the staggering and set out to repair his "lost life," as he thought of it. What could he do instead? He looked all around at the work available to such as himself and found nothing to engage his passion. He decided to do nothing. Supporting himself in a minimal style with odd jobs and manual labour, he began to travel and drifted hither and yon across the globe. He found adventures, engaging people, even friends here and there, but nothing assuaged his sense of "lost life," and so he drifted on for years and years. Finally he was an old man and felt his last hours drawing near.

What, he asked himself, have I done with my life? What have I accomplished, and what do I leave behind as my legacy?

Not much, he thought to himself. A big disappointment, drifting and meandering, and finally, a settling into apathy and decline. What a pity, he thought. If I had my life to live over again, I would certainly do it differently! I would embrace the drifting and meandering as my life's work, and embrace the plans and disappointments as life's vagaries, and chuckle and laugh at every unexpected turn in the path. That's what I would do.

Suddenly, an angel appeared to the old man and spoke to him: Your wish is granted. You shall have another life, starting over from scratch, and you had better use it more wisely than the last. Now get up and get on with it, and don't let me catch you repeating your old ways.

The angel disappeared, and the old man sprang up and found himself young and vigorous. Gleefully, he ran out the door and immediately stepped into a puddle.

Oh, for heaven's sakes, he said to himself. Is this how it's going to be? No sooner have I started a new life than I step into a puddle and get muddy? What kind of life is this?

He sat down on the nearest curb and shook his head. Why would he start another life, anyway, if everything was going to turn out puddles and mud? Why not end it, be done with it, get it over with?

As he sat there wondering and pondering, he saw a dog sidewinding along the gutter, sniffing here and there, pausing to enjoy a scent, to bless it with his offering, then move on. The old young man watched the dog for quite a while. The dog seemed to be having a nice easy relaxed time of it, walking along, sniffing, and peeing. The dog was, in fact, enjoying life.

Now, why haven't I ever noticed that before, said the old young man. I could have asked the angel, when he was around, to make me a dog so I could enjoy life! Too bad I didn't think of it. It certainly is no fun sitting here on the curb watching a dog enjoying his life while I have nothing but regret about what I didn't know and didn't ask of the angel.

The old young man sighed. The dog was disappearing around a corner. The street was empty except for a little boy, approaching from the left. He was kicking a stone as he went and humming a monotonous tune. Once in a while, the boy looked up into the sky as though to check something there, then returned to kicking the stone and walking along, humming. The old young man watched until the boy was just in front of him and then he asked the child: Excuse me, why are you looking up into the sky? What are you looking for up there?

The boy, startled, stopped and turned to the man. I'm not looking *for* something, he said. I'm looking *at* something.

And what's that you're looking at? asked the old new man. I don't see anything up there except the blue sky, a few clouds, sometimes a bird…

The little boy stared at the man. For a while he said nothing, looking astonished and puzzled, then he shrugged his shoulders, looked up at the sky once more, sighed and smiled, and walked on, kicking his stone and humming his monotonous tune.

The old new man looked up at the sky. At the blue of it, at the few clouds slowly moving across it and changing as they went, so that he became fascinated by the ever-shifting shapes and textures, and then he saw a bird—no, two birds—swooping and circling each other and disappearing suddenly, as though swallowed by the tiger cloud just opening its mouth, then reappearing out of the flaming, smoking dragon cloud…

On and on the man watched the sky, on and on he sat, fascinated and unwilling to stop watching the display of ongoing life, and finally, tired out and smiling blissfully, he fell asleep right there on the curb.

A bum, said the voice of a man getting out of a taxi. How many of these bums can we afford to support? he asked his companion. Why don't they get up and start doing something worthwhile with their lives? Here we are, working hard, and there is that bum, just sleeping away as he pleases, doing no work, contributing nothing. It riles me, I tell you. Now, when I was young, I had a project in mind and I set myself to accomplish the work, and by golly, I did it, too! You see that smokestack over there? That's mine and so is that one beside it. Whenever I look at those smokestacks emitting and spitting, I am proud of what I have accomplished with my life. But how you can teach somebody like that bum about ambition and achievement and the better things in life, I really don't know anymore.

Off went the two men, talking away, and on slept the old new man, dreaming of angels and birds in the sky and the scent of blossoms in a morning meadow.

And when he woke up, that's what he set out to do: find the meadow, follow the scent, watch the clouds in the sky, and be forever shifting shape as he wandered and meandered through the sky-blue, silver-lined, feather-light air.

129

Golyga as told to Lilly Barnes

LILLY: *Thank you very much, Beeswax.*

GOLYGA: *You are very welcome, my dear. We are glad to see that you enjoy our stories and that you see their application in your life. We also assure you that these stories are equally applicable in the lives of many many others and that they will be part of our book for that reason. Because of your love of stories and parables, we are able to send you our messages in this delightful form and we know the ancient art of storytelling still speaks to humans more powerfully than mere lectures. It sets up a resonance in the psyche that reverberates long after the story is told and affects the lives of the reader/listener whenever a situation arises in which the story's message is appropriate. And so we close for the day, having had a good long session without taxing your health, and having enjoyed the work together as always.*

LILLY: *Thank you again, Beeswax. Until soon.*

GOLYGA: *Yes. Until very soon, and with pleasure.*

* * *

GOLYGA: *Here is the next instalment then.*

We are always amused, in a kindly way, by the human propensity for creating difficulties, each individual in his or her own path. The most frequent method for creating such obstacles is the repeated use of tape loops, which are useless, obsolete, and often deleterious. They pertain to the perception of the Universe as a hostile, difficult, and suffering-inducing place where vigilance is always necessary and the best defence is mistrust and self-induced reckless defence-building. Reckless, in that they bring so very much the opposite effect from the desired one.

Most defences are of the nature of ongoing mistaken perception of the steps one ought to undertake to be safe, to advance, and to be at ease in the world. For example: you desire a house. The only way you can perceive of getting one is to buy one. Which means earning the money for it. So you work for money. Your life, for years and years, becomes a tied-up affair, with little left for joyous living. It's a tough life, you say. And so it goes on.

If someone were to tell you, There is a simpler, easier, more efficient way of going about reaching that goal, would you listen? If someone were to say, Pray for it and trust it will be yours, would you scoff? If someone were to give you a house, would you think it a miracle? If

130

you lost the desire for a house, would you feel cheated of a goal? If you achieved a house and it was taken from you, would you fall back on the universe-as-suffering and start over? Or give up and be defeated by life?

Extrapolate from the above many other goals people set for themselves and then pursue in a dogged and often joyless manner. When, in fact, all they need to do is to have the confidence and the courage to be a child of the Universe, to allow the energies of creation and joy and fulfillment to course through their beings, to rest easy in their minds that the goals that are for their greatest good will come about.

One little concrete step at a time, and a period to follow of detachment from the desired goal while the Universe sorts out the various entangled strands to weave the shape of your goal. The next concrete step will present itself anon and again, a period of "just living" while it all moves forward for your benefit.

Our suggestion is: pick a goal and try our method as outlined above. See what happens. And then be appreciative—of the ease, the assistance every step of the way from any source, and of the enjoyment brought to you with the results.

And here is the short version: Pick a goal. Make a first concrete step toward it. Allow it to float off into the ether until the next concrete step presents itself.

Continue until achieved, giving appreciations all along the way to every helpful source.

GOLYGA: Clear?
LILLY: Very clear, Thank you.

✳ ✳ ✳

GOLYGA: Thank you for being ready, able, and happy to be working again. Didn't take long, considering your transition and your energy. Didn't take long, also considering we had to transfer our entire intent to another plane altogether because the obvious conclusion, after Mexico, is that you need to work on a regular basis and have work of your own going on in order to feel happy. So we suggest that we make a schedule for this work of ours so you have a clear idea of what time we need for our together-work in order to move it forward at a satisfactory rate—for all of us—and what time is available to you to do research for your own work and to live and enjoy the spring.

As for today, we do have a short session in mind because you are so eager and because we can make it useful to the general tenure of the work.

One fine day, as I was walking along a stream, listening to the waters and the rocks murmuring sweet nothings to each other, I spied a green apple floating on the waves, circumventing the larger rocks, until it came to a smooth flat rock and there it hopped up and landed right in the middle of the rock.

My, my, said the green apple to itself. This is a fine how-de-do. Nowhere do I see a watering mouth in sight, nowhere even a horse to be finding me delicious, nothing but water, trees lining the stream, and other such non-apple-eating paraphernalia of life. What will I do to fulfill the function of my being, which is to give nourishment and pleasure, both at once, to a sentient being or otherwise warm-blooded or at least breathing creature on this Earth?

The apple looked around but saw nothing it could describe as useful to its function. Finally, the apple gave up and moved on—floating again on the surface of the water, until it came to a bend in the stream, and there, in front of its apple-green eyes, it saw a meadow. And in the meadow stood a single cow. And the cow had no shade anywhere in the meadow and was pitifully mooing because it was hot and thirsty. It couldn't reach the stream because a fence had been built there with the express purpose of keeping this one cow away from it and from polluting the water that served as drinking water to many people just around the next bend.

Moo, said the cow, sounding very unhappy.

Right away, the apple started thinking about how it might help that poor cow. To get some water, to get some shade, to get some pleasure out of life. But what could a green apple do, all by itself? Not much, concluded the apple. Hardly anything at all. So it decided it would be best to engage in a campaign of gathering helpfulness from all around.

Help! Help! called the apple, from its floating position on the waters of the stream. Help! Help! A poor cow is in trouble, all by herself in the meadow, hot and thirsty and very unhappy to boot.

Somebody heard the apple. It was the farmer who owned the cow and who had never actually thought about his cow's life, all by itself out in the meadow.

Goodness, the farmer said to himself. Maybe that's why this cow has produced so little milk and isn't getting any fatter, and refuses to get pregnant whenever we bring the bull around. What can I do about this?

The farmer went home to his wife and told her about the cow in the meadow. The wife took a look at this husband of hers who seemed concerned only for the cow's productiveness and she told him: What if I decided you were not productive enough? Do you think I would stop loving you if, for example, you had a tractor accident and lost the use of your limbs and had to sit around all day getting looked after and contributing nothing at all to our livelihood?

The farmer was so startled, he couldn't even open his mouth. How did they get from the cow in the meadow to him sitting in a wheelchair, being a parasite but nevertheless loved?

The wife laughed to see his face. He looked so startled, so surprised, and so confused, she took pity on him.

Think a minute, she said. Mozart makes a cow give more milk. Does that tell you anything? Pleasure is what makes the milk come down. Now, how about a little pleasure before I bake apple pie for our dinner?

The wife took the farmer by the hand and led him up the stairs to the bedroom, where they both sampled some new delights with great pleasure.

After that, the farmer went out into the meadow, stood beside his cow, stroking her back, and promised he would get her company, shade, and lots and lots of water.

Moo, said the cow, in a very different tone. Appreciated, is what she meant.

The green apple, meanwhile, was still floating downstream, wondering whether its life purpose would be fulfilled before it began to rot and fall apart. Rot and fall apart, it heard as a refrain playing in its tiny brain over and over again. Rot and fall apart, that's going to be your destiny if you don't get somebody to eat you soon.

And then, suddenly, the green apple heard a wild noise from up above. In the branches of a tree sat a bird, laughing its head off. Not a nice gentle musical laugh, I'll tell you, but a raucous almost nasty laugh, loud as can be.

What are you laughing about, asked the green apple, annoyed.

About you, of course, laughed the bird, shaking its feathers and hooting out loud all over again.

"Rot and fall apart" is not exactly a bad fate for somebody who has seeds inside. Seeds that, when you fall apart, will sprout and grow into apple trees! I mean, what do you think happens at the end of that other route you seem to prefer so very much: somebody eats you, then shits out the seeds, pardon the language, and then, if you're lucky and they land in the right spot, they sprout and grow into apple trees.

Omigosh, said the green apple, I never thought of that. And, of course, the apple trees grow apples and they get eaten for sure, right?

The bird didn't get a chance to answer that one. It flew off because just then the farmer's wife came walking along the stream, humming and swinging a basket.

The farmer's wife saw the apple bopping on the waters of the stream and it looked like a right delicious apple to her, so she took off her shoes and socks, hitched up her jeans, and waded into the stream to catch the apple floating by.

Goodness, she said, looking closely at the apple. You look so fresh and delicious, I don't think you're going to make it all the way into our apple pie. I believe I am going to eat you right here and now!

So the farmer's wife did that. Ate the apple, resumed her walking to the village store, where she bought the apples for her apple pie, and eventually, years and years later, she and her entire family were happy to say they never had to buy apples at all. Because there were six apple trees right behind their house, where the old outhouse used to be, and they were growing and producing the most delicious green apples every year.

GOLYGA: *And that's our story for today. Get it, dear Lilly?*
LILLY: *Yes, I sure do get it, dear Beeswax. Thank you very much. This story is going to be part of the book, isn't it?*
GOLYGA: *Oh yes. You don't think you're the only one who needs to hear it, do you?*
LILLY: *True. Well, I thank you, we all thank you. Until soon!*

GOLYGA: Yes, very soon. Until then, dear Lilly, much pleasure and delight!

LILLY: Could I ask you a question, please? What did you mean by "shifting your intent to another plane altogether"? What did you have in mind that isn't going to work?

GOLYGA: Well, we thought that leaving the times of work entirely open would facilitate your engaging in it as a pleasurable interlude in your life. A kind of oasis you would stumble across more or less regularly. But we see that whenever time has passed without a work session, you begin to get worried about it, as though you were at fault or were not fulfilling some quota, so we decided it might serve you better if you had a schedule.

LILLY: Yes, but that doesn't sound like "another plane altogether." It sounds more like a change in method.

GOLYGA: No, it's more than that. If you could be floating on the waters of life with no thought about product, time spent working, schedules, etc., then we would go on as we were, taking advantage of the energies as they flow. As it is, your ongoing need for feeling "productive"—as if living isn't being productive enough—makes us sure that a routine of sorts will benefit your sense of accomplishment. Which you still need at this time.

LILLY: Okay. I concede it's true. Perhaps up at the lake I can try being alive, period, with oases and islands of work.

GOLYGA: Perhaps. Meantime, we'll do the schedule thing, with the injunction that you really try to be enjoying life every which way.

GOLYGA: Now: here is another short addition for one of the episodes.

When humans decide to change their lives in some way, they go about it cerebrally first. They decide, they challenge themselves, they weigh pros and cons, they delineate a course of action. Then, once embarked, they observe themselves with a sharp and critical eye, take note every time they fail in the smallest detail, and generally harass themselves until they—usually—lose heart and give up. If they continue doggedly toward their goal, they pride themselves on overcoming obstacles, perhaps even exaggerating the obstacles so they have more reason for pride, and they bring themselves to the brink of failure over and over, only to push on, push harder, bring more and more energy to bear on the entire process.

What this results in, sooner or later, is the abandoning or achieving of a goal. What the price was is rarely included in the calculations of success or failure. The agenda, the program, the undertaking for change is everything. This, it seems to us, applies to people who aim for losing weight, building a career, having a new carpet, car, house, or achieving health, happiness, a new and wonderful relationship. In other words: everywhere and to everything is this method of achieving goals and changes the modus operandi. We would like to suggest a very different kettle of fish and hope you will be intrigued enough to give it a try. Really, experientially, without too much intellectualizing. Simply:

Be clear about what your goal is. Never mind whether we think it's a worthwhile goal, whether anyone, in fact, thinks it's worthwhile except your own self.

Once clear that it is, indeed, what you want, say so out loud. In a quiet moment, with full concentration, with energy and breath behind it, say out loud what your goal is.

Now think of the first move you can make toward that goal. Something practical, simple, but clearly oriented toward the goal—if the goal is a change of habit, say, undertake one act that your future self-with-changed-habit would execute.

And now—the hardest part—let it go. Move through your day as though the goal is assured, the change is underway, everything you do is informed by the change, the imminent achievement of your goal. "Just a matter of time" is the attitude, and "goody, it's on the way."

Those are the steps of manifesting, you'll say. What's the difference, why tell me this again?

Well, for one thing, it seems that humans do need to be hearing some things over and over again before they give credence and actually undertake checking it out in action. For another, there is a subtle difference between manifesting a thing, a goal of desired results in the physical realm, and the changing of a habit, including changing the habits of thought-forms running through your heads.

The difference is this: when you want to manifest something like a car, say, you have a concrete, simple goal. When you want to manifest a change of habit, you have a complex system of energy manifestation to deal with and need all the help you can get on a repeated basis. So the difference in accomplishing the latter is the way you go about defining the goal, stating it and then bringing yourself to the attitude of success.

Thus: let us take the example of wishing to stop smoking tobacco.

You have been vaguely wanting to quit. You now really think it's time. The old way of going for the goal entails an enormous output of energy, self-recriminations for failure, constant monitoring of your addiction-related thoughts, etc. The new way brings you quickly through the stated goal to the first step. Then it gets complicated because your entire system will be coming up with tried-and-true ways to sabotage yourself. If, instead, you walk about with the assurance in your mind that non-smoking is just around the corner, then your energy carries you forward to that goal instead of jerking you backwards and forwards with every thought, act, moment.

As for a more complicated goal—say, better relationships—you have to spend a bit of effort on seeing where and how your relationships can be improved from your end so you can formulate a clear goal to state. Possibly approach such a goal one step at a time. After that statement and a first step, everything is easier because your awareness will be so increased that old patterns of relationships will fall away on their own.

Get it?

LILLY: Yes, I do. Thank you very much. But wait a minute. Remind me what the steps are for physical manifestation. Or, rather, object manifestation.

Okay, the car. You want one, you decide what kind, you take a step, you let go. There is little in the way of self-monitoring. You simply put your attention on noting the events that come to you that pertain to the object of your desire. Whereas with manifesting change, or the more subtle goals pertaining to your attitudes and perceptions of life, there you have more internal focus and have to keep the "goal just around the corner" feel with you, lest it get drowned in old thought forms. As we said, a subtle difference, but very important.

And so we conclude today's segment with the one-two steps of the exercise:

1. Think clearly and succinctly until you have established what the goal is.
2. State the goal out loud.
3. Take a first, practical step toward that goal.
4. Let go.
5. But be constantly aware of the attitude and conviction that achievement of the goal is just around the corner and that you are directly headed that way.
6. Add, if you like, appreciations every time you note the least change heading you in the right direction.

And that's it. Happy hunting!

LILLY: Thank you very much.
GOLYGA: You are welcome, my dear, and we'll be with you again soon.

* * *

GOLYGA: Yes, we are here, ready to work, glad to be doing it with you, rarin' to get on with finishing the book so we can do another one. Okay?
LILLY: Yes, okay. Let's go.
GOLYGA: Alright. As we can see, Lilly dear, you are thrilled and utterly delighted with all the hard work we are suggesting to our readers. Why should you be the only one partaking of so hard a journey, right?
LILLY: Actually, that notion had not yet occurred to me. I would dearly love to meet somebody who is serious about the journey.
GOLYGA: You have met such people, but they are each involved in their own particular route and so there is little time or expansion to include others such as yourself unless you go "professional."
LILLY: You mean become a specialist in one area and provide a service in it?
GOLYGA: That would do it. Of course, channelling a book can be seen as a specialist's undertaking, wouldn't you say?
LILLY: Yes, but it's solitary work, as is my "day gig" of writing. It would be great to do some of the travelling with others.
GOLYGA: All right then. Here is our suggestion: start doing some of the manifesting work we have outlined in our material. That is the one area of work you tend to shy away from. Not deserving? Not feeling it's right that you "take advantage" of this

*knowledge? Bullswoggle. You deserve and you are supposed to take advantage of this
knowledge as much as anyone!*
LILLY: Are we going to include all this in the book?
GOLYGA: Yes. We are.

There are others who feel undeserving for no good reason. Besides, as an introduction to this section of the book, what better subject than whether or not people are doing the work. We want to remind people that just reading this book will bring you enormous pleasure, it's true (there goes your modesty again), but notwithstanding Lilly's Canadian diffidence about self-promotion, if you, the reader, want more lasting results from this reading than momentary pleasure, we recommend most highly that you do some work. Choose according to your own sights what you most need in your life—whether it be peace from worry, joy, or some control over unwanted mental habits. Be assured that whatever goal you set yourself as a beginning, "all roads lead to Rome," or, in this case, to increased joy in your life.

Anyway, you have nothing to lose. Not even a perspective on the universe. In other words, keep your belief system intact except for one small opening facing the possibility of something new. Through this opening, exercise your "benefit of the doubt" muscle to do some work on any of the aspects we recommend. Then keep track of how you feel. See if experience itself brings you some degree of certainty that our claims are reasonable. See if, by doing any of the exercises or activities we recommend, you achieve a greater degree of enjoyment of life. Be truthful, observant, and clear in an experiential way, about the results of any exercise you have undertaken and stuck with for a time. Then, if you can, hold on to your old way of thinking, believing, doing, living. Experiencing increased joy of life brings with it its own momentum and motivation: who doesn't want to feel better?

Then, add a second exercise or mental skill to the first, and again, follow the results. And begin appreciating the work you are doing on your own behalf, giving yourself kudos every time you become aware of how much you have improved your own life, by your own doing.

So the operative word here is *doing* in addition to reading. And this preachy interlude is now giving way to more of the fun and games you have been enjoying in this book.

LILLY: Is that it for today?

GOLYGA: It is. Though we do want to add how glad we are that you have decided to take a week off your workaday life and devote all of it to our book. Soon we'll be talking about getting this book out to publishers. For now, enjoy the creative flow and life!

* * *

LILLY: Am I reading you right that you want to work now, before yoga or meditation, etc.?

GOLYGA: You are reading us right, yes. Let's do it and then you have the rest of the day to relax and do things you need without energy concerns for our purposes.

LILLY: Good idea.

GOLYGA: Please remember that when you are working on the new phase of this book, which is our project together, I, Golyga, am very much involved as well. The directing intelligence is a composite or group entity, such as the one you met through Diana, when learning to channel with the help of her group-entity guide Mathew. We are together as a group to facilitate the ongoing project with as much efficiency— as regards your energy—as possible, and with as much effectiveness in the way of communication as possible. And so, let's get on with a Golyga instalment, shall we?

Golyga was sitting with his head in his hands, contemplating the very nature of thinking. This didn't come easily to him since he was a man of action, but it was necessary. His beloved Lillykins was so addicted to thinking that he had to engage in it periodically to prove to her he was not incapable of it.

What shall I think about today? he asked himself. What exactly could I think about that would result in an improvement of anything? Ah, I know! I'll think about the mess the world is in. No, wait. That doesn't serve any purpose at all unless followed by action, and any action taken will have consequences both unforeseen and unpredictable and possibly with opposite results than those intended. Let me rather think about something else. How about my own state? Am I happy, am I sad, am I doing the right thing?—that sort of thinking. Except that leads to nothing so much as a bellyache, in my experience. Goodness, said Golyga to himself. I had better ask Lillykins what sort of thing she thinks about when she is thinking.

So he did. And Lillykins told him the following: Why, anything at all and everything. One has to think, otherwise one is not human, after all.

And what exactly do you know about being human? asked Golyga of Lillykins, whose claims to being human or even knowing the state of being human were, of course, entirely theoretical. Lillykins, if you remember, was, like Golyga, a creature of many possibilities, one of them embodying herself in human shape, but neither of them was human per se.

Lillykins didn't let that stop her from believing herself knowledgeable. I've been in human form often enough and long enough, she said, to know that thinking is an important and omnipresent part of it. It precedes any action—unless the human is blowing up with anger or bitterly crying or laughing like a hyena with some explosion of joy. Thinking is the prelude and often the determining factor of what action humans take. It also determines the mood, the beginning and end of all relationships, the engagement with the rest of the world. So you see that humans spend a great deal of time and energy and effort in thinking, and that it is of utmost importance.

Golyga sat and thought some more. Tell me, he finally said. If thinking is so all-important, why are humans so negligent about the contents of their thoughts? Why do they allow thoughts so randomly to pass through, to determine mood, to influence action in an almost haphazard way? If thinking is so all-important, why do they not pay the most diligent attention to the nature of their thoughts?

Lillykins was silent. She hadn't encountered this puzzle before. It was true, when in human form she had often been beset by thoughts and wondered at their power, but never had she considered that she might determine, even when in human form, the content and intent and outcome of those thoughts. She considered it all now and felt herself rapidly getting sick to her stomach.

This isn't something I care to think about right now, she told Golyga. I will, however, think about it once I am in human form again. It's the sort of thing one should think about while in human form, I am sure, but right now I am more inclined toward taking the form of a butterfly.

141

Golyga was delighted. Butterflies were one of his favourite forms, especially if Lillykins was one, too. So they popped themselves into butterfly mode, shook their beautiful wings, looked to the right and to the left, and took off into the air, circling one another, sliding downhill on streams of air, singing with their spirits and their beauty and their wings of gossamer, emitting tiny sounds of joy.

Oh look, a butterfly! Two butterflies! said a child sitting on the seashore, hoping to be allowed into the water. I wish I could fly…

GOLYGA: And that, my dear, is the end of today's Golyga episode.

LILLY: Not as action-filled as most, but I see where you're going with this, I think.

GOLYGA: You do, do you? Well, we're glad to hear it. The "where we are going with it" will follow another day, but yes, you are right: thought-form work is what it's about. Shaping your universe is what it pertains to. And allowing the joy of butterfly laughter into your lives is what we hope to achieve.

Joy, you see, is not merely a state of feeling delighted, feeling uplifted, feeling "fine." Joy is a form of energy that is closer to the light energy you want to aim for. It is the form of energy available to humans that brings you closest to the spirit of the benevolent universe—remember that term? Joy is the Lightness of Being, the importance of being not-Earnest, the very delight of it is a transformation of energy that leads humans into their highest form possible while in body. When we say, "Seek joy," we are not urging a path of selfish indulgence or toward pleasures of the flesh, or any other misinterpretation of that phrase. When we say, "Seek joy," we mean that state of being that is most akin to the light, fine energies of the kindred spirits in our dimension. We are linked with you by way of joy energy more than in any other mode. The earnest seeker on a spiritual quest is far behind the butterfly wings of joy of those who seek delight and de light. Get it?

LILLY: Got it, yes. Thank you very much.

GOLYGA: Now all you need to do is find out how to spend more and more time in a state of joy.

LILLY: Exactly.

GOLYGA: Well, you do know some of the ways already and you will learn more and more as we go along here. We wanted to be sure that you, Lilly, and the reader, of course, understands that joy is no word to be bandied lightly, that it is of paramount importance—without sounding too earnest, we hope—and that thought-form work is one of the most important routes to being in as great a state of joy as is humanly possible.

We'll return to thought-form work anon. For today, we salute you, we commend you, we love you and care for you, and we'll see you sooner than you think! Yours in joy, Beeswax.

LILLY: Thank you, Beeswax and Golyga and, of course, MarTee.

* * *

GOLYGA: Yes, we are here and ready to work and we do want to congratulate you on your loveliness. See how close that word is to loneliness? How little it takes to change one to the other? Our little self-indulgence for the day. Now, to work…

Lillykins was sitting and thinking. What, again! Still? When is the woman going to stop thinking and start living?

Golyga was the one asking himself that question but decided to be fair and remember that Lillykins was not always thinking, and that thinking was part of living.

Now, Golyga asked Lillykins, would you say that some kinds of thinking are part of living and some are anti-life?

Yes, I would, said Lillykins. But there is a simple way of checking which is which. All you have to do—in case you ever engage in thinking yourself, dear Golyga—is close your eyes and get a feel for what is going on in your body. If your body is responding with a hum of harmony, of excitement even, then the thinking is life-enhancing. If the body is emitting a tense, shallow-breath, high-pitched whine, you are probably engaged in the kind of thinking that goes around and around or zig zags all over the map but accomplishes nothing.

Interesting, said Golyga. And what might there be in the way of content of the first and latter kind of thinking?

Lillykins shook her head. Some things, she said, you do have to think about and figure out for yourself. Or at least try. If you don't get it, I'll help you out.

Golyga snorted. What arrogance! What insufferable cheek! Then he saw that Lillykins was smiling and teasing him, so he forgave her and went leaping off into the blue, whistling like a banshee.

Never mind what banshee-whistling sounds like. The point is: when if ever is Golyga going to do some of that useful and life-enhancing thinking? The point also is: why is that anybody's affair except Golyga's? After all, he's done very well for all this time without sitting down and doing any heavy-duty thinking, right? Wrong. Golyga has done more than a little of such thinking as is useful and delightful and therefore not usually seen as "heavy thinking." He has even been able to invent, to produce, to alleviate, to succour, to be a mentor and pal, and to bring joy and comfort to others by way of his thinking. The reason Golyga is not often perceived—by his readers, that is—as a thinking creature is that he spends as much time as possible enjoying life, and that, as humans seem to think, denotes a non-thinking being.

The best balance between thinking mode and non-thinking mode varies from situation to situation, from one time of life to another, from job to job, from person to person. So there are no overall rules or generalities we can recite to help you find that balance. Most humans are overbalanced on the side of useless thinking. So we recommend you apply Lillykins' checking method as often as possible to eliminate the energy-sucking, joy-destroying kind of thinking.

GOLYGA: Get it?
LILLY: Yes, thank you.
GOLYGA: Now, lest you think we have decided on dour lectures in place of our delightful tales of adventure, let's go back to Lillykins and Golyga and find out what they are up to.

Lillykins has decided to take a shower. She has gone to the waterfall, turned herself into a duck, and is sitting under the spray, content to feel the crystal waters cascading off her back. Golyga is watching her, full of admiration for her beauty, contentment, and the sheer colourfulness of the scene. However, their contentment was short-lived. Along came an interruption neither could have anticipated because they thought themselves in one of those tranquil moments of life when, for a time, it seems as though tranquility is our natural state. Not so, the two of them found out. Tranquility also has its tides and flow. And just now, it was definitely ebbing rapidly.

Lillykins as duck is sitting under the waterfall, Golyga is watching with delight, and now, suddenly and unexpectedly, a canoe comes zooming over the falls and lands on Lillykins. Smack dab on top of her. All Golyga could see was the canoe, a scared-looking figure inside it, and no Lillykins anywhere, duck or otherwise.

Well!

With one mighty leap, Golyga was on top of that canoe and lifted it bodily out of the water, tossing it aside as though it were so much duck feathers. Then he stared at the spot where Lillykins had been only moments before but he saw nothing. Nothing but water, that is. Not even a feather floating or a quack.

Golyga was aghast and dumbfounded. He was also pissed off, devastated, and confused. The usual sorts of feelings when a mate suddenly has his sweetie disappear on him. What to do? What to do? went his mind, in a useless repetition. Meantime, his feet were probing the bottom, his eyes searching as far as they could roam, his arms and hands feeling everywhere for any shape at all that could be Lillykins'.

Nothing. No sign of her, no hide nor hair or feather either. Golyga groaned. Right out loud and with great gusto. Then he heard a giggle. Lillykins' giggle.

Golyga couldn't see her, but now that he knew Lillykins was safe—who else would give off such a giggle except a safe creature?—he could relax and apply himself to the next thing. Which was to check the canoe and its hapless owner, which he had both together tossed aside.

The canoe lay on its side, looking worse for wear but not entirely broken, and a hand was slowly reaching out from beneath it. A huge hand, the size of a barrel. Fascinated, Golyga watched what else emerged: an arm the size of a tree, then the head. A pinhead. Well, maybe a head the size of a pea. Definitely unexpectedly small.

Well, no wonder, Golyga said—unfortunately not to himself but out loud—no wonder this creature went over a falls and landed on anything that happened to be around. A pea brain!

Meantime, the creature's body was following the rest out from under the canoe, and Golyga realized this was a creature he had never before seen. Neither human nor fowl nor any other living being he had ever encountered.

Meet my cousin Mercybelle, said Lillykins' voice in his ear. I do believe I have told you about her in the past.

Golyga was astounded. *This* is your cousin Mercybelle? You never described her, but goodness, don't you think you should have?

Lillykins laughed. Golyga didn't like the sound of that laughter, so he looked around for her to tell her so to her face. Lillykins, however, had no face at this time. She was a rock—though no rock face included—and fairly immune to the kind of looks Golyga was trying to impress on her. Meaning: Really, Lillykins. You might have warned me!

Meantime, Mercybelle was arriving in front of Golyga, who held out his hand for shaking, hoping it wouldn't be crushed by Mercybelle's enormous paw because his hand was rather delicate at that moment, having just been used to toss a canoe.

Mercybelle stared at the hand Golyga extended to her.

Lillykins giggled again and then said: Forget it, Golyga. Handshaking is not a known courtesy where my cousin comes from.

And where might that be? asked Golyga, studying Mercybelle with undisguised curiosity.

From the beyond, said the tiny pea-sized head in front of him. I'm not one of your earthlings, I'll have you know. There will be no entertaining me with your silly tales and cautionary woes.

"Cautionary woes"! Golyga was incensed. Whoever called my delightful adventure stories cautionary woes? Lillykins?

Pish-posh, tish-tosh, said an entirely new voice from beneath the waterfall. Could you all move somewhere else please to hold these endless and useless social chats? I am unable to breathe with all that inanity flying about. Push off, will you?

And then the voice added: Please!

Changing everyone's response from annoyance and hostility to curiosity. Where did that voice come from and who was it?

Well, I'm afraid we'll have to leave the answer to that question to another time, but we can tell you right here and now what Lillykins' cousin Mercybelle was after, coming to see her in such a dramatic fashion: she was after Baby. Yes, she had heard about Baby and wanted to take him with her to the land of her origin and abode. You can imagine the feathers flying once she made this known to Golyga and Lillykins, but you'll hear all about its outcome at another time.

Meanwhile, here is the lesson for today:

Expect the unexpected not by preparing for any eventuality but by sitting easy in the stream of life, by noting all its pleasant twists and turns—and the not so pleasant ones, too—and know that life will always always bring the unexpected and you will always always benefit from riding lightly and easily, letting everything splash like the crystal waters of a waterfall—even a canoe landing—because life is what there is, is all there is, and how you take it on is the "how" of living.

GOLYGA: No, Lilly dear, this is not a warning that a canoe is going to land on your head. Nothing is landing on your head. The canoe is symbolic and the landing metaphorical.

LILLY: I knew that even while the split second of fear surfaced, fear of the unknown future being a very persistent tape loop, I guess.

GOLYGA: You guessed right. So beware. And be as happy as a duck under the waterfall, without canoes dropping on her head, because what's the point of going through life anticipating canoes on the head that might never come and, even if they do one day, will have ruined every bit of the good times leading up to it.

You may think this is old news, dear Lilly, but you'll be surprised by the number of humans who cling to that tape loop because they see no alternative.

That's it for today, my dear. Enjoy, enjoy, enjoy, and have a swim on us!

* * *

GOLYGA: Long time, yes? You feel it so? Well, we're glad you have missed our work together, and here we are, together and doing it again. And so: we have loose ends to tie up.

Lillykins' cousin Mercybelle, or whatever her name was, planned to take the baby/boy with her. She fully intended to spirit him away, so to speak, so she could bring him up in her domain, the domain of the rich and famous. Hollywood, if you like. There, in a huge mansion with several swimming pools, some kidney-shaped, some piano-shaped, and some swimming-pool-shaped, Mercybelle lived with a hundred or so dolphins. (Hence all the pools, you see.)

147

Her dolphins had been after her to bring them a human child to play with because they are fond of humans, you know, and like getting to know them better. They also secretly hoped to persuade the human child to set them free so they could return to their ocean home.

Thus Mercybelle was on an errand for her dolphins but, seeing Golyga and Lillykins and the boy child, she wasn't sure she ought to come right out and state her plan to take the boy with her. She had the notion that there might be objections. And being rich and famous as she was, and not particularly bright, as it happened, she decided the way to get her will was to use subterfuge. One fine morning of her visit, she waylaid the boy and began telling him all the things he would enjoy if he were to come home with her: chauffeur-driven car rides, shopping in the finest toy stores, Disneyland visits any time he pleased, etc., etc.

The boy listened, his eyes widening. He had no idea what this aunt of his was talking about. He had never seen anyone quite so huge in his life and had to raise his head and tilt it back so far that his mouth just naturally fell open.

Mercybelle immediately assumed that he was impressed by all she was offering and so she went straight to Lillykins and Golyga and told them the boy wanted to come home with her, and who were they to stand in his way toward the good life.

Golyga and Lillykins looked at each other and broke out into laughter. This laughter brought the boy over quick as can be and, because he liked laughing, he joined in. Mercybelle was not amused.

I don't see at all what's funny, she said, puffed up and huge. It's not as though I can't offer him the finest things in life. Anyway, my dolphins want to get to know a human child.

Dolphins? asked the boy. Real live ones? Do you live on a ship?

Mercybelle knew how Lillykins felt about her dolphins in the pools so she only said: No, but my house is on the ocean beach.

You mean they come and visit you? asked the boy, more and more intrigued.

No, said Lillykins. She keeps them in jails. Pools by the ocean. They can see their home but they can't get back to it.

The boy's mouth fell open again. He looked at Mercybelle, aghast. Finally, he asked: Why do you do that? Why don't you let them go back to the ocean?

Because then they might swim away and not come back, Mercybelle, said, beginning to sob. I love those dolphins. She rubbed her eyes with fists the size of Ottawa. I love them, but if I let them go, I'm not sure they'd even come back to visit me. I'd be all alone.

The boy looked at Golyga and Lillykins. Both waited to see what he would say.

The boy shook his head. So, he said, thinking. You would rather be a jailer than lonely. Do you enjoy being a jailer?

Actually, I hate it, said Mercybelle. They're always looking at me with those eyes, and they hardly talk to me anymore. I think they resent me and they're not friendly, and... No. I really don't like being a jailer.

Well then, said the boy. Why don't I come along with you to your place and help you free all the dolphins? Would that be all right?

Golyga and Lillykins were still thinking it over when Mercybelle said: Well, actually, if I'm going to let the dolphins go, I don't need you to come. And to tell the truth, I don't really like having little boys around. Never did. Which is why I got those dolphins in the first place. Maybe I'll get a dog.

Mercybelle heaved a great sigh, heaved herself up and into the canoe, and whooshed herself out of sight.

LILLY: Wasn't the canoe smashed to smithereens?
GOLYGA: Okay, Ms. Logical, insert the phrase "repaired her canoe" into the previous sentence.

* * *

GOLYGA: Yes, my dear, you tripped and stepped into your lovely dress, but no, it had nothing to do with us. As Micah once said when you assumed dark forces at work: "Reality check, Mom, you tripped." And so we suggest that you be very aware of the kind of happening in your life that is simply ongoing life, and, on the other hand, the "messages." Whenever a negative message comes up, double-check, because it is not likely to be from us. Such as: "You would not have tripped if you had sat right

149

down at the computer instead of pulling open the blinds first." Does that sound like us? Of course not. So: double-check all negative messages.

And be aware of the energy tone whenever you are tempted to think, Is this a message? There is a decidedly different energy tone around those events, people, and anything else that comes to you as messages from us. You have only to stop for a moment in whatever you are doing in order to sense it, and we are willing to bet you'll be correct most of the time in your assessment.

You can also try that old standby: attempt to put it out of your head. If it goes, it was you. If it's hard to dislodge, it was one of us trying to reach you. Okay?

LILLY: Okay, thank you, Beeswax. I have a tendency to see omens, which has more to do with superstition and doomsaying than with getting help.

GOLYGA: Especially lately again, and you might want to do something about it. Your mother's voice can be dismissed as inappropriate for you in many instances, and you have been able to get rid of much, but there's obviously more. Stay aware, and perhaps give yourself more appreciation for catching that voice when you do. Practise and you will be rid of everything that is doomsaying-to-no-avail. All right. Now to work…

LILLY: Thank you, Beeswax.

We were going to do a very long session today, about the efficacy of swimming in the cosmos, but we will do something else instead. Something much more specific in its application. We will suggest ways and means and methods of going about allaying unnecessary fears for those of you on the planet Earth who are given to worrying uselessly, simply out of habit. Lilly calls it "keeping the plane in the air," this kind of worry that can do no conceivable good but nevertheless occupies much time and sucks much energy from so many of you. It seems to be something you engage in willy-nilly, with a mistaken notion of "caring" involved, and a fearful hanging on lest you fail to fulfill some mysterious obligation to some mysterious force of retribution.

There are, of course, enormous forces arraigned behind such a manner of going through life. "Original sin" is one, "the sins of the father" is another, endless warnings in childhood about the doom and gloom sure to follow later in life, well-meant advice about every manner of action and thought that will have dire consequences unless a narrowly proscribed course is followed to a T. And on and on.

There are, as we say, many forces at play to keep you worried and anxious for the rest of your lives on Earth. After that, of course, you'd be asking yourself: Did I really waste all that time worrying to no avail? Well, why not get rid of the habit now so you can enjoy life whenever not actually in pain or hungry (we don't mean for two hours) or homeless and in danger.

You know some of the methods through hearsay, and some of you have been practising ways of staying in the now, which keeps you worry-free at least for the duration of, say, meditation. Unless, of course, you are worried about not doing your meditation well enough, thinking instead of achieving mindlessness—sorry, mindfulness. Let us assume you know nothing about how to reduce and perhaps banish useless worry and anxiety from your life. Take it from us, it's not going to be easy. It will take practice and more practice, and you will backslide and find yourselves going over the same old ground again and again, but you will improve your life from the very first moment you engage in the practice. For at the very same moment when you say: "I don't need to worry about that" or "It's useless to worry about that, so I won't"—from that moment on you begin to lighten your life of burdens, to make room for joy.

There is nothing simpler than the yardstick for measuring anything you might feel inclined to worry about: "Is worrying about it going to help at all in any way?" If the answer is "no," stop worrying. Assessing the worrisome situation makes sense, devising ways of changing the situation, finding alleviation, anything at all that changes the situation for the better—those are not "useless worrying mode." Those are useful and should be engaged in. We are talking about useless worry and anxiety here, the ruminating of the mind and the roiling of emotions that have no useful outlet because there is none to be had.

Drop those and you'll be amazed at all the time and energy you used to waste on them.

Ask Lilly. She was once a worrier supreme. She could worry about a hundred things at once, skipping from one to the other without pause. Somebody close to her taught her the lesson well: "If there's nothing you can do about it, take it out of your head." She's been practising ever since, and lo! She's down to very few worries these days, and their days are numbered. Good for you, Lilly!

Now, let's briefly list some of the worries you might be hugging to your bosoms to no avail: somebody's health. If you've done all you can do to help them, let it go. Allow them their path. Another one: somebody's relationship to you. There isn't much one can do about somebody else's feelings. Only superficial changes can be made—in behaviour, in attitude. But if somebody's energy is not forthcoming in a positive way, then let go of worry about that.

You can, of course, do something about your own energy in relation to that person, that's definitely useful. But that's not what we're talking about. Worrying about relationships is usually worrying about the other, and largely useless.

Then there is worrying about your child: is it safe, are you doing the right thing, will it grow up to be the kind of person you want it to be? Check it out: do everything you can to do the right and loving thing by that child, then quit your worrying. Once you have taught, let it go. Worrying that your child has packed the right socks for a trip, worrying that the plane will carry it there (keeping the plane in the air), or worrying that somebody will treat the child well—all useless. Do what you can in any situation to make it the best you can, then let it go.

On the one hand, this sounds simple, on the other it sounds difficult, and in the end the proof is in the pudding. Some of you will find it easier than others to distinguish between useless worry and preparation for action. Others will find it almost impossible not to worry because they have equated worry with love, or with "doing something." For every single one of you, practice is the way to get where you are going (even if it isn't to Carnegie Hall, as the old joke has it).

Here is the simple step-by-step version:

1. Catch yourself worrying. (To get that process started, simply check in with yourself periodically to see whether you were, in fact, worrying. You'll find that often you were.)
2. Ask yourself whether there is anything you can do about the situation or person, to help improve matters. If the answer is "yes," then do it.

3. If the answer is "no, there is nothing I can do about it," then shift your focus to something else. Simply move your thoughts to another subject. And yes, it's possible to do that, even if somebody is dying, even if *you* are dying. If there is nothing you can do about it, why waste last times worrying?

4. If you have moved your thoughts and they have landed on other worries, repeat above process, until your thoughts land on something useful or delightful or, goodness, they leave you alone for just a bit to enjoy simply "being."

Lest you think the hard work involved in the above practice is hardly worth it, you're all right, Jack, or even if you do worry, let us tell you this: every time you worry or are anxious, you restrict your energy flow, reduce your life force, submerge your life joy, and are generally a drag on the Light-Love-Energy we seek to improve for everyone's sake. So not only is your own life reduced, you also drag down the overall up-energy available on the planet. And you are set up to be more easily battered by the changing vibrations in these days of the shifting, more easily swamped by all the "bad news," more easily drowned in the darkness and shadow side of all our natures.

LILLY: Excuse me, Beeswax, are you saying that you, Entities beyond the veil, and Beings of Light, also have shadow sides to your natures?
GOLYGA: No, we are saying the shadow side of existence on Earth, in physical bodies, can easily swamp the Light and Love Energy we hope to bring and increase in and for you.
LILLY: Thank you.
GOLYGA: All right, we could have said "all your natures," but you know perfectly well you'd all read it as an accusation. When, in fact, it's just a fact. You are on Earth, after all, to do just that work of transmuting darkness and negative energy into Light and Love Energy.
LILLY: Where does the negative energy come from?
GOLYGA: Another subject entirely and one we shall most certainly address in the future. For today, Lilly dear, we want to thank you and bid you farewell.

* * *

GOLYGA: Yes, we are ready and pleased to be working with you today, since all the previous obstacles—such as computer problems and contract negotiations—have been removed or put aside, and we are happy to tell you this is going to be a segment you will enjoy!
LILLY: Can't think of one I haven't enjoyed.
GOLYGA: Well, some more than others, shall we say. Here goes…

Once upon a time, there was a great big bear called Big Bear. He hung out around the dump near a lake in Muskoka and foraged there for the goodies thrown out by cottagers and locals alike. A particular favourite of his was bags full of feathers. Yes, feathers. Mouldy or wet or thrown out because of allergies, several bags of feathers were tossed out every summer, and Big Bear loved every one of them. He checked every soft bag he could find and when he discovered yet another bag of feathers, he dragged it off to his den, to line it and make it soft and cozy for the winter.

Why shouldn't a bear have a soft and cozy lair for his hibernation? he used to think as he dragged his feathers homeward. Why should I rely on the fat of my body to be comfortable? Humans don't do that. I've looked into their homes and they are filled with various degrees of comfort, but every one of them has something softer to sleep on than a hard floor. So, it's feathers for me and that's that.

Well, one day, Big Bear was dragging home another bag full of feathers when he ran into Fox, who asked him what was in the bag. Feathers, said Big Bear. Want to make something of it?

Fox took a couple of steps backward. Why would I want to make something of it? he asked, puzzled by Big Bear's belligerent tone.

Because you probably think I should be sleeping on a hard floor, just because I'm a creature of the wild, and big and fat to boot. At least during fall and early winter I am. After that, of course, it gets harder and harder to be comfortable because I get skinnier and skinnier and my bones begin to ache and complain so that I can hardly snore.

Fox was still puzzled. And why, he asked, do you suppose I have objections to your bags of feathers and soft sleeping? Why do you suppose it's any concern of mine how well or bony your ass is during hibernation? Why are you even telling me all this?

Big Bear stopped with his mouth wide open. Are you trying to suggest this is nobody's business but my own?

Exactly, said Fox. And nobody's business is what I would call your snoring, too, unless, of course, you have a partner complaining about it.

Now it was Big Bear's turn to be amazed.

How did you know that? he asked Fox. Has she said anything to you?

Fox let out a nasty-sounding snicker and went off down the path toward the blueberry patch, hoping to find a tasty lunch for himself among those who like blueberries.

Big Bear looked up into the sky. He was apoplectic and asking the Great Spirit for advice on how to handle his temper before he blew himself up into smithereens. Here he had done everything in his power to please his mate, had even lined the cave with all these bags of feathers to make the place comfortable for her, and the thanks he got in return was complaints about his snoring.

Big Bear managed to calm himself sufficiently to go home, drop his newest bag of feathers on the floor, and set out in search of his mate. He finally found her in the blueberry patch and there he confronted her with her tattle-telling ways, embarrassing him in front of one and all about his snoring.

Embarrass? said his mate, Medium Bear. Why would it embarrass you if I tell people about your snoring? Doesn't everybody snore sometimes? I know I do. What's the matter with you, anyhow, always so concerned with what people will think of you. It'll drive you bananas.

Big Bear was not mollified or pleased to hear his mate go on like this. All very well for her, she was from other parts and could afford to seem a little odd or unconventional to the folks around here, but he was born and bred and raised here and lived here all his life and would until the day he died and went to the big berry patch in the sky. So whenever he said or did anything, he was very aware, very tuned-in, he liked to think, of everything everybody around thought about that sort of thing. True, it was a nuisance sometimes, because there were so many things he would like to try doing sometime but never did have the courage to undertake lest somebody would think it odd or funny or silly.

Silly was the worst. Big Bear couldn't bear to be thought silly. So he always bore himself with great dignity and lost many opportunities to have fun. His mate, on the other hand, never passed up an opportunity to have fun, and, Bear thought to himself, nobody ever thought her anything but a fun-loving, generous, delightful companion and friend. He had never heard of anyone who didn't enjoy her peccadilloes and didn't envy him his lovely mate, Medium Bear.

After thinking about it for several months, as was his way, Big Bear went to his mate and said: You are right, my dear. I shall endeavour to change my ways. Henceforth I intend to care not a whit whether I appear dignified or even sober. I shall cavort and delight and have a whole lot of fun.

Yippee, said Medium Bear. Let's start doing it together. Today, there is a hayride for children over at Concession Road 35 and I was planning to hide in the hay and have a ride, too. Want to come?

Sure, said Big Bear. Can we both hide under the hay?

We'll see, said Medium Bear, and she chuckled at the thought of them hidden in the hay, underneath all those children who would jump with glee for the entire duration of the hayride.

So off the two went to Concession Road 35, and secretly and silently they climbed onto the wagon and hid under the hay. Soon, a whole herd of children came running and clambered all over the wagon, the farmer said, "Giddy-up," to the horses, and off they went.

At the beginning, it was fun. The bumping and the yelling and the jumping up and down of the children, and even the smell of the hay, strong though it was. But after a while, Big Bear found the hay tickled his nose and soon he felt an enormous urge to sneeze.

Don't do that, said his mate, trying to hold his nose for him. If you sneeze, they'll hear us, and I happen to know, that farmer does not like bears, especially under his hayride children.

Well, they tried and tried to keep that sneeze in Big Bear's nose, but finally it did come bursting out, in a great big booming *kaaachooomp*, and hay flew everywhere and children tumbled all over, and Medium Bear curled up laughing, so that only the farmer and Big Bear were actually facing each other to deal with this development.

Big Bear was the first to speak.

Now, before you get all upset, he said to the farmer, and maybe even irate, allow me to introduce myself: I am Big Bear. The bear rolling and laughing her head off over here is my mate, Medium Bear.

Yeah, right, said the farmer, and I am Goldilocks. Where is Little Tiny Bear?

Big Bear was puzzled. There was no Little Tiny Bear as yet, and why in the world would this farmer with his big boots on and his bald head be called Goldilocks?

This is very interesting, said Big Bear. Tell me why you think we already have a baby when we don't, and why you have been named Goldilocks.

The farmer, however, had run out of what little humour he had in him and was now getting seriously aggrieved.

You ruined our hayride and, what's more, you scared all the children to death.

Don't be silly, said Medium Bear, finally sitting up and partaking of the conversation. Not one of them is scared. Just look at them!

The farmer looked around to where the children were standing, surrounding the wagon, and listening with great interest and not one bit of fright. Now it was his turn to be puzzled.

Has nobody ever taught you to be afraid of bears? he asked the children.

The children looked at each other and nodded. Oh yes, they said. We *are* afraid of bears. But surely these two are not real bears, are they? I mean, here they are, speaking English and sneezing and laughing. We assumed they are part of the entertainment for this hayride and we must say, it's quite a wonderful aspect of the entire adventure.

The farmer stared at the children who spoke like no children he had ever heard, but then they were city folk and there was no accounting for the ways of city folk, even the littlest of them.

No, he said, these bears are not part of any entertainment. They are indeed real bears. But it's too late now to be afraid of them because we are all stuck in so unusual a situation that old accustomed responses are not about to help us out of it.

Help us out of it? said the children, aghast. We don't want out of it. We want more. More hayride, more bears sneezing and giggling, and certainly more of this unusual conversation we are all having.

There was no sound at all for about ten seconds, after which Medium Bear began giggling again, and the children clambered up on the hay wagon, and Big Bear decided to sit up front with the farmer to pursue their conversation while everybody else was singing lustily and jumping up and down on the hay.

And thus it was that Big Bear changed his entire life during one hayride and became a well-beloved figure, an eccentric, a fun companion, and happy mate. Not to mention his unsurpassed ability to snore his head off among the bags full of feathers in his winter cave.

LILLY: Thank you, yes. I did enjoy this a great deal.
GOLYGA: And despite interruptions, we completed the segment, and so, in the future, you'll know not to worry about uninterrupted working sessions, all right?
LILLY: All right, yes. Thank you.
GOLYGA: Now eat, rest, enjoy, have a giggle and a hayride, or whatever is going to give you joy.

* * *

GOLYGA: And so we return to our odyssey and our adventures and our little get-togethers. I know you are pleased, and so am I. We have much work ahead, all of it fun, and so your eagerness to resume is appreciated.

Lillykins, as we all know by now, is a curious being. Curiosity, in fact, rides her like the proverbial monkey on the back. Curiosity also gets her into the oddest situations and encounters. Here is the next one…

Lillykins sat on a rock, contemplating the sky. Clouds were moving across the bluest of skies, some quickly, some slowly, all of them in shades of grey. No silver lining was discernible anywhere. Lillykins pondered the sayings about silver linings and why they were so pervasive in all human cultures and languages. Was it perennial optimism and the determined soul's orientation toward the light, or simply humanity's inability to go on unless there was hope to cling to and an instinctual tinting of rosy hue inside every cloud of grey. So Lillykins was idly musing, as she looked up into the sky.

Meantime, a creature was approaching. A tiny creature, silently and smoothly gliding up the rock upon which Lillykins sat pondering.

The creature was nearing Lillykins' derriere by now, not at all sure what lay before its darting eyes. Immobile? Not quite. Vibrations were discernible in the lumpish shape ahead. Alive, then, with the distinctive energy vibrations of a warm-blooded creature, and the assumed ability to move, perhaps suddenly and dangerously.

The creature advanced more cautiously, keeping its clear sharp eyes focused on the lump that was Lilykin's derriere—seen from the creature's perspective, of course. Far be it from us to so describe the shapely, slim, firm buttocks of our heroine.

Suddenly, the lump moved. A second creature—or should we say third?—attached itself to the lump and scrambled and scrabbled back and forth on a small part of it, scrabbling and rustling and rubbing all its legs or tentacles on the big lump. And just as suddenly, the second creature stopped, moved off through the air, and was gone.

Our slow-approaching creature had, of course, stopped to watch the activity in front of its long nose. Frozen in the stance of a forward-pointing arrow, it now relaxed enough to start breathing again and even shot out its long tongue, to make sure it was still working and capable of its intended actions in the world. After a short while, the creature began inching forward again, forward toward the vibrating mass on top of the rock.

And then something else happened. The creature detected motion at the top of the lump and looked up. And almost fell over in astonishment. This lump the creature had been watching so carefully and closely extended upward for a long way! It had other lumpy masses on top of it. It was a most misshapen congregate of lumps, in fact, and horrific in its ugliness.

The creature froze again. Did it even want to get any nearer to this ugly thing? Would this amount of ugliness turn out to be dangerous for a creature as sleek and beautiful as itself? Could it be that ugliness of such mammoth proportions emitted poisonous gas, or evil intent with barbs, or any other kind of danger to the beautiful of this world?

I mean look, the creature said to itself, with my beautiful colours, patterns of scales, articulated body of great suppleness and slithering graceful movement, and with my long elegant tongue and shapely legs and toes—what in the world could I do to protect myself if this ugly thing were to emit ugliness rays? I'd be in danger of lumpiness and near-immobility, and subject to scrabbling creatures all over me. No, the horror of it all was too much for the creature, so it fainted. And fell off the rock.

The motion of the creature's sudden fall penetrated the awareness of the top lump of the aggregate. It moved. It turned. It shone its eye rays onto the creature lying beside the rock in a dead faint. The entire lot of lumps suddenly rushed upward and emitted not poison rays but sounds of a horrendous timbre. Like grates of iron being banged and scraped against each other. Luckily, no one was around to hear the sound; it would have paralyzed any listeners in their tracks.

Well, of course there *was* one listener: Lillykins. She who made the awful sounds. She who was, in fact, the aggregate of lumps, now upright and staring with its light globes at the fainted creature lying there: a snake she knew to be dangerous and even lethal.

Lillykins emitted a different sound. A small, whiny, scared sound in the throat. At the same time, she moved backwards, away from the fainted snake, and she wondered—she couldn't help it—what in the world would make a snake faint like that? Never suspecting for a moment that it was the sight of her own rump, being scratched by her own hand, in combination with the sight of her body towering above her own rump. Never suspecting that the snake was an aesthete, swooning at the sight of so much ugliness, and it would never quite recover from the experience, even once it came out of its faint, and would, for the rest of its days, slink about trying not to see too much. Would never ever raise its eyes to the sky, let alone ponder the existence or non-existence of silver linings and humanity's persistent adherence to the belief in their existence.

Lillykins backed away from the rock, glued her eyes to the path her feet were taking, and went off, under the impression that the snake had never actually seen her. The snake recovered, found the lumps gone, and slunk away, convinced it had been a nightmare, and yet…and yet… influenced forever more by its judgment of what was ugly and its belief that ugliness is evil and dangerous.

LILLY: Have I been particularly judgmental lately?

GOLYGA: No, my dear, except against yourself. You have judged yourself on every thought, action, endeavour—good or bad, mostly bad—and so you are worn down by the assault of judgmental pronouncements on yourself. How about letting yourself be—a lump or a bee or just a vibration on a rock. How about that for a break?
LILLY: Thank you, Golyga. I do see, suddenly, that I've been nattering at myself about every little thing. Any pointers for reducing that natter?
GOLYGA: For one, be alert to your thought processes. Then, when the habit asserts itself, observe something without judgment. Whether it be a finger on your hand, a leaf in the snow, or the dance of a dust mite—just observe and make no other comment. Then try to do the same thing for your own actions, thoughts, musings: observe them, do not judge them, let them move on like the clouds in the sky. Don't even check to see whether or not there is a silver lining. Observe what is in front of your nose and be.
LILLY: Thank you very much.
GOLYGA: You are very welcome. Until soon, Lilly dear. Be well, be happy, be our valentine and our snot-nosed rebellious kid and our creative partner, and our delight on the path.

* * *

GOLYGA: And so we resume and continue. Please relax and be not worried about interruptions, we won't go away. Also, take a pace you can sustain without tension, and when needed, take a short break.

Once upon a time, there was a stalwart sort of man who always knew what was right. Goodness, he often said to himself, if only the world knew what I know, everything would run smoothly and everyone would be happy. Unfortunately, practically no one listens to me, and those who do disagree with me.

And so the stalwart man went about his life in a sour fashion, always mumbling to himself about what he knew better than everyone else.

Came the day when the stalwart man was ready to leave this Earth and his body and enter into the kingdom of heaven. He arrived at the notorious pearly gates and expected entrance. However, first he had to pass entrance qualifications by the minions sent to do this preliminary work.

What have you been doing with your life? asked the first one. Have you been enjoying it?

Good heavens, no, said the stalwart man. How can one possibly enjoy life on Earth? Just have a look at it. Everything about it is wrong and everyone on it is doing everything all wrong.

The examining angel was astounded. Everything? Everyone? How can this be? Did you never run into anything or anybody right?

Not once, said the stalwart man.

Well, in that case, said the angel, you'll hardly find anything right here either, so what's the point of coming in? I suggest you find a place that agrees with you and is agreeable to you. Go ahead, and have a good time searching for it.

The stalwart man was astounded. But I thought heaven was the place where everything was going to be right and I would finally be understood and appreciated!

Not here, said the angel. In here, everyone is right in their own way and everything goes forward in the best way possible. So you see, this is definitely not the place for you.

Well, where shall I look? asked the stalwart man. What other places are there, besides Earth and heaven?

The angel started to laugh. Every other examining angel came around to laugh as well. Pretty soon the sound of delighted laughter echoed throughout the heavens and was possibly even heard on Earth.

Only the stalwart man didn't join in. He huffed and puffed and took himself off to seek those other places. Unfortunately, he was soon lost from view and no one knows to this day where he is. Furthermore, no one is out looking for him. After all, if that is his task, his path, his endeavour, who is anyone else to deprive him of it?

And there you have it: another fable to add to the many you have read, Lilly dear, have written yourself, and have encountered through Golyga and his wonderful adventures. We brought you this one at this time to facilitate something for the reader of this book: if you find it all nonsense, or "off," or in any way offensive to your certain knowledge of how things really are, remember the stalwart man. Or, on the other side of the coin, be assured that you'll be quite fine without reading this book and perhaps even doing some of the work.

162

Oh yes, you'll be fine.

Whether as fine as you can be, whether as delighted with living as you might be—all that is another question. So there you are: free will does pertain to many aspects of life on Earth, and you are definitely free to avail yourself of it. If, however, you are curious and want to continue reading, be assured that the best route is to make certain you are enjoying it. In other words, play with those notions that seem entirely foreign or unacceptable to you. Play with them as you would with juggling balls or balloons. Throw them up into the air, let the light shine through, flick one up, catch one and hold it for a while, maybe even cuddle it through the night. And when you're done playing, see what has pleased you about it all. And see what it is you'd like to have stick around. All right?

GOLYGA: In future, we will pick segments of the Golyga material to help us elucidate certain notions and ideas. In the meantime, however, we are going to keep suggesting a method of working that is easiest on all of us. Your body, Lilly, is doing fine—remember to rest, please—and we are looking forward to regular sessions. On the other hand, we are not going to be impatient if you take off on a trip or do other work, as it suits you. We are well on the way and have no need or will to put you under pressure.

LILLY: Thank you. I look forward to our sessions.

GOLYGA: We know you do. That's it for today, my dear. Be well, be happy, be joyous, be beloved.

✳ ✳ ✳

Yes, we will have a short working session together today. Short because the material is concentrated and meant to be worked with and digested over time. There is no point in galloping ahead with this book, dear reader—unless you mean to read it again more thoroughly—without attention to the work to be done. However, the work need not be a burden or a great source of "shoulds." It can be accomplished easily and with good results if you but pay attention to your daily life with this new perspective in awareness whenever you remember it:

You are not here on Earth to struggle and have a tough time of it. You are passing through, as you have passed through other lives and will pass through more in the future—whether on Earth or elsewhere—and you will learn what you can while here, then continue learning when elsewhere. So do not make your lives miserable for fear of missing a moment's learning or seeing only half the picture unless you strive and wrestle with yourself every moment of your waking life. (By the way, much of your learning takes place during sleep.)

We recommend that henceforth you stop periodically as you go through your day in order to check in with your internal goings-on and to reassure yourselves: There is no need to be struggling and striving.

You will have met this notion before and perhaps even believed it and set it in motion in your lives. If so, let this serve as a reminder.

For most of you, however, even if the notion came to you in some form or other, the actual practice of the new paradigm has been abandoned. It's just too foreign an approach, after all these generations of Sturm und Drang, of struggle and dark expectations of pain and doom and gloom and difficulties and problems. Humans have been perpetuating that universe of doom and gloom for so long, it's truly difficult to perceive of life on Earth as being a stage flooded with light and laughter, with joy and love, if only you will buy the ticket to the show.

Not the best metaphor, perhaps, because you are, in fact, a participant rather than audience, but how one views life is the single most important factor in how one lives it, experiences it, and leaves it. Whether your life lessons are difficult and even horrible, or whether they are merely troublesome, your view and perspective will make more difference than any circumstance.

Take death.

Lilly has just this morning heard of the death of a friend. A quick death that she deems a good one. However, the larger picture might well show that this friend, not having prepared himself, will have more learning ahead than if he'd had a slow death. However, again, none of this matters if you simply remember that learning is what we are all here for, that time is a limited and limiting concept, and that going through life on Earth will be most "productive" if you are able to see it as your "course" for this semester.

We, too, are in motion in that we are learning still and, even while teaching and bringing increased knowledge to those of you in body, we are being helped and taught by more knowledgeable beings. A chain of learning, in other words, and the major difference is that we know it all the time and engage in it with joy and delight and much playful creativity. A way of learning and being that is available to you as well and *it's up to you* whether you choose it or whether you continue to struggle and push and make hard-nosed demands on yourself.

We can feel that Lilly is at this very moment letting go of the sadness for Bill's death. Not only because he would have preferred a quick death to a slow one from cancer—which he had—but because she can sense/ feel that the transition Bill is undergoing can only be for the better. "Go joyous into that dark night" is not given to all of us, so "go quickly" is considered the next best thing. Go forth, in every case, means going forward, moving on, and entering a universe where struggle and pain and hurdles that threaten broken limbs or spirits simply do not exist. There are other shadows, there is no light without shadows, but none of the sheer misery that so many of you insist on surrounding yourselves with on a daily basis.

Try it:

Periodically, as you go through your day, stop and ask yourself: Am I making a struggle where there need be none? Am I in need of this worry, this anxiety, this anticipation of misery, this fear of anything? And then let it go, whatever darkness you find. Let it go as though it's a cloud that is supposed to pass on, move away, and leave the light shining in the sky and all over your day, your life, your steadily increasing joy.

* * *

GOLYGA: All right then, we'll do a session we shall both enjoy. We'll travel far and wide and then return to our beginning, having learned and laughed and cried. Shall we?
LILLY: Yes, please.

Here we are, said Golyga to his mate and delight Lillykins. Here we are, sitting by the river, wondering what next. After all, since this baby arrived, we've hardly had time to see to our own pleasure, let alone our own adventures. So let's take the opportunity and do something wild and wonderful.

Like what, for example, said Lillykins, secretly thrilled at the prospect.

Well, for instance, we could fly to the Himalayas and ride a snowcapped mountain peak and slope on our bottoms.

Brrrr, said Lillykins.

All right then, we could swim in the Amazon River.

And be food for goodness knows what creatures in it?

All right, said Golyga, you make a suggestion.

Lillykins thought about possibilities she would enjoy. How about sailing off the coast of the Hawaiian Islands?

Fine, said Golyga. Let's go.

But first, said Lillykins, we should—

No, no, no, said Golyga. I know you and your "first we shoulds." First we should just go and do it. Then we'll contemplate the rest. Come on.

Okay, said Lillykins, to Golyga's surprise, and off they flew, the two of them, on huge wings, soaring high and riding the wind, until they arrived at one of the Hawaiian Islands. There they stopped to figure out how to procure a sailboat. And how to sail it, once they had one.

Golyga suggested they simply watch the seas until they saw a sailboat, and then they could get on board, observe how sailing is done, and perhaps even practise on that boat before procuring their own.

Again he was surprised by Lillykins' immediate acquiescence.

What's happening with you? asked Golyga. You're altogether too agreeable. Is there something afoot I should know about? A volcanic eruption? A tidal wave?

Lillykins laughed. Don't be daft, she said. I am merely in a good mood and ready to enjoy myself. Let's go. I see a sailboat on the horizon.

Golyga and Lillykins flew over to the sailboat, then changed into pelicans and followed the boat for a while. Nobody seemed to be aboard this craft and nobody seemed to be sailing it, which amazed and mystified Golyga and Lillykins.

Could this be a famous ghost ship?

Ghosts don't sail in sailboats, said Golyga. It would be too "coals to Newcastle," if you know what I mean.

Lillykins disagreed. It would be entirely appropriate and quite wonderful, if you ask me. When I'm a ghost, I would certainly like to feel I can fill the sail of a sailboat and take off on the seas any time I please. I would, in fact, much rather do that, as a ghost, than haunt or rattle or scare or even star in movies. Wouldn't you?

Yes, said Golyga, you're right, I would. However, if this is a ghost ship, it would be entirely easy to ask permission to learn how to sail it. Come on, let's get on board and find out.

Lillykins and Golyga changed into ants. Two little black ants who walked side by side—an unusual sight, if anyone had been there to see— and explored the deck. Nobody there. Not even the ghost of anything, as far as they could tell.

Then who is sailing this boat? Lillykins wondered aloud.

We are! Golyga and Lillykins heard. We are and you had better heed because we do not take kindly to ants trying to take over our sailboat.

Sorry, said Golyga. We won't even try. But who are you and where are you? Are you ghosts?

Certainly not, said the voice. I am the wind, and this is my boat, and I play with it whenever the notion takes me. So bug off.

Rude, said Golyga. Isn't he rude?

Lillykins shook her head: Shhhh, she said. Don't annoy him. He could wreak havoc with our plans to learn to sail a boat—once we have one.

So true, said the wind. Glad to hear one of you is sensible. So I'll tell you what I'll do: I'll teach you to sail. Then you can bug off and get your own sailboat. Okay?

Sure, said Golyga. Great. Let's do it.

And they did. The wind taught Golyga and Lillykins to sail—and what better teacher could there possibly be?—and as soon as they had the hang of it, the two of them thanked the wind profoundly and left.

Now, said Lillykins. Let's look around and find a boat just the right size for the two of us.

That would be the boat I see over there, in the natural harbour. See it?

Lillykins did. As soon as they boarded this boat, being ants again, they encountered a most amazing sight. A huge rat was packing her belongings, preparing to leave the boat.

It's all yours, she said. I've had it with this boat. It rocks and it sways but it never goes anywhere. It's all yours and may you enjoy it!

Off went the rat, swinging her suitcase.

Why do you suppose the boat never went anywhere? said Lillykins. It looks like a perfectly good boat to me.

Oh, it is, said Golyga. Look here. This is the reason the boat never went anywhere. Golyga pointed down, and when Lillykins looked, she saw a huge anchor lying on the bottom of the sea, tied to the ship by enormous chains, keeping it from ever leaving the spot.

No wonder, said Lillykins. For heaven's sake. Do you think that rat didn't know about the anchor?

Who can tell, said Golyga. All I know is we now have a boat to go sailing on and we're going to do it right now.

Together they lifted the anchor by means of a winch, and they sailed the boat along the coasts of the Hawaiian Islands, enjoying every minute of it. Finally they came back, dropped the anchor, and sat side by side, resting.

What we have to do now, said Golyga, is figure out what to name the anchor.

Whatever for? asked Lillykins. Why would we want to do that?

Well, said Golyga, if you know what to call your anchor, it's easier to hoist it off the bottom and begin whatever journey you may want to go on.

Ah yes, said Lillykins. That makes perfect sense, my wise and delightful companion and mate. First mate.

And captain, said Golyga.

Ha! said Lillykins.

But that isn't a conversation we're going to follow to its end today. Because for today it's quite enough to know that our task is to name the anchor. Name it, hoist it, and sail the seas.

LILLY: Is that it for today, Golyga?
GOLYGA: Yes, it is.

LILLY: Thank you for a most enjoyable tale as well as a valuable lesson.

GOLYGA: You are most welcome, Lilly dear. And thank you for the respect and consideration you gave yesterday in preferring to ask me first whether or not to divulge my name in conversation.

LILLY: Yes, I felt a resistance toward divulging it and didn't know whether it was my own or whether it was coming from you.

GOLYGA: It was coming from you. On the other hand, I do believe nothing is gained at this time by talking casually about names and tasks.

LILLY: Are you saying I shouldn't mention this book to anyone?

GOLYGA: Not at all. It gives me pleasure to hear you describe it. But names, and tasks of a specific nature such as retrieval work, should be talked of only in the context of learning, not casual conversation.

LILLY: All right. I'll remember that. But in the case of someone asking questions, as M. did, in order to learn more about the subject of channelling—is that casual conversation or learning?

GOLYGA: In that case it's learning. You'll find it easy to tell the difference by simply checking whether it's ego talking. Generally, you are not prone to boasting or ego talk on the subject, so this is not a wagging finger you're getting here. All right?

LILLY: Thank you, yes. And thank you for the answer.

* * *

GOLYGA: Yes, my dear, we are here and glad to be talking to you. You need a talking to. You are so hard on yourself. Where is the compassion you have for others? Where is the care and attention to yourself and for yourself? You are running when you should be pausing to ask yourself: What can I do for myself that would truly be helpful both in the short and the long run. Nothing you can do about the weather, so it might be easier to pack up and go for the season. Lots you can do for the internal weather. For instance: be with us. Ask us for help. Ask for love and compassion. Give yourself the gift of love and compassion. Bring into your life whatever gives you solace.

LILLY: Seems to me I still tend to go for escapism, thus prolonging the agony.

GOLYGA: To some extent. But you also allow yourself to deal with feelings by way of tears and staying with solitude, though it would be easy to go to Toronto and bear solitude there, among distractions. You are actually carrying a rather larger burden than usual these days—though not for much longer—larger than for seasonal change and old abandonment issues—which you have largely conquered or, rather, healed. You are carrying the burden of many energies that are in agony—the Russians, yes, but also *T, S, R,* and others. *M*, also, is not having an easy time right now. So think of yourself as an overburdened donkey—no, better make that some creature you can be more sympathetic with: say a chipmunk—an overburdened chipmunk, and give it a great deal of sympathy and caring attention. Okay?

LILLY: *I'll try. I'm rather large to identify as a chipmunk.*

GOLYGA: *The ratio of body and burdens is good, though. Remember that you are but one body, carrying far too much right now. Do the protective evocations and keep on doing them because that way you won't be burdened with the energies of people you can't really help anyway.*

LILLY: *Thank you very much, I can begin to feel the relief now.*

GOLYGA: *You are welcome, my dear. The other suggestion we would make is to bring fear under control. There is nothing really to fear—whatever comes up by way of weather or company, you can counter it with a solution. You are not stuck. So banish fears and you'll find it easier to give yourself love and protection. Okay?*

LILLY: *Okay. Thank you again. You have already been most helpful.*

GOLYGA: *Good. Shall we do a work session then?*

LILLY: *Yes, please.*

All right, here is some material for the book that you will insert into the second part. It has as its subject, or topic, the tendency of humans to hang on to material from their past even when it is neither helpful nor pleasant nor even useful in any way. For example: say a traumatic event in childhood has left a person with a tendency toward depression or anxiety that gets activated whenever certain triggers occur. Well, the triggers will occur, willy-nilly, in the course of a lifetime. And to ignore them is to give in to victimhood on the subject of whatever the traumatic events were. On the other hand, to unearth the triggers and endeavour to avoid them does not work any better, because then the fear of the triggers determines decisions in one's life, and that's definitely as bad as any so-called solution involving avoidance, escapism, or any other form of sidestepping emotions that are painful.

So here is what we recommend: become clear on the traumatic events and on the triggers. Then observe yourself. The moment you feel yourself touched by the traumatic past, the moment you become aware of the old syndrome, pause. Pause and take stock. Make clear again what it's about, what happened, what havoc it wrought, and then: kiss it goodbye. Not forever, because such material tends to have a long life and sharp nails with which to hang on to you, but goodbye for this time around. That way, instead of ruining your life again for a considerable length of time, it will be a shortened period and will, because of the pause, the acknowledgment, even a few tears, perhaps, have cleared out some of the trauma and made it less virulent in the next recurrence.

Think of the traumatic material as having a life of its own, a character, a symbolic representation, a very large will to live. Then think of yourself as being far more complex, more clever, more complete a being than the creature you have just envisioned. Constantly remind yourself, when it appears, that it is but a shadowy representation of something that was once traumatic and powerful while you were a victim. Make clear to yourself and to the creature that you are far from being a victim now. That you are willing to be empathetic, even compassionate, but then the creature is to remember its diminished state in relation to your now powerful self and is to be gone.

In the process of dealing with this creature you have clothed in a body and given a name, you are already demonstrating your dominion and immediately, you will find, a great reduction of the pain involved. Because the pain resides largely in the victimhood of the original events.

So, to recap:

Allow the traumatic material to come up into awareness once triggered into your emotions and give it a body and/or a name.

Also give it compassion.

And then assert your powers of self to bid it begone.

There is nothing to be gained by hanging on to the emotions past the point of awareness and acknowledgment and compassionate understanding. Because then it's a self-indulgence and counterproductive in every way.

If you want to be sure that enough compassion has been given, ask the creature whether it has received your heartfelt sympathy. If it says no, give it more. If it says yes, that's your cue to bid it a courteous and loving goodbye. And feel/watch it retreat, leave, diminish in size and power, and, in fact, become smaller and smaller each time you experience the above sequence.

GOLYGA: Yes, Lilly dear, we can hear a question coming on.

LILLY: Say the trauma is abandonment. To give it a body, I envisioned a very dark, fluid shape of a large humanoid and found it scary. I can also give abandonment the shape of an abandoned baby, but then I can't really tell it "goodbye" with any good conscience. What am I doing wrong here?

GOLYGA: You are intellectualizing. Try pausing and letting a shape come up for abandonment—whatever it may be.

LILLY: It's a clay-coloured lumpish creature, moving in place, roughly rectangular but alive, though I see no legs or other features.

GOLYGA: Excellent. Now, can you find sympathy for this creature?

LILLY: Yes. It seems to feel very exposed outside like that. It's used to being inside me, especially in the upper part of my body and the throat area. Now it's exposed and helpless out there. I don't want it back in my body, but on the other hand it's hard to tell it to bug off altogether. There seems to be some attachment between us.

GOLYGA: Well, of course there is. A lifetime of living together, for one. And thus the feeling that if you don't give the creature a home, it's abandoned, as you were. A horrible fate you wouldn't want to impose on anyone, right? So what solution is possible here and now?

LILLY: I don't know.

GOLYGA: We recommend the following: bid the creature goodbye and see where it goes.

LILLY: Okay, I'll try that. It seems to have changed shape gradually to become a long creature, a giant worm or such, moving out into the universe, becoming fainter in colour and substance.

GOLYGA: It's not feeling any pain, as far as you know?

LILLY: No. It seems to have gone off seeking, but it's not in pain and I don't feel bad as a result of bidding it goodbye.

GOLYGA: Good for you, my dear. That creature will change shape many times yet, and it will likely reappear in/with you in future, but now you know exactly what to do if you want to rid yourself of this traumatic material from your past. The same method applies to any traumatic events anyone has ever had: make it conscious, give it a body and/or name, give it sympathy, bid it goodbye. Over and over, if necessary, but you will definitely see and feel the diminishing size and power of the creature and the traumatic material.

Now: all of the above is to be included in the book, in section 2, all right?

LILLY: All right. And thank you so much. I finally feel relief from the present bout of agony. May I ask you something unrelated to the book?

GOLYGA: *Of course, my dear. Anything at all—though we doubt it would be entirely unrelated.*

LILLY: *It's about my friendships. While considering how difficult it is for me to give myself love and empathy when I'm down, I started to think about my friends and whether they are able to love themselves. I have not exhausted the list of them, but so far, not one is good at loving herself or himself. Will I be able to have friends who can love—themselves and others?*

GOLYGA: *Yes, you will. But there is that practice you have to engage in that we have mentioned before: go for the unfamiliar energy. Not the ones who call on your pity and empathy and understanding. Find those who delight in your company rather than seeking it to supply their needs. And the best way for you to catch that unfamiliar energy is to be very observant—of others and of your own energetic reaction. Beware old reactions, knee-jerk responses. Beware even negative responses to someone's energy. Keep checking out what goes on when you meet people and eventually you will learn what it feels like to have your energy not sucked and depleted but enhanced and replenished. Okay?*

LILLY: *Thank you, yes. I'll do that as soon as I meet some people. At the moment, it's more chipmunks and such.*

GOYGA: *Well, make sure they are not the overburdened kind. Much love, as always.*

LILLY: *Thank you, thank you, thank you.*

GOLYGA: *You are welcome, my dear. All the best until soon.*

$$* * *$$

GOLYGA: *We are pleased to be with you and working again and to find you in good shape despite all the holiday indulgences that inevitably beset humans. Odd, isn't it, that celebrating includes so much self-destruction in your present state. Though you, dear Lilly, did keep it to the chocolate realm rather than expanding into the many other indulgences favoured by holiday celebrants. Good for you, anyway, because here you are, ready and willing and able, and so here we go.*

Once upon a time, there was a great big famous ball of yarn that people actually went to visit and admire. What exactly they found admirable about this great big ball of yarn was infinitely fascinating to Golyga, who'd heard of the ball's existence from Baby. No longer a baby, of course, but still in the habit of being amazed and astonished on a daily basis.

Curious, isn't it? he asked Golyga. That a ball of yarn would elicit admiration because of its size alone, though it sits there, doing nothing at all?

Golyga agreed and immediately set off to study the kind of people who would go and gawk—as he put it—at a ball of yarn as though it had some intrinsic value.

When he arrived at the ball, he saw it surrounded by bread crumbs, and these crumbs were being gobbled up quickly by a whole host of little creatures he had never before seen on the planet Earth.

Curiouser and curiouser, Golyga said to himself, quoting he knew not whom, and stayed there to watch the creatures gobbling crumbs. Soon it became obvious that the creatures were actually not so strange as he thought. They were ants but looked rather different than other ants because each wore a tiny woollen coat, a little hat with a peak, and gloves on all extremities. This astonished Golyga further. Enough so that he whistled his secret communication whistle to call his friend and beloved mate Lillykins to come and be astonished, too.

Lillykins appeared in a flash, having tired of her current interest, and she was duly astonished.

It must have something to do with the proximity of this ball of yarn, she thought, watching the ants scurry back and forth, carrying crumbs in their mouths to wherever their home was.

But who could have knitted those tiny garments for the ants?

To his annoyance, Golyga had no answers. It was ever thus: when he was alone he could simply be astonished without having to explain. When Lillykins joined him, he had to rummage around in his mind for possible explanations. This time, nothing satisfying came up, which was annoying, Golyga felt, and rather demeaning, since his great powers were such that he could see farther, know more, be far more aware and knowledgeable than most.

Most what? he suddenly thought to himself. Most what, indeed?

Lillykins, meanwhile, had laid herself flat upon her stomach and was studying the ants from as close quarters as possible without disturbing their route and activities. She immediately saw that their garments were perfectly constructed, perfectly tailored, and had been created not from wool but from some unknown material.

Lillykins beckoned to Golyga and pointed out her findings. Golyga was astonished all over again and this time forgot to get hung up on explanations and feelings of inadequacy.

That's it, he told Lillykins. This is so amazing a find that we must simply live with the fact of its existence and be relieved of any endeavour to pin an explanation on the phenomenon.

Lillykins, however, disagreed. Be practical, she said. What we have here could have marvellous application in many ways for the good of all kinds of creatures. Think of all that might be involved in the true proliferation of knowledge behind this phenomenon. The question is: how do we find out what it is?

Golyga thought for a moment and then agreed: We should try to find out what is behind this astonishing phenomenon. Why don't we ask the ants?

Lillykins was startled. This had not occurred to her. However, she was not startled for long. Still on her stomach, she addressed the nearest ant: Excuse me, she said. Could you please stop a moment and tell us something?

The ant did not stop, however. It continued on its way as though Lillykins had not spoken, or at least not to it.

Well! said Lillykins. I'm not sure what this means, but it isn't going to help us, is it?

Golyga asked the next ant: Could you please give us some information? We would appreciate it...

The ant kept going as though deaf.

Lillykins and Golyga looked at each other. What else could they do to get the ants' attention?

Aha! said Golyga. Let's try doing it by way of their beloved crumbs. Ready?

Golyga quickly started sweeping up crumbs with his arms, shaping them into great heaps on the ground. Lillykins joined in, and soon most of the crumbs were in front of them, in two great heaps, and the ants ran around like mad, confused and upset. Not one of them seemed to realize the crumbs were still there, but in another configuration. They even ran around and over the heaps, not realizing these were the same crumbs as those that had been scattered all over the ground beforehand.

175

Again, Lillykins and Golyga looked at each other and once more they were astonished.

Now what? they wondered, watching the ants scurry in confusion.

Finally, Golyga tried once more to address an ant directly. Excuse me, he said. Stop a minute, will you? We have a question to put to you.

Again, the ant didn't seem to hear him. Or understand what it heard. One of those. It just continued on its way as though no one had said a word. Which irritated Golyga to the point of picking up the ant—gently, mind you, but bodily—and lifting it to his nose—his eyes crossing as a result—and speaking directly into the ant's tiny face.

What in blazes is going on here? he asked the little ant face, and the ant, to his surprise, answered him. In a tiny voice full of astonishment, the ant said: What do you mean, "What's going on here?" Can't you see that a great tragedy has overcome us? All our food has disappeared, we'll soon be starving to death, and there's nothing we can do about it. That's what's going on.

Golyga shook his head. No, no, he said. I'm not asking about that. I'm asking about the tiny clothes you are all wearing and what material it is made of and who made it, and I'm asking about how the crumbs came to be here, and the whole ball of yarn.

Now it was the ant's turn to shake its tiny head, and it sure did, almost flinging its tiny hat off in the process.

What a stupid lot of questions, the ant said, disgusted. We are starving and you are asking stupid questions. However, I might as well answer them rather than faint right here from the fear of hunger. The crumbs are brought by people who come to admire that ball of yarn. They stand around here and eat, you see, and drop crumbs. Then, as they leave, they drop other stuff as well—wrapping, containers, utensils, that sort of thing. We chew it all down to something we can use and we have hired a hound dog who can knit and who makes us our clothes. Simple. Nothing astonishing about it.

Really! said Lillykins sarcastically. A hound dog knitting tiny perfect garments out of chewed-over garbage is not astonishing? All right then, tell us this: why did none of you stop to answer our questions before, when we tried to get some information?

We were busy getting our food supply laid in against a rainy day, so to speak. No time for philosophical discussion when you are busy providing for the future.

Well then, Golyga challenged the ant, you must have plenty laid by for this time of need!

The ant stopped its wiggly movements and thought out loud: Yeah, you're right. What happened to all the crumbs we laid by for this eventuality? Let me go, will you? I want to check out where the store of crumbs is.

Didn't you help build up that store of crumbs? Where did you take them? Lillykins was not about to let the ant tootle off until more questions were answered. She was not in the least satisfied they had done with the ant. The ant started wiggling in Golyga's grasp, almost managing to free itself because Golyga was holding it gently so as not to squash it.

Stop wiggling, said Golyga. We'll let you go soon enough and we'll even tell you of an enormous heap of crumbs, if you answer a few more questions. Like: what about this great big ball of yarn. What's it for? Why do people come to see it?

The ant shook its tiny head. No idea, it said. No idea at all. We only know that those people bring food and the stuff for making clothes and that's all we need to know.

What about that hound dog, Lillykins wanted to know. How did he learn to knit?

The ant shook its head again. No idea, it said. Never even thought about it. All I know is, he makes our garments and we're cozy warm. That's it. Now can I go?

Golyga sighed. This ant was not going to answer any questions, that was clear enough. Might as well let it go.

Wait a minute, one more, said Lillykins. Tell us why you run around looking for the crumbs, all upset, and don't recognize the heap of them in front of your nose, right there. Lillykins pointed to the nearest heap of crumbs.

The ant looked and shook its head. How can you even pretend those are crumbs? Look at it. It's a hill. Hills are not made of crumbs. Crumbs lie about on the ground. You two really don't know anything, do you?

At this point, Golyga sighed and let the ant go. It scurried off, in search of the store of crumbs laid by for this time of need.

Well, said Lillykins. We are no further ahead on any of our questions, are we?

Oh yes, we are, said Golyga. Think about it: we have encountered creatures who, while warm and well-fed, ask no questions at all. Their horizon so close and narrow they don't even recognize a hill of crumbs. And while we have no answers to the "why" of that great big ball of yarn or the people who come to view it, we do, thank goodness, have our questions. Nice word that, *questions.* It includes *quest* and *ions* and promises, to those of us in the swing, eons of questing after knowledge, endless moments of astonishment and curiosity, and of making connections, playing with notions, enjoying the search for answers.

Goodnesss, said Lillykins. That ball of yarn is quite wonderful in its way, isn't it? And so they stood up, Golyga and Lillykins, and gazed at the great ball of yarn, scattering a few crumbs here and there. Then they turned and left, never noticing that the ants had begun to follow the trail of scattered crumbs right to the heap of crumbs and there began a whole new undertaking: to scatter the hill until the crumbs were all over everywhere and could be taken home and stored against a rainy day.

GOLYGA: What do you think, Lilly dear?
LILLY: I think it's another charming and useful fable and I enjoyed adding it to our store.
GOLYGA: Until soon then. Be well, be happy, be amazed!

* * *

In case you, dear reader, have not drawn your conclusions on a vast enough scale, we want to bring you some points to contemplate and to initiate in your own life. Whenever there is a good idea floating around that entices you in some way, but then you decide to dismiss it for lack of time or energy or preparation or overloadedness, please pause and reflect:

If you are too overloaded to pay heed to a good idea, what kind of life are you living? If you are too overloaded to take on anything new— exciting though it may be—what kind of life are you living? If you are too overloaded to experiment, enjoy, branch out—whether mentally or physically or any other way—what kind of life are you living?

Once you have answered these questions for yourself, sit down and determine what in your life you can drop or change or streamline or compress to make time and energy for implementing good new ideas for your life. There is bound to be something you can do without. For one example: time and energy spent on worrying needlessly. For another example: time and energy spent on outdated useless activities, relationships, tasks of any kind. Habit and inertia are the reasons many people waste time and energy for no good reason at all.

Now, supposing you have found time and energy for incorporating some good new idea or other into your life: be vigilant for all the time it takes to make this new idea a habitual part of your life. For example, if you have decided to take up yoga, do it regularly until you have established it as part of your life without constant debate over whether or not to engage in it.

After it has become a habit, pay attention in a different way: habits have the insidious effect of reducing the activity involved to its least effective scale. Awareness alone brings with it the full benefit of any activity.

So here you are: you have incorporated a new idea into your life, you are paying attention to an activity even though it has become habitual, and presto! you are well on the way to paying attention to every part of your daily life. Which is a goal to be desired with great fervour, but can be implemented only by action. By the doing. And therefore in the very process of achieving the goal, bringing you incremental improvements and many surprises about old habits, and many little joys of discovery.

This is the addendum for today, and we recommend that you be ready and open to whatever good new idea comes into your life. Why not make your life an exciting adventure, à la Golyga and Lillykins, rather than drudgery, monotony, stress, and exhaustion?

Here is the short version:

Encounter a new idea that entices you
Sit and reflect on all you do in your life
Find something you can eliminate

Institute the new idea until the activity becomes habitual

Pay attention to the new activity—its ramification in your life and its influence around you.

Spread the habit of paying attention to the rest of your daily activities.

As you can see, dear reader, this is once again a lesson in doing. Not much good comes of merely reading about this one. You'll have moments of remembering what you have read, and perhaps even moments of trying out the notions spread out for you here, but gradually you'll forget all about it and go on as you always have. Pity, because this simple sequence of intention-activity-practice can actually change your life for the better.

However, as always, free will is yours and many will avail themselves of it in order to make no changes at all. Those of you who do, thank yourselves for the initiative until the rewards of your work come pouring in.

All the very best.

GOLYGA: That's all for now, my dear. Rest soon and be well.
LILLY: Thank you very much.

* * *

GOLYGA: We are not only ready to work, but also to congratulate you, Lilly dear, for the tone of fun and frivolity you brought to it. Let's remember always that Sturm und Drang is rarely a better mode than fun and that frivolity is rarely just that. We mean: is it frivolous to enjoy the sunshine, at any time and especially in November? Is it frivolous to enjoy jumping in and out of clothes until satisfied that yes, this feels comfortable and attractive—as long as it's undertaken in the spirit of fun and not with that old bugaboo "the right thing." You, Lilly dear, go ahead and indulge your formerly deprived child in the ways of play as much as you like and you'll never hear a word of censure from us. Given that you are far more likely to be serious and driven to produce than you are to overdo the fun and games. Though, we must say after New Mexico, you are achieving a far better balance than ever before.

And now, to work.

All right, here we are then: Golyga once more in charge of the baby, now a growing boy, but, since we are not naming him, always in danger of getting "Baby" stuck on him. Golyga is devising a means whereby the boy can ride on Golyga's back without being deprived of the view. As a dragon or swan, Golyga's head and neck tended to block the view, so he was now trying the shape of a broomstick, with the brush at the back. Rudder-like, he thought, and was rather pleased with the notion until, once the two of them settled on the stick, with Golyga in front, as befits the parent figure, the boy could see nothing at all ahead. So they changed places and the boy rode as if on the front of a bike, Golyga holding him in place with one arm while the other held fast to the broom handle.

Eventually, his arms got tired and he decided to switch their position. And as he did so, the boy slipped right off the broom handle and fell, fell, fell toward the ground. Luckily for both of them—just think what Lillykins would have done to Golyga had anything happened to the boy—they were so high up above any ground that there was plenty of time for Golyga to shape-shift himself into the form of a wide-backed rhinoceros with the wings of a giant dove—lovely image that, eh?—and to dive under the falling boy and catch him.

Phew, said Golyga with a great snort of relief. This is going to take a bit of doing, I suppose, but you really will have to learn how to fly on your own, my boy.

What do you mean? said the boy. I know how to fly. I've been flying for ages. I love flying. I fly all the time, when you don't insist on carting me around like a piece of luggage.

Golyga's mouth fell open—not a pretty sight on a rhinoceros—and he said, with a groan: Why in the world didn't you tell me that, my boy? Why have you never let me see you fly?

Actually, you probably have, said the boy, but didn't want to remember it. Sure, I've been flying for ages. Watch!

And as Golyga looked on, the boy transformed himself into a dragonfly, batted his wings a few times just to show off his style, and took off into the air. Flying just like a dragonfly, which is to say: hither and yon in swoops and loops, with great speed and agility and grace. A dancing on air, in fact, so lovely to watch that Golyga quite forgot that was his own boy, flying those loops and swoops. Until the dragonfly landed on top of his rhinoceros head and squeaked something into his ear.

What? What? said Golyga. Repeat, please. My hearing isn't what it might be, inside this thick skull.

Well, get out of it, yelled the dragonfly, loud as he could. Let's take off and fly somewhere really fun together!

Now, nobody had ever had to say that sort of thing twice to Golyga, so quick as a rhinoceros's wink he became a whistling swan—the kind that flies long distances without ever tiring and looks elegant as hell—and off he went, up into the sky. The boy was not about to try keeping up as a dragonfly but he couldn't quite get the hang of shape-shifting himself into a whistling swan. Somehow, he kept turning into a duck, flapping and squawking in the wake of Golyga the swan, and finally yelling, Stop! Stop! You have to stop and teach me how to do that whistling swan thing!

Golyga stopped. Oh, he said, smug and insufferable. So there *is* something more I can teach you, you whippersnapper. Okay, come here. See these long feathers and how they're lined up? That's what you have to concentrate on when you're turning yourself into a whistling swan.

Got it, said the boy, and he did indeed, and turned himself into a whistling swan in the blink of a duck's eye—if there is such a thing—and away he went, soaring high and using his mighty wings and strength to ride the wind, whistling as he went.

Golyga watched with pride. Then he took after the boy, and nobody has seen either of them since. Well, that's not true, of course—we just wanted to leave you with a lovely visual image on this sunny day. Actually, both Golyga and the boy ran into some foul weather pretty soon and decided to land, which brought about a whole other adventure, one for another day.

Now, what we would like to point out, before we go, is that that little story is meant to be applicable to any relationship—not just parent and child—to all the myriad encounters of any kind with "the other." In other words: since nothing stands still and unaltered, check it out! Is "the other" in the same place where you last encountered it? Are you the same? Not likely. Which means the relationship also needs adjusting.

And this applies whether it's with a human, an "entity," an animal or plant, an inner voice, a long-made plan or agenda—everything and anything needs mindful attention if one is to be in the true heart of experience.

Much communication fails for the simple reason that people run on automatic. Having once decided what a person is like, or what their reaction is to a person or situation, nothing is ever re-examined and so it becomes not only stale but also untrue, insubstantial because based on false premises, unlike life, which is always fluid and moving.

So here is a little exercise you can undertake in relation to everything and anything you encounter this day—and any other:

Observe yourself
observe the other
observe the changes
act on them.

GOLYGA: That's it for today, my dear. Enjoy the sunshine. Be with us again soon.
LILLY: Thank you, I will be.

* * *

We have left our dear Golyga and the baby landing and running into an adventure without ever telling you what the adventure they encountered was. Here it is:

As Golyga and Baby set foot on the ground, a huge eiderdown came squawking across their path and, in moments, had engulfed them altogether so only Golyga's nose showed.

Grrr, hrmph, drrw, Golyga said, meaning: Where are you, Baby, and are you all right?

He could neither see nor hear Baby but he could now feel his little hand sliding into his own, and so they held each other by the hand and Golyga turned to the eiderdown.

Listen, he said. I'm not sure how to address a squawking eiderdown and I don't want to be rude, but we can hardly breathe and, besides, we're fine and cozy without getting all covered up by you, so would you squawk off, please, and leave us be?

183

Well, squawked the eiderdown. If you call that not being rude, I do wonder what you'd sound like if you *were* to be rude. So let's hear you be rude.

Now Golyga was stumped. I mean, how much ruder could you be than to tell somebody to bug off?

All right, he said. I'll try. I don't like you being made of the itty-bitty feathers plucked out of living creatures. I don't like you squawking, as if you have a right to a squawk. And I don't like anything descending on me without so much as a "may I," so bug off and get away from us. How is that for rudeness?

The eiderdown shook its head, causing Golyga and the baby to sneeze several times.

Not nearly rude enough, said the eiderdown. You were actually being honest—if in a somewhat aggressive way—and if I were not so sensitive a creature, I'd hardly take notice of your blathering, but since I am sensitive and soft and warm and useful to many many not so hoity-toity creatures as you are, I'll tell you this: you smell bad and you're ugly and you sound like a foghorn with a cold in the head. How's that for being rude?

Pretty good, Golyga had to admit. Not bad at all. What do you think, Baby?

Baby, much shorter and therefore getting less air to breathe, decided all this blather about being rude was getting him nowhere and started to kick at the eiderdown. A not very hard but very steady rhythm of kicking out in all directions.

Ow, ow, ow, squawked the eiderdown. Quit that, you little turd. Want me to smother you altogether?

Well, no sooner had the eiderdown threatened Baby than Golyga heaved the child from under the eiderdown to his shoulders, kicked his way out of the eiderdown until he stood free beside it, and told the eiderdown in no uncertain terms where it should go and in what company.

The eiderdown gasped. And gasped again. And then let out a little sob. And a bigger one. And finally, a long howl of sorrow and anguish came from the eiderdown, until both Golyga and Baby were aghast at what they had caused.

184

Listen, said Golyga. I'm sorry. I'm afraid this whole altercation should have been handled much differently and much better and I blame myself for this. After all, I am an adult, and I should be able to—

Golyga was interrupted by a big guffaw of laughter. A big puffy guffaw, which emerged from the eiderdown, and then a feathery giggle that went on and on.

Finally, the eiderdown spoke: Gotcha, didn't I? I really gotcha. You had no idea what I was up to, so I gotcha big-time. This is my little bit of fun, see? I come squawking all over somebody and see how they take it. Then I play games with them till they lose it and then I play all hurt and suffering till they feel guilty as hell. Then I have a good laugh. It's a great game, you should try it sometime. I have to keep finding new people to play it with because some get fed up once they know the game. And the ones who enjoy getting it played on them—well, they're no fun after a while. So I keep having to look for new people—do you know anybody I can play my game on?

Golyga and Baby looked at each other. They looked at the eiderdown. Then both of them took a mighty leap, right over the top of the eiderdown, and they walked away. Saying not another word to the surprised-looking eiderdown and not even looking back to see its little huddled shape on the ground.

Well, that'll teach you to recognize that little game, said Golyga to Baby. A good lesson, wasn't it?

Baby looked at Golyga and was about to say something but then he just nodded.

Yep, he said. A really good lesson for all who can't see through games like that right off. Now what about something to eat?

GOLYGA: And that is the end of that loose end, all tied up. What do you think?
LILLY: Very useful lesson, thank you.
GOLYGA: And thank you for holding the channel open and clear and free of interference. Until soon, Lilly dear.

* * *

GOLYGA: Hello, my dear. Good to be with you again, though you are not yet ready to see the overall benefit of our joint venture, I know you enjoy the entertainment of it

and the sense of "having some work done" by the time we have finished our session. In actual fact, of course, the work is mine and you are merely the receptor.
LILLY: "Merely"? This doesn't sound like you, Golyga.
GOLYGA: True. I'm not myself—you have no idea how funny that statement is, because you have been assuming that I am one and you are another. Not so. I am many and so are you and at some point we intersect. It is at this point that our adventure story emerges as the creation of yours truly, emerging through the receptive open channel of you and with the aid of your vast and varied imaginative capacities. Your imagination must be capable of opening to mine or of combining with mine and thus we can co-create. Is that getting clearer?
LILLY: Yes, thank you, it is. So let's co-create!

Golyga was sitting somewhere or other and Lillykins was amazed at something or other, but today we will concentrate on the tale of Hylu. Hylu, brother of Lillykins and overly fond of practical jokes, was becoming a great nuisance. He and Baby were in cahoots, playing a game of hide-and-seek that Golyga and Lillykins had not yet become aware of. Those two were canoodling. We'll leave to your imagination what exactly this means—whether canoeing on the river with noodles for paddles, or noodling at each other's orifices with sensitive tongues, or simply meandering through memory lane. Let your own experience and desires be your guide. The purpose of this canoodling in our tale is that both were occupied in something other than baby-watching, having handed that task temporarily and with some relief to Hylu. Who proceeded to interpret the task as enjoying himself with Baby. Not an uncommon perception of child-minding in some societies, though in others it seems to be taken as a serious and taxing endeavour.

Hylu was calling Baby to come look for him. Every time Baby came close, Hylu changed shape to something Baby couldn't even guess, such as a fleck of dust, a feather drifting down from a branch, a great blue splotch in the sky. Baby enjoyed the game at first but was getting frustrated and calling for some rules and boundaries around what was permitted.

I can't find anything called Hylu if the shape and definition of Hylu keeps changing even as I approach him, said Baby, pouting and sucking on his big toe. I'm not going to play unless you specify three shapes that are to be yours during this game and from which you will not depart, no matter how close I come to finding you.

All right, said Hylu. Three shapes and no more.

But you have to tell me those shapes in advance, said Baby, suspecting foul play.

No problem, said Hylu. No problem at all. Here they are: The shape of a cloud, any cloud shape. The shape of a great blue heron. And the shape of a little blind mouse.

Oh, for heaven's sake, said Baby. You are making it too easy for me. Okay. Go ahead and hide, and I'll find you.

Whoosh, went Hylu, and he was gone.

Baby began looking everywhere for a cloud, a blue heron, a mouse. He saw all three almost immediately: a mouse-shaped cloud, blindly meandering across the sky; a blue heron flying straight into a tree and perching as no blue heron had ever been seen to perch—had to be Hylu, right?—and finally Baby saw a great blue cloud, on tall legs, standing and fishing by the river.

Great, said Baby. These rules are not going to work at all, and I am the one who asked for them, so now what do I do? Aha! I have it. I'll wait out my turn for looking by having a nap and then, when Hylu gets impatient and comes looking for *me*, I'll nab him.

Which is exactly what happened, so why go into details. Let's rather examine the assumptions Baby made about the rules he laid down:

- That shapes are recognizably one thing and not another and do not transmute from one to another.
- That shapes are determined by space, or in a spatial relationship, and are the visibly recognizable part of an entity.

Neither of which were true and neither of which therefore were of any help to Baby in his game with Hylu.

If you think about it, said Hylu, you caught me by being not right about anything but by letting it all go, giving yourself over to the moment, not hanging on to anything like rules or even the game. How amazingly clever of you, he said to Baby. Stop seeking and you shall be found. Or, put another way, drop the whole game and the win is yours.

Baby gave a little snore. He didn't know yet that he'd "caught" Hylu and won anything. And so, as soon as he opened his eyes, saw Hylu there, and put out his hand to grab him—poof—Hylu was gone again and Baby was back at the beginning: seeking, seeking, seeking shapes he could recognize and perhaps catch hold of.

Ah yes, so it goes.

Be but for a moment tired of the game and let it all go and you shall win it all. Be but for a moment back in the seeking and everything will escape your grasp. How to tell Baby such a thing? Don't even try. Simply cradle it into letting all go as often as you can and hope one day he'll awaken to know the state of grace he's in while not seeking to grasp.

And now we'll let Baby take another little nap and wish him well in his winning of the game.

GOLYGA: Yes, Lilly dear, you take it correctly that this is the end of today's episode.
LILLY: Thank you for the lesson, so delightfully presented as always. And suspensefully, too.
GOLYGA: You are most welcome, and I hope you will thank your own imagination for its wide receptivity.
LILLY: How can I widen it further?
GOLYGA: Let go of shapes and games. Play in the realm of infinite variations, combinations, and creativity. Roam freely in the land of any-shape and no-shape. Be not bound by seeking nor by finding. Etc,. etc., etc.
LILLY: Thank you.
GOLYGA: Until soon, my dear. Be joyous.

* * *

GOLYGA: And so we resume our tale, knowing full well that our endeavours include not only enjoyment but also learning and the eventual sharing thereof. Have you, Lilly, given thought to the eventual sharing and what avenues might be open to it?
LILLY: Vaguely. I assumed you would suggest what to do with the manuscript when the time was right.
GOLYGA: How discerning of you. Yes, indeed, I have a plan of action mapped out that will result in publication and much delight all around. As you said: when the time is right. At the present rate of progress, this time should be not too far in

the future, since we can certainly make our first contacts before the manuscript is completed.

LILLY: I'll leave the timing in your hands then, shall I?

GOLYGA: Lazy thing, you. But yes, do. You have your own book to be concerned over, so I shall happily take over the routing of this one. With an occasional hint, as well, about what to do with the other one. All right?

LILLY: I'll be more than happy to get hints, advice, and help there.

GOLYGA: And you shall have it. Now: time to get on with it.

Golyga, the hero of our tale, is amazed. He has never heard such chatter and such rushing about in the realms of everlasting goings-on. He has never, in fact, been involved in such a commotion as he is encountering at this moment. It seems to him that a flock of geese has brought all this about, but it has not. What the cause of the commotion is, in reality, will escape our hero for some time. We, however, being blessed with the overview Golyga is lacking, as well as the hindsight he has yet to develop, know that the cause of all this commotion is Baby.

Baby, you see, has been left alone with Hylu for too long and he is objecting vehemently and loudly to Hylu's latest plan for amusement. Hylu wants to go swimming in a cold mountain stream. Baby does not enjoy cold water. So Baby alerted the fish, the fowl, and all the creatures of the area to prevent Hylu from entering the cold waters of the stream. Birds are swarming around Hylu's head at this very moment, fish are jumping and splashing, and ants are crawling up his legs. Not to speak of the worms underfoot and between his toes, of the slugs slipping in and out of his nostrils...

Oh, please! Stop it! This is truly horrible, and I, Hylu, will never ever again entertain the notion of cold-stream swimming together with you, Baby.

Which made Baby desist and dismiss all the creatures who had come to his aid. But not before they demanded their share of the rewards.

What rewards? said Baby. There are no rewards. Just that I don't have to get into ice-cold water and pretend it's fun. That's the only reward here.

The creatures who had been ready and eager to help Baby, thinking he was in dire danger, became upset.

You were yelling and carrying on, they said, as though a major catastrophe was about to happen, and we had to rush to your aid lest it befall you personally, and so we did. Now we find out it's only your reluctance to get into cold water that was at the core of your fussing, and we must say, this was a complete misrepresentation of the truth. So, to teach you a lesson, we shall now demand rewards, each of us according to our want.

All right, sighed Baby. What is it you want?

Well. Next thing you know the commotion and noisy goings-on were increased tenfold over the earlier eruptions, and nobody could hear anything at all. Baby seriously considered escaping in the midst of the confusion and thus also escaping the consequences of his actions and promises, but Hylu was not willing to let Baby off quite so easily. After all, he had been deprived of his swim in the cold stream water that Hylu loved and so he was happy to see Baby discomfited as well.

I want sugar, said the ants.

Me, I want soft cheese, said the slugs, being French. Something mouldy and smelly would be best.

And we would like to have a great big stand upon which to display ourselves to advantage, said the great blue Heron.

How did *you* get into this? asked Baby. I didn't notice you before, when everybody was trying to help me.

Of course not, said the Heron. It would never occur to me that somebody truly objects to entering the fresh waters of a stream. I was certain from the beginning that it was all a misunderstanding, and so it turned out to be, didn't it?

Baby had to admit that Heron was right. He had never meant to suggest it was a matter of life and death, but the fuss he made was taken as "Big Deal and Dangerous."

Yes, said Baby, that's what it was. A misunderstanding. Can you explain it to the others?

No way, said the Heron. They are hell-bent on reaping the rewards that might accrue from this misunderstanding and don't want to hear from me that it's all over, forget it, nothing to be gained.

Well, where am I going to get sugar and soft smelly mouldy cheese, not to speak of all the other things I might be asked for?

I suggest you just enter the stream. Think about it. If they have not saved you from the cold waters, nobody can demand rewards for it.

Baby had to admit that that would solve everything, and so, reluctantly and with many expressions of suffering and anger, he entered the stream's cold water.

Hylu sat on the banks and watched.

What are you doing out there—watching? asked Baby. Why aren't you coming in, too? After all, it was your desire to get in here in the first place, not mine.

My desire was for having some fun, said Hylu. Jumping and splashing and screaming out loud—that sort of thing. I certainly never had any desire to clench my face into a fist and stick myself in there like a thumb into screws. No thanks. That's not my idea of fun or, for that matter, of the way to do anything. I'd rather not do it at all.

Which is what I had in mind when all this started. I just didn't want to. And look how it turned out: I'm in the cold water, you're not, and everybody's mad at me.

Think about it, said Hylu. A plain "I don't want to" will usually do in place of all the fuss and commotion people get up to trying to avoid something.

You are so right, said Golyga, who had come to join them, curious about the commotion. Now get out of there, Baby, before you catch your death of cold. And remember today as one of the lessons in the school of life that Lillykins and I are determined you shall attend.

Oh, gee, said Baby. Couldn't I just go and sit at a desk somewhere and colour in pictures?

Certainly not, said Golyga. Now dry yourself off and come with me. Lillykins must be impatiently awaiting our return by now.

But Lillykins, if truth be known—and it will inevitably become known, in our next instalment—Lillykins was busy. Much too busy to be aware of the time passing or anything else besides the dragon before her. Breathing not fire but ashes. And bringing about not the burning we expect from a fire-breathing dragon, but a burying-under-ashes. Intoning, as he went:

Ashes to ashes, ashes to ashes.

Though mentioning neither the origins nor the destination of the ashes. So, as you can imagine, Lillykins was ready with any number of questions...

GOLYGA: *All of which we'll get to hear the next time we get together. Until then, all the best to you.*

* * *

We left Lillykins standing, facing a dragon of strange habits: the breathing of ashes. Whatever, Lillykins wondered, should I make of this? And can I simply ask the creature what it's doing and why?

The dragon, meantime, was observing Lillykins with equal fascination. After all, he had never in his life seen so beautiful and ephemeral and earthy a creature as this human-shaped womanly one in front of him.

What exactly might you be? asked the dragon. Surely you are too beautiful to be an ordinary human?

Oh, gee, thanks, said Lillykins. In fact, I am far from ordinary, and I am human only at this particular moment in time. And, now and again, I repeat the experience because it is truly fascinating. But there are so many other modes of experience that I sometimes have a hard time deciding which to choose.

Have you ever been an ash-breathing dragon? said the dragon, utterly taken by the creature in front of him.

No, as a matter of fact, not yet, said Lillykins. Do you recommend it?

No, said the dragon. Actually, you'd be better off choosing to be a fire-breathing dragon. More fun, more scary, more useful all around. But I had no choice. By the time I was born, there was no fire-breathing dragoneering available, you see. The fires were gone, the only thing left were the ashes.

How sad, said Lillykins. Will fire-breathing dragoneering ever be available again?

Well, yes, said the dragon. If you, for example, wanted to become a fire-breathing dragon, you need only apply. As for me, it's too late. Once an ash-breather, always an ash-breather.

Are you sure? asked Lillykins. Is there nothing you can do that would turn you into a fire-breather?

Oh well, said the dragon, there is, but I would have to be willing to leave behind my entire ash-breathing self and take on an entirely unknown entity, and who knows what that unknown entity would turn out like? What if the fire-breather I became was an intolerable snit of a thing? A holier-than-thou otherworldly preachy kind of dragon? What if the new me was to turn out to be a fire-breather who left all else in ashes? No, no, I'd better stick with my old ash-breathing self. At least I know what I'm up to. See what I mean?

I do, said Lillykins. But I still think it's sad. Say, ash-breathing dragon, would you like me to turn into a fire-breathing dragon for a bit so you can see me at it and get a clearer notion of yourself as fire breather?

No good, said the ash-breather. You as fire-breather and me as fire-breather could well be two entirely different kettle of fish.

Yes, said Lillykins, I do see what you mean. You are determined to stick to breathing ashes because you know all about ash-breathing and you're too damned scared to leap into the unknown and become a fire-breather because, well, you have no guarantees what you'd be like. Am I right?

Put like that, I must say: yes, that's right. So bug off, out of my way, and don't darken my path again, you snotty, judgmental little shit.

Lillykins jumped out of the way, and the dragon stomped off, down the path and into the distance. Lillykins watched him go, then sat down to think. Yes, she had been judgmental and snotty, but she had also felt sorry for the poor stuck dragon and still did. She decided to turn herself into a fire-breathing dragon, right then and there, and go after the ash-breathing dragon to apologize. But before she could so much as draw another breath, she was taken by a new thought: what if it was in the nature of dragons to be stuck? Fire-breather or ash-breather and never anything else again? Oh my. Was she destined to become a fire-breathing dragon and get stuck there? Or to be Lillykins, afraid to change into a fire-breathing dragon lest she get stuck there and therefore stuck in being Lillykins?

No, no, no, no, said Lillykins to herself. I have been many a creature in my life so far and I shall continue to change and become and change again, as I choose, and I refuse entirely to be determined by the fear of change or the fear of getting stuck, so here I go. Zip zap, and Lillykins was a fire-breathing dragon. And we shall hear all about that in our next session.

LILLY: Thank you, Golyga.
GOLYGA: You are welcome, my dear. Until next time.

* * *

Once upon a time, there was a very strange sight to be seen, standing in the path of our dear Lillykins. It was that old ash-breathing dragon we have met before, and he was not a happy ash-breather either. What with one thing and another, he felt aggrieved, hard put upon, and discombobulated because he had been ambling down the path, away from Lillykins, when he had chosen to turn and see what effect his departure had on her—and lo! Lillykins was a fire-breathing dragon. Just like that. Something he had considered throughout his complaining life, she had accomplished in the blink of an eye.

Not fair, he thought.

Not fair! he shouted at Lillykins, and turned to face her and have it out with her, this affront and upsetting turn she had caused in his thinking. Because was change not something to be considered seriously and at length before actually taking a timid first step toward it? Was change not something to be put off until one was entirely sure of all its consequences and possible developments? Was change not something to be feared and avoided if possible, and to be dragged into if not? Was change, in other words, not something entirely difficult to deal with?

The ash-breathing dragon turned, walked back to Lillykins, and said: Look here. I want to ask you some questions. Can you hear me over all that noise you're making with your fire-breathing?

Oh sure, said Lillykins, breathing flames and smoke into the air and watching the wildly exciting, beautiful sight of it. I can hear you. But what you have to say had better be good because I am enjoying myself and would rather not be interrupted just now.

The ash-breathing dragon was even more affronted and annoyed. Are you telling me you would rather have fun and games than deal with the serious issue of change? Or the various possible approaches to it? Or the—

Oh, come to the point, said Lillykins. Don't go blathering on and on. Yes, fun and games are preferable to the endless shillyshallying you call serious consideration of a subject. And no, I do not recommend you become a fire-breathing dragon—that is the point here, isn't it? Because unless you can really focus and be alert and sharp in the NOW, without shillyshallying all over the place, you'll be a bag of cinders before the hour is out. See what I mean? So let me concentrate here and enjoy these flames shooting forth and sparks flying and—

Fine, said the ash-breathing dragon. Go ahead. Have your fun. Leave the rest of us in our miserable ash-breathing existence.

Come off it, said Lillykins the fire-breathing dragon. You chose to be your miserable self and, as far as I know, you are the only ash-breathing dragon around here. Anyway, you said yourself that change isn't something you want to engage in lest the unknown bring you a worse fate than your known and familiar misery. So bug off and be miserable somewhere else, okay?

The ash-breathing dragon had never been so insulted, nor spoken to in such a fashion, ever. It was enough to make him perk up his furry little ears—yes, furry, my dear. Feathery ears on a dragon would look altogether silly and they might catch fire or be covered in ashes and then what good are feathers?—so: ash-breather perked up his furry ears and suddenly he sat right down on the ground to think. Trying to keep his head up so he wouldn't choke on his own ashes with every inhalation.

There he sat, and there stood Lillykins the fire-breathing dragon, enjoying the beauty of the flames she was producing and the sharply focused state of awareness she needed to maintain to avoid danger from her own breath.

And next thing you know, the entire scene changed drastically. A huge rain cloud came zipping along overhead, opened its enormous maw, and spewed forth gallons of pinkish rainwater. Pinkish only at first, when the flames could still be seen. Smokish as soon as the flames were drenched. And just plain rainwater-coloured and cool and refreshing for the rest of the time it lasted. Which was not long. The cloud sailed on and left, and Lillykins watched it float away. The ash-breathing dragon, however, jeered and smirked.

Ha! he snorted. Now where are your beautiful flames, eh? Where are your beautiful flames now? All gone, I guess, those beautiful flames of yours.

Lillykins turned to ash-breather and shook her head. You poor old thing, she said. You poor, miserable old ash-breather. I guess you never heard of "better to have enjoyed and lost than never to have enjoyed at all"? And I guess you have never experienced something and decided that, whenever you felt like it, you would experience that wonderful thing again? And I guess you're just too plain stuck to move out of your miserable state and you'll keep blaming everyone and everything for it rather than make a move and change. You, ash-breather, are to be pitied and avoided. Because there surely is no point in trying to help you, is there?

Ash-breathing dragon, still sitting with his head raised high, now let it droop down. Soon he began to cough, choking on his own ashes so he had to jump up and shake his head from side to side, ridding himself of them. And next thing you know, he got so dizzy he just had to sit down again.

Lillykins watched the ash-breather, fascinated, not at all sure she should simply leave him there, though that is what she intended to do eventually.

Oh well, she thought. I guess I can give this miserable sod another little bit of my time and attention—always knowing that when I feel like it, I can once again become a fire-breathing dragon for as long as I choose. Or anything else, for that matter.

***

GOLYGA: *It's been a while, but who is counting. Now that we are back at our work together, let's enjoy every moment of it, shall we?*
LILLY: *Yes, indeed.*

Lillykins, as we know, was facing a dragon. A very unusual dragon in that it was breathing not fire but ashes. And Lillykins was, as is her nature, feeling sorry for this dragon and his inability to be a more flamboyant, fear-generating dragon. After all, how terrible to be spewing ashes where colour, heat, and dancing flames might have been.

Never mind, said Lillykins. I am sure your ashes have their uses. Think of their advantage in a garden, on the paths, to keep weeds from coming up, on the edges of garden beds to keep bugs out, and so on. Think of the uses of ashes in preparing various materials—don't ask me for too many details, said Lillykins, but I am sure ashes have many uses.

Oh sure, said the dragon. Compare ashes and fire, will you? What a list we could make with the supreme importance of fire on one side and the minuscule list on the other side. And even if you were to put aside any usefulness and simply concentrate on the beauty, well… Let's just forget comparisons altogether, shall we? Let's just say I'm deprived, underprivileged, and certainly deserve every bit of sympathy anybody can come up with for my sorry state.

Oh gee, said Lillykins. I wouldn't go about asking for it like that. Sympathy is definitely more easily forthcoming when not solicited so blatantly.

Are you saying I'm a whiner?

Well, you're not far from it, are you? I mean, look at you: you are healthy, you are not unattractive except for that grey stuff coming out of your mouth, and I don't just mean the ashes, and you are probably capable of many things, if you only stop whining about what you cannot do—breathe fire.

Whoa, said the dragon. Did I ask for a lecture? Did I even ask you personally for sympathy? I thought we were having a discussion on the comparative values of being a fire-breathing dragon and an ash-breathing dragon. And yes, perhaps we did stray a bit into the personal, but it was certainly not my intention to get abuse from the likes of you, breathing neither ashes nor fire but just hot air.

Lillykins shook her head. My own fault, she thought. I've let myself get sucked into his game of sympathy or abuse. I'm supposed to be an all-giving friend or else I'm the enemy. Well, forget it, dragon, Lillykins thought. I'm going to be neither because I'm out of here.

Bye, said Lillykins to the dragon, and off she went, leaving him to stare after her with a puzzled expression. After all, everybody else so far had played this game with him—back and forth, back and forth, friend or enemy in turns, and this one just went one round and took off. Was this a new species evolving on the planet? If so, dragon didn't think much of it. What was a body to do if everyone stopped playing the old games and just took off whenever they weren't pleased with developments in a relationship? Divorce everywhere—that's what it would lead to, and what chaos that would create for the children of the world, and for the world itself.

So thinking, dragon ambled off, shaking his head and thereby strewing ashes all around.

On the other hand, he suddenly thought, what if everybody walks away from the old games and starts playing new ones? Fun games? Together instead of against each other?

Dragon shook his head. It would never work, he thought. There'd always be some playing old games and some playing new ones and the twain would confuse each other all to hell. Unless there was a code, of course. Blue for the old games, red for the new. No, better make that not a colour code—in case of colour-blindness—but a code based on the feel of the game. If it feels good, it's the new kind. If it feels bad, it's the old stuff. That should be easy enough; all we need to do, thought the dragon, is pay attention to how we feel, right? Goodness, can't get much easier than that, can it?

And so, humming happily and simply buzzing the ashes in all directions, the dragon tromped off with a lively step and began looking for that Lillykins, to tell her the good news.

GOLYGA: We, meantime, shall hop or fly or simply whee-whoosh to where Lillykins is sitting on her favourite rock. Next time.
LILLY: Thank you, Golyga. You seem always to know just what's on my mind and then to address whatever it is with episodes of your tale.
GOLYGA: I wonder how I am able to know what's in your mind? Or what's on your plate? Or what's up for the next step of your journey?
LILLY: A vast overview?
GOLYGA: That's part of it. But also vast experience with the human condition, as seen from our vantage point, and a clear understanding of what it takes to proceed

*on the path you're on. I would like to congratulate you, Lilly dear, on your progress,
as evinced by the way you feel these days.*

LILLY: *Thank you very much. For the congratulations and also for the help you
have given me—and continue to give me—toward this progress.*

GOLYGA: *Most appreciated. All the best till next time. And love.*

LILLY: *Thank you, Golyga. Love mucho.*

* * *

We were about to see the large dragon amble off into the sunset when
lo!—a great crane came along and said to him:

Hey, ash-breather. No need to go searching for Lillykins to tell your
tale. She's kind of busy, anyway. Why not tell it to me and I'll listen very
very carefully and then tell you how interesting it was and how much I
learned from it, and we can all go home happy.

The dragon was astonished. Why would you want to do that? You
don't even know if my tale is interesting or not. What's in it for you?

The crane laughed. Aha! There we have it. The ash-breathing
dragon assumes everyone is out for something. No possibility that
someone might be happy doing kind and helpful things for others. No
wonder you're breathing ashes.

Now, wait a minute, said the dragon. It isn't as though I've never
done any random acts of kindness, you know.

Yes? Tell me one, said the crane. I'm listening.

The dragon tried to think of an act of kindness he had done without
thought of reward and, you know, he couldn't come up with one. His
head sank lower and lower, and his ashes tasted bitter.

Ah well, said the crane. Don't feel so bad. If you want to, you can
start in right now, doing acts of kindness wherever you go, making up
for lost time, and you'll see: even your ashes will taste like honey!

With that the crane flew off, large wings beating the rhythm, a song
high on the wind.

The dragon watched the crane go and wished he'd had time to ask
how one goes about this business of "doing random acts of kindness."
He wished he could call back that crane and practise on him. Now, right
here, there was absolutely nobody around he could practise on. Nobody
anywhere he could see—except himself, of course.

Suddenly, the dragon had a thought: why not practise on myself? Let's see…what can I do for myself that would be kind…

The dragon was deep in thought. This wasn't easy, coming up with something completely new like this, but he was determined. Meantime, without noticing, he had opened his tiny wings—well, tiny compared to the size of his body—and they flapped a bit as though excited, and pretty soon they flapped harder as the dragon thought harder about what kindness he could do for himself…and next thing he knew, he was rising off the ground and flying!

Well, to tell the truth, at the beginning it was more like a run-hop-sail-a-bit sequence, but the sail part got longer and longer and the dragon got more and more excited because he'd never been able to fly before, and his wings flapped faster and faster, and suddenly he was sailing up up to the top of the nearest tree.

There he sat, like a giant roosting bird, grinning like mad. Grinning because he was thinking: If even *searching* for a way of being kind results in this, imagine what actually being kind will bring about!

We'll leave the dragon sitting in the tree, grinning, and we'll just assume, shall we, that the dragon henceforth changed his ways and became a happy flying dragon given to many acts of kindness and much flapping about.

GOLYGA: *Yes, we are here, we care for you, and we do want to work together today but first: remember to do your thought-form work whenever opportunity arises. Even such a useless thought as whether or not you have enough time up here to accomplish everything you hope to—you will or won't, but meanwhile you'll ruin the enjoyment of being here. Looking back on this summer, you want to be able to say, Yes, I made the most of it. I didn't waste time or energy on "should" or anything else that did not contribute to the joy of being here.*

LILLY: *Yes, thank you.*

GOLYGA: *Now, as to today's session: what with wind and headache, we are going to keep it fairly short. We'll clean up some loose ends and make suggestions about fitting segments together. All right?*

Once upon a time, an ash-breathing dragon stood in Lillykins' path, and another time it left her standing there being a fire-breathing dragon, and then again, there came that same dragon—or was it perhaps a different one? Whatever the dragon story is, the message is clear: if you have a dragon in your path, engage it. Find out what it's about. What it wants from you and what you might want from it. Talk until the two of you have everything sorted out and then—alone or together—travel on your path with a new-found peace and enjoyment.

Dragons are only obstructing your path or threatening you in any way if you have not made clear the nature of your dragon and the nature of your relationship. Once that is clear, you—each one of you—can be confident that a dragon is, after all, an imaginary construct. As they say. Its power derives from its mystery.

Demystify by clear communication with the dragon, and presto: you have either an ally or a departing, deflated imaginary construct. So that's the story of the dragons, whichever kind they are.

GOLYGA: All right?
LILLY: Oh yes. Fine. Thank you.

* * *

WHAT HAVE WE HERE? A FONT TWICE THE SIZE OF THE USUAL? AN ACCIDENT?

WE BEG TO DIFFER. WE WANT TO BE SURE THAT IT IS CLEAR TO YOU, LILLY DEAR, AND TO EVERYONE, THAT COMPUTERS ARE A FORM OF ENERGY BOTH FAMILIAR AND EASY AND THAT WE HAVE NO NEED OF THEM.

AH WELL, THE BEST ADVANCES OF HUMANS ON EARTH WILL SEEM AS TOYS ONCE THE SCIENTIFIC MODE IS NO LONGER WORSHIPPED IN THE ANNALS OF KNOWLEDGE, AND A WIDER PERCEPTION OF THE UNIVERSE BECOMES ACCEPTABLE.

To get to the work for the day, here is our dilemma: Lilly dear is low in energy but eager to work. Do we deplete her further or recommend waiting until tomorrow? Lilly awaits our decision, holding herself still.

Good for you, Lilly, it shows that you trust we intend you no harm. On the contrary, unless some good will come of this work for you personally, we cannot undertake it with you. There is no difference, you see, between "doing good" for humanity or any other life forms—rocks included here—and doing good for you, personally. There is neither separation nor something good for one and not for another when it comes to this material we are working with.

True, the colour green might look better on one than on another, and the hat you wear might not suit everyone, but when it comes to the matter of energy, you cannot have something good for one and bad for another.

Energy is.

How it is used can be good or bad, and here we do make a distinction. But energy used badly is bad for everyone, and energy used lovingly, positively, productively, creatively, is good for everyone.

So you see, when you indulge in thoughts of recrimination or blame toward anyone, you create energy that leaks in gobs, brings negative results for everyone concerned, and increases the pool of negative energy in your "neighbourhood," your field. And so we recommend to every one of you that you be aware and constantly conscious of what you are doing with your thoughts, your acts, and your intentions. We are not asking you to be holier than thou. We are not asking you to be angels on Earth—though you would, we dare say, enjoy that a great deal—we ask only that you be aware and conscious.

The next time you are tired for no good reason you can see, check your last hours for thoughts, acts, and intentions and see whether your preoccupations were of the energy-draining kind.

For example: Lilly has been dealing with something quite new to her, a human who has no conception of the creative process, no desire to see anyone else in their own nature, and has not even come across the kind of spiritual quest in which Lilly is engaged. Not an easy task, to make the situation workable. Living together, finding uninterrupted work time, continuing her training in stilling the mind, etc., etc., all in the face of a force negating her very existence and endeavours. The usual response is to be preoccupied, to blame, to be recriminatory, day and night. To recount the endless ways of having disrespect and inconsideration thrust one's way.

Well, Lilly has been doing that but not nearly as much as she might have—thanks in part to our help. She is endeavouring, after all, to be above that sort of thing.

We suggest there is a better way to defend oneself against such energy drain. Looking after your own thoughts, acts, and intentions in a scrupulous way and using your energies consciously will be your best defence. Appreciations of what is good in your life—those help, too. And checking your reactions for old ones, no longer appropriate, also helps. But above all, keep your mind on the flow, and the moment you sense an outward drain, surround yourself with light—a form of energy most conducive to replenishment—and watch the energy flow reverse itself and increase in your body and spirit. You can feel yourself swell with its warmth, the expansion of the rich, delicious feeling of connecting to the universal energy flow available to all who call on it. And next thing you know, the little draining habits of mind will cease to have power in your life.

So there is actually a simple formula to remember for this entire syndrome, and it goes as follows:

Focus your awareness on the flow of energy in your body. The more you practise this, the more you will be able to discern subtle differences and comings and goings of energy and its nature. You will discern immediately whether somebody drains your energy or increases it. You will discern whether your thoughts, acts, and intentions are of the kind that drain or increase energy. And you will be able to change the drain to increase in positive energy in a flash. Merely be aware, and the moment you feel drain, make the change.

The change you will need to make most often is in you. Rarely, you might need to remove yourself from a situation or person(s). Usually, you need only change the content of your mind to reverse the energy drain.

Think of it: control over your degree of energy, your mind's content, and the amount of joy in your life. Because, with the in-flow of positive, creative energy, your joy will increase immediately and thus your energy will glow and radiate and bring in warm presence of joy.

203

GOLYGA It seems we have gone ahead and worked today. How is your energy, Lilly dear?

LILLY: No loss at all, thank you.

GOLYGA: Good news all around.

LILLY: And thank you for the lesson.

GOLYGA: You are most welcome. Let us close here for today. We'll be together again soon.

* * *

GOLYGA: Hello, my dear. Long time, no instalments. You have been busy, encountering and duelling with the dragon, and here you are, tip-tip-tapping again, to beat the band. And the critic/editor firmly in place, too.

LILLY: Sorry. I'll get her out of the way.

GOLYGA: Good. We've been waiting to tell you this part of our story ever since we heard about your undertaking the Ritual of the Voices. You see, there are many ways of going about ceremonies and rituals that are powerful and have lasting effect. There are other ways that, like child's play, are lasting in their afterglow because they are done with such immediate and unselfconscious flowing and deep integrity. To demonstrate such an episode, here is another instalment of our adventure.

Lillykins had been ever so enthralled by the various and delightful hues all around her on the island that she was simply shocked to find herself marooned on a rock while high tide cut her off from the mainland and everybody on it. No one even knew where she was, you see. She had flown to the island in a fit of glee over her victorious encounter with the dragon and had not paid attention to the rising waters.

Now she was stuck.

But what about flying off the island? you say. After all, she flew there, didn't she? Well yes, of course she did and she could easily fly off again as well, but *she didn't! Remember that!*

Once she saw the water had risen so high as to trap her on the island, she completely forgot that she could shape-shift into a flying creature—a fly, a dragon, a butterfly, a hawk—and simply take off. Yes, she'd forgotten that. She sat there, trapped by unfounded fears, and wondered what next. Should she try to swim ashore? To holler? Send smoke signals and be rescued? Or simply wait until the water receded and she could once more cross… How? Lillykins couldn't remember a land bridge or even how she came to be where she was. The trip here had been wiped from her memory!

Now Lillykins was really succumbing to worry and fear. Was her memory going? Was she about to find herself starving without the skills to feed herself? Was she going to be wearing dirty underwear and not know it? It was a horrible prospect, and Lillykins shivered in her skin to contemplate all the horrifying possibilities that came with being marooned on an island, without others, without memory, without, without, without…

Then something happened. (About time, don't you think?)

Lillykins looked up at the sky, having heard something there, and she saw a circling blob of something. At first it was not clear whether it even had wings. Gradually, Lillykins could see that the blob was blue, a very deep and vibrant blue, and then she saw that it had eyes. No wings were visible, however, and when she heard the sound repeated, it had a note of wind-rushing-through-embers. (If you are wondering what that sound might be, imagine a quiet scene: fireplace, cottage, sitting and reading, and then a sudden rush of wind coming down the chimney and hissing into the fire, into the coals and embers, spreading them wildly, but there is a screen in front of the fire, as there should be, so nothing dangerous is occurring.)

However, to hear such a sound coming from a blue blob in the sky was mystifying, so Lillykins trained her eyes on said blob and never took them off it.

The blob circled. High above in the sky, it circled several times, then came down to Earth. Sliding and gliding through the air, gracefully, in a lovely, almost dancing manner, but entirely without wings.

Lillykins got up and headed for the spot where the blue blob had landed. It looked, from her vantage point, to be about three metres in diameter, round in circumference but flattened. It hummed. It emitted a gentle glow. And from that glow came rays of warmth and, if Lillykins could believe it, rays of joy.

Lillykins came closer. Nothing and nobody but the blob and herself, on a rock island surrounded by water. Should she be afraid? Lillykins found herself incapable of fear. The warmth, the rays of joy, the colour of the blob, all combined to make her feel not only safe but positively courageous. She walked right up to the blob and stood beside it, bathed in warmth and joy.

Hello? she said, tentatively and gently, just in case the blob had ears to hear. She couldn't see any ears. All she could see was eyes, and they turned out to be fakes. In other words, as some butterflies have eyes on their wings to fool predators into thinking them huge, so this blue blob had eyes that were not real seeing eyes at all. Nevertheless, Lillykins felt that the blob was a living creature and perhaps it could hear her.

Hello? she said again. And then she jumped back.

The blob had suddenly emitted a high screech and hopped about a metre to the left.

It looked scared—shrinking into itself and shivering. The rays of warmth and joy shrank, too, until they were a thin layer, barely discernible.

Now what? Lillykins didn't dare open her mouth again lest she scare the blob further. How to reassure the poor thing that she meant it no harm and would, in fact, do anything she could to help it in any way it might need help—having landed on this marooned rock.

What to do, what to do?

Lillykins sat down to think. Sounds were out—they scared the blob. Touch? Would the blob let her come close enough to touch it ever so gently and reassuringly?

She took a tiny step closer to the blob. The blob shivered but didn't move away. She stepped closer again and slowly, slowly stretched out her hand.

The blob waited. Shivered but waited.

Then Lillykins ever so gently touched the blob's side and slowly stroked it with one finger.

The blob held still and stopped shivering.

So Lillykins stroked it with her full hand, around its side, across its top, all over the blue surface of the blob, and now the blob started humming—a lovely little tune—and it started expanding, getting larger and lighter at the same time, like a soap bubble blown by a wondrous child, and then, suddenly, it began floating. Up off the ground it floated and hung there, shimmering, sending out rays of warmth and joy—and two arms!

Two arms that reached out to embrace Lillykins and hug her to its blue middle.

Lillykins was delighted. Embraced by the warm, joyous blue blob, she danced, floating up above the ground, and soon the two of them floated higher and higher, circling above the rock and the water, and finally taking off into the high wide sky.

Lillykins looked down. Oh my, she thought. What a ridiculously small spot that is, the rock in the water. And how close to the mainland! I could have jumped across, if I'd turned myself into a cheetah. Or flown across, of course, or swum across, or glided across like a regal loon. What was I thinking of, sitting there and worrying?

Lillykins looked down again and this time she saw Golyga and the baby on the mainland, and they were making a fire. They seemed to be having a good time, and she thought she might go and join them.

But first, she would stay with her blue blob for a little longer, just floating in the warmth of its blue embrace. No questions, no talking, no names—nothing but the lovely blue blob in the sky.

GOLYGA: Yes, that's it for today, dear Lilly.
LILLY: Thank you, Golyga. Yes, I could have benefited from this tale some time ago. And will now, you can be sure. Thank you very much.
GOLYGA: You are most welcome. Think about it, my dear—soon the novel will be done and then we can have fun together on a regular basis!
LILLY: I really really look forward to that!

* * *

GOLYGA: A long time has passed, in Earth time, but we are nevertheless happy to be welcome again.
LILLY: You are most welcome. Much has happened, in the meantime.
GOLYGA: Yes, we know. I am including the entity you call MarTee in the "we" because, of course, nothing happens without him, in your case. He is the conduit par excellence for you and thus for me as well. However, I shall henceforth assume that his presence is taken as always with us and go back to referring to myself in the singular. I might mention, however, that I, too, am not exactly an entity separate

and unconnected to many others. *In fact, my communication with you is a sort of relay in the energy flow, bringing you the end result of intended communications from far away.*

There, again, the Earth necessity for referring to time and space has allowed imprecision, but there's nothing to be done about it, since you are on Earth, part of the Earth existence or manifestation, and can't be expected to understand what is beyond that state of being.

LILLY: *Anything you can tell me about your nature and/or the nature of other entities would be most welcome. In terms I, the earthling, can understand, of course.*

GOLYGA: *We do not miss the sarcastic undertone, but we choose to ignore it. The fact is, my dear Lilly, you'll one day be looking at this state of being from a far different perspective and with all the understanding lacking—necessarily—at this time, and you'll chuckle at the memory of sarcasm. There are such vast areas you cannot fathom right now and yet…you understand more than so many earthlings. Why not concentrate on that?*

LILLY: *And please be assured, while I can't truly comprehend the vastness of the universe or its complexity, I do have inklings of it and know my mind would be overwhelmed if, at this point, I was thrown into knowing much more.*

GOLYGA: *Yes. We know that. You are right, too, to undertake each step on your journey with thoroughness rather than zipping through the universe with all faculties at once, giving yourself, in the end, only confusion and perhaps even anxiety. Now. Shall we do some work together?*

Lillykins was asking herself questions. She was always doing that, of course, because it was an important part of her nature, but just then, she was intrigued by specific questions that had brought her to the brink of disaster more than once. Why, for example, was she not able to fly in her usual shape but had to turn herself into a winged creature first? Why was she not able to read Golyga's mind all the time but had to be satisfied with guessing when it was she intuited his thoughts and when she was bringing her own wishes to bear, distorting her understanding? And furthermore, when was she going to understand what the most resolute thinking could not bring to a satisfactory conclusion: that she had all the abilities of a human and yet was unable to attach herself with complete faith and trust to anyone else? Did others manage to do it and her failure was due to an unperceived lack in relating?

Wait a minute, Lillykins suddenly said to herself. Perhaps the baby will prove helpful to me in this. After all, until now I was concerned only with how I could be helpful to Baby, but perhaps, after all, this could be a two-way learning situation?

Lillykins went searching for Baby, but Baby was nowhere to be found. Only a snake crossed her path—intent on its own business.

No, said the snake when Lillykins asked it for information. I have not seen or heard a baby. There was, however, a child on the path just below the large rock. Perhaps he knows where this baby is.

Lillykins continued on the path the snake had indicated and, sure enough, found the big rock. And the child, too. And, quite clearly, the child was Baby, grown to a sturdy-legged little boy, amusing himself with a game with pebbles.

There you are, said Lillykins. How did you grow so fast? Where is Golyga? Have you had anything to eat?

The boy looked at Lillykins and laughed. Do I look starved? he said. Do I even look hungry? I know how to feed myself, you know. I even know where to find food and how to prepare it. Want to watch me?

Lillykins was about to stop him so she could ask more questions, but the boy suddenly became active. Zip—he fished some shrimp out of the river. Zap—he threw them on a fire. Zip-zap—he hauled them out again, without burning his fingers or the shrimp, and offered them to Lillykins.

They're delicious, he said. Try some.

Lillykins did. She was delighted, astounded at the competence of this child, and utterly amazed at his generosity.

So you've been okay then while I was...er...away?

The child looked at her. I didn't even know you were away, he said. I thought of you every day and knew you'd be back soon, and in the meantime, I learned what I could so I'd be able to help you out when you returned.

Lillykins could hardly believe her ears. Where had this considerate child learned his ways? How did he come to have so much heart-love to give? And, me oh my, had he any idea how wonderful it felt to be thus loved?

To find out the answers to these questions, Lillykins intended to sit and talk to the boy, but he was busy gathering more wood for the little fire, and then made her a cup of tea. Not that Lillykins was a tea drinker, but she sure did appreciate his loving care.

What did you do all the time I was away? she asked. She wanted to hear again that he thought of her every day.

Instead, the boy said: I looked for you in my heart and there you were, so I didn't really know you were away.

Lillykins burst into tears. She had never been so surprised, so happily surprised, in her life. She was thrilled. But not sure this was all real and would continue. Could it be a dream and she'd awaken to find herself once more feeling alone?

Don't you have me in your heart? the little boy suddenly asked. It was a question that had never before occurred to him, and he was anxious, suddenly, about the answer. Lillykins looked inside her own heart. And lo!—there he was: the baby, and beside him the little boy. And also, lo!—there was Golyga, and goodness, any number of others. So many that Lillykins thought she would have to make some time, soon, to get acquainted with each one of them. Meantime, she was here with the boy.

Goodness, yes, she told him. You most certainly are in my heart. I can feel you breathing in there, and I can feel your own heartbeat in mine, too.

Oh, good, said the little boy, relieved. Then you'll have me with you wherever you are and you'll never be alone either. Isn't that a wonderful feeling in your heart?

Yes, said Lillykins. Yes, it is. And thank you for bringing it to my attention. Now, how about some more of those shrimp?

And so, on that day, one of Lillykins' questions was answered, and since it was a very important one, she decided to postpone all others until she felt utterly confident that the answer to this question was securely fastened. In her heart, in her bones and sinews, in her mind and in her dreams, too. And that's where we shall leave Lillykins today.

LILLY: Thank you, Golyga. Thank you very much.
GOLYGA: You are welcome, my dear. We'll be together again soon. After all, your mother is safely on this side of the veil and in our care, and your life is resuming its rhythm, so we'll be able to stay in contact more frequently again. Until then.

LILLY: Until then. And thank you again.

* * *

GOLYGA: Yes, we are ready and pleased to be going at it again, though we do realize your first concern must be your health. The pain in your hip will not improve until you rest thoroughly, and so we feel confident that sitting here, writing, will not deprive you of any fun and games you might want to engage in on this beautiful day. However, we also realize that pain takes up energy, so we will not be dictating for very long today. Let's get to it.

Once again, it occurred to Golyga that Lillykins had better become more aware of his own undertakings, if he could put it that way, because otherwise she might be tempted to think him frivolous and of no serious intent. When, actually, that was far from the truth. The truth, as he saw it, was that his life was one large, long endeavour to increase joy in the world, and he considered that a worthy and eminently serious undertaking. The fact that it was accomplished by feeling, producing, experiencing joy in himself, was quite beside the point, he was going to tell Lillykins. The point was that his endeavours were indeed increasing the joy quotient in life as a whole and making available more and more joy to any and all who availed themselves of this most wonderful experience.

Now, where was Lillykins so he could once again try to make clear how dedicated and wonderful a being Golyga really was? Where indeed?

Lillykins was sitting and thinking. No chuckles, please; Lillykins would not appreciate it.

She was sitting and thinking about something very specific and worthwhile: the education of Baby. What, again?!

Well, actually, the education of "the child verging on young adulthood who used to be Baby," as he was now known.

The child had little or no notion of how to engage in social discourse with peers, and this part of his education would have to be supplied post-haste since he was approaching that age where peer pressure is a major factor in life decisions. How would he fare, if no such education was provided, when he did encounter peer pressure? Badly, feared

211

Lillykins, and so she was determined to do her best to come up with something useful.

Bussing in children his age was not going to work because the child—let's call him Frederic—was likely to change himself into any number of creatures between the time she ordered a bus and chose the children and their arrival time. Bringing Frederic into a social situation with children presented the problem of where/when/who, but, it seemed to Lillykins, would be more easily arranged. So she changed herself into a swan and set off, on mighty wings, to find a situation on Earth to suit her purposes.

Soon she landed in a town called Bracebridge. A small North American town with little diversity that tended toward conservative views, but had pockets of enlightened beings. Lillykins thought this place would serve well indeed because peer pressure to conform would be strong and the choices of association rather limited.

Yes, she thought. I'll bring Frederic here and we'll see how he gets along and what he lets himself be talked into by his peers.

Frederic, meanwhile, was amusing himself as an inchworm, studying the veins of a leaf and how its life blood was distributed to each of its cells. He liked, at the same time, to tickle the leaf and give it a giggle.

So when Lillykins descended on him and asked him to take on human form and come with her, he was not immediately thrilled to give up his inchworm state of being. However, curiosity—ever a spur to his learning—soon had him obliging Lillykins' wishes, and off the two went, to Bracebridge. Right into the middle of a skateboarding competition that was taking place in the park.

Wow, said Frederic, thus immediately fitting in and becoming a member of the peer group Lillykins had in mind. Cool! And then he asked whether he might try skateboarding, or was it something only Earth children were capable of doing?

Go ahead, said Lillykins, try it. And then there's roller blading, too. Your equipment is right over there, in that backpack. Go for it!

Lillykins withdrew to the sidelines and watched while Frederic donned the requisite protective gear and hopped onto his skateboard.

Wheee, he went, pushing off and whizzing along the straight ramp leading to the highest jump-off point. Straight it was, but also steep, and before Frederic had reached halfway up, his skateboard ran out of steam and started going down again, backwards.

Boos were heard all over the park.

What was that? Frederic asked himself. *Boo* is not a word I have encountered. I expect it's an encouragement to try again.

So off went Frederic again, this time pushing off much harder, reaching the top, and launching from the jump-off point like an eagle. As he hit the air and began to feel its buoyancy, he spread his arms as though they were wings, flapped them a couple of times, and lo—landed far far beyond anyone else's point of descent.

Clapping, yelling, and much commotion followed.

Frederic was surrounded. Smiling faces, unmistakably adoring. Much ado about the nature of his skateboard, and where was he from, anyway—the big city? And would he do it again!

That, all of that, from the girls. The boys, on the other hand, were clumped together at the far end of the runway looking pissed off. Grumbling and making gestures easily recognizable as unfriendly.

Frederic, curious about what they were saying, made his way over there to say "Hi" and "What's up?"

Nobody told him. Nobody, in fact, said a word to anyone from the moment Frederic got close enough to hear. Thinking they might be shy, he started a conversation.

Skateboarding sure is cool, he said. I never tried it before but it's going to be my favourite way of getting around. Unless roller-blading is as much fun, too. You guys ever roller-blade?

Sure, said one kid, a little taller than the others. All the time.

Would you show me how to do that? asked Frederic innocently.

Sure, okay, said the tall kid, who put on his roller-blades and took off.

Wow, said Frederic. And cool! Then he quickly put on his own roller-blades and followed the tall kid, imitating his movements and doing very well indeed, until he came to the road and had to stop. And didn't know how.

Help! Help! yelled Frederic. How do I stop?

At this point we must segue to Lillykins, still on the sidelines but now galvanized into action by Frederic's calls. She flew—well, ran—over to Frederic and caught him in her arms.

213

Big groans went up everywhere among the kids. Meaning: the poor guy—he's got one of *those* mothers! Oh boy, oh boy. Better get him away from her so he can get a life! Well, it didn't take more than a moment, after that, for every kid—girl and boy—to be on Frederic's side and for Frederic to be included in every activity he chose to join. And it didn't take him long to figure out just exactly which activities he did want to join and which were not his cup of tea. The deciding factor was always: was it going to be fun for everybody concerned or was somebody going to be the loser, the victim, the outcast, the recipient of anything nasty or even unfriendly? Because the lesson he learned most thoroughly at Golyga's knee was that joy and joy alone had the power to distinguish between the good and the bad.

If there's no joy in it, it's not for me, Golyga was wont to say, and Frederic had listened well and learned to distinguish which undertakings caused joy and which didn't.

And so, Lillykins concluded, they had done their bit and exposed the boy to learning situations long enough for now. Time to get back to the island, to inchwormhood, to rushing about as dandelion fluff in the wind, to whatever took their fancy for that moment. Because she herself was learning the lesson of joy—from Golyga by way of Frederic—and was becoming partial to experiencing joy rather than any "shoulds." She was, in other words, "getting there"!

LILLY: So, we are talking here about a step beyond "harmlessness."
GOLYGA: Yes, we are. Harmlessness is, of course, included. There is no joy if you are knowingly harming someone or something along the way. Including harm to yourself.
LILLY: Thank you very much.

* * *

GOLYGA: Yes, we are here, ready to work, and delighted that you are ready and eager, too. However, lest this work of ours become one of your "shoulds"—of which you still have rather more than you need or can be comfortable with, we suggest that today's session be one of those seemingly "just for fun" ones. So here goes…

Golyga was sitting on a rock. His favourite rock, in fact, one he had imported all the way from New Mexico to place in the middle of his favourite lake, sticking out of the water so he and others could sit on it and survey the lovely scene. Loons, ducks, great blue herons, as well as seagulls and various other less mystically elevated fowl and feathered creatures. Golyga could also see clouds, islands, water all around whipped by wind into waves of the most delightful patterns, trees bending and bowing, leaves dancing... Goodness, Golyga could hardly keep up, there was so much to watch and enjoy.

Which is when he said to himself: I need to clone myself in order to enjoy everything there is to enjoy, to do everything I want to do, and to be as accomplished, productive, and successful as I plan to be.

Ho-ho! he then said to himself. Where in the world did that come from? Since when have I been eager to be successful or productive or anything of the sort? This doesn't sound like me at all!

True, said a voice he didn't recognize. Not the sort of thing you have ever concerned yourself with, but... Here the voice paused and cleared its throat in a portentous manner. ...but, you see, you have reached a certain age and need to be conscious of that and of what-all you intend to accomplish in your lifetime.

My lifetime? Golyga raised his eyebrows, for he did have some at this moment, having taken a relatively human form for a change. What do you mean by "lifetime"? Golyga asked the voice. And who are you and where are you and let's have a look at you, shall we?

The Voice laughed. Nothing to see, it said. I'm a voice in your head and I'm having one of those conversations with you that will be etched in your memory and haunt you evermore.

Oh yeah? said Golyga. I don't like haunting and etching and such to do with my mind. I call it messing with my head. So get thee hence and avaunt, he said, turned himself into a swan, and swam off toward Lillykins, who was just coming his way, also gliding on the surface of the water like a majestic white swan.

What ho! said Golyga-swan. Where have you been then? Stratford? Russell Hill Road? Where?

Lillykins appeared surprised, which on a swan looks very odd indeed, swans being ever intent on looking anything but surprised.

Where do you suppose I've been? asked Lillykins, a bit indignant because what business was it of anybody's. Except, as she had to concede, it was a question she herself had often asked of Golyga, so it wasn't something she would object to out loud. I've been looking after our child, that fickle and obstreperous critter. Right now he is sitting on a rooftop, listening to a newscast emitted by a wire sticking up into the sky, making plans to rescue some country or other devastated by a hurricane. You can't spend your life rescuing humans, I said to him. It never ends and your life will be over before you see any progress. Just forget about it. Go skiing or something.

Golyga laughed, loudly and longly. Until Lillykins became annoyed enough to turn herself into a broomstick and threaten to swat him.

Golyga continued laughing. He knew that threaten was all she'd ever do, and the broomstick, furthermore, was made of rushes that whispered and bent with every breath.

All right, said Lillykins. Better tell me what's so funny before I really get mad.

You, laughed Golyga. Obviously, you no longer remember the first time you and I had a conversation along these lines: that humanity was forever in need of rescue and we could never ever do enough to make a difference.

Are you suggesting we stand by indifferently if there is something helpful we can do?

Not at all, said Golyga. I am suggesting that to make "rescue" your life's work is to be condemned to failure. So unless you want to spend a lifetime frustrated and end up feeling that you've wasted it, I suggest you do what you can when you can and, for the rest, live your life with as much fun and delight as possible. The less Sturm und Drang, the better.

Not very idealistic, said Lillykins.

No, said Golyga, alas. Idealists either have to close their eyes at least halfway to stay idealists or open both eyes and turn bitter. Disappointed in humanity, in their own ability to make a difference on a big scale. I say: do what you can when you can do it and then go about your own business with the aim of harming no one and of increasing the world's joy quotient.

To Lillykins' surprise, she laughed and laughed, until tears rolled down the length of her broomhandle.

How absurd, she gasped. That's exactly what I was trying to tell our son and then, here with you, I'm defending his position. One likes one's offspring to be at least somewhat idealistic, I suppose.

One likes that self-image is what you mean. The all-giving, all-concerned, ever ready to sacrifice, to dedicate, to argue and fight on behalf of humanity. It's admirable in anyone's eyes, even the cynic who professes to disagree with such notions. Admirable, but wrong. It's impossible to solve anything for anyone who isn't "there." All you can do, my dear, is what you can when you can and enjoy your life.

Well, said Lillykins, I think you had better be the one to convince our son of this attitude.

Not me, said Golyga. I've been telling you about how I live and how I think everybody should live, but far be it from me to tell anybody that.

You just told me, didn't you?

Golyga started laughing.

Not again, said Lillykins. You're not having another laughing bout without me! And quick as can be, Lillykins joined in the laughter until both were hooting and hollering all over the lake. And next thing they knew, there was the son, sitting on the rock in the middle of the lake, observing his parents' hilarity, and surely and happily getting sucked into it until he, too, was laughing most heartily all over the lake, and no one had to say one word to him about the best way to increase joy in the world.

Not that he was entirely cured of his messianic bent, mind you, but that is a subject for another day.

* * *

GOLYGA: Yes, we are here and ready to work, and good for you, Lilly dear, to divest yourself of the mundane, as you call it, which has been all too prevalent with you these days. Such matters as whether your friends have transportation up to the lake or not really can be left in their hands, don't you think?

LILLY: Yes, I think you're right.

GOLYGA: So, now that we are on our own lofty plane, what shall we engage in today?

LILLY: Why the sarcasm?

GOLYGA: *To point out to you that there is another way of looking at the entire scenario: you were kind enough to spend time and long-distance money on solving your friends' problem, but then you spent time and energy berating yourself for this kind act. Why is that, do you think?*

LILLY: *Old habit of self-berating, I assume.*

GOLYGA: *Yes, old habit. But also a new kind of expectation of yourself to be above the mundane. You see, there is a misperception of the realms of "lofty." We are not removed, above, or lofty in any way. We are amazed and full of great admiration for the ways of humans, given what they have to deal with. We believe the mundane is the realm where all human action proves itself either munificent and beneficial or disturbing and negative in outcome. Whether you buy recycled toilet paper or just appreciate the fact that a tree has been felled to give you paper, the least consciousness about your planet—even in regards to the everyday affairs of living—is an advance of positive energies.*

As for your preoccupation with divisions such as "mundane" and "lofty"—or however you want to put it—it's the preoccupation itself that is the bogeyman. Whenever you engage in divisive categorization, beware that it isn't spawned by the judgmental attitudes you want to be rid of. So let us review what is useful in your present situation for the purposes of this book...

By dividing your life into the mundane and the lofty, you create a barrier to the free flow of energy throughout all your life. If you can allow the flow to enter and leave all your endeavours, whatever category, there is no such thing as the mundane. Then, also, everyday life will flow smoothly in all its details and aspects because even glitches will benefit from the flow and be seen in their most useful light. Get it?

LILLY: *I certainly do.*

GOLYGA: *So instead of leaving behind this aspect of your life while your cottage is full of people—friends and relations—bring yourself to the situation with an unimpeded energy flow. And practise your "I receive all positive energies" whenever it occurs to you that it might be useful. Okay?*

LILLY: *Okay. And thank you.*

GOLYGA: *All right now, we go on to the lesson for the day, which has nothing whatsoever to do with your personal life, Lilly dear.*

LILLY: *I doubt that.*

GOLYGA: *You are right, it will be a boon to your life as well.*

You have noticed by now that whatever subject we choose, it has relevance to your life. We are choosing the subjects for their relevance to humans in general, so it isn't too surprising, you being human, that these subjects resonate. However, there is a further point to be made and that is the very receptive attitude you bring to our endeavour. You do not shirk or evade the sometimes unpleasant truths we reveal—such as mental habits, judgmental attitudes, etc., etc.—and you do not feel attacked or derided but only helped and glad to be chosen to learn all this in a concentrated course.

You have noted, we suppose, that this session is to be a general overview rather than an episode in "the adventures of," and so we'll simply add two more observations and one suggestion.

First observation: humans are very dense.

We are talking here of the material that makes their bodies appear, to us, of a denser fabric than our own. Therefore, humans have some necessary dealings that are unique to their state of denseness. Such as gravity, and illness of the body, and being easily captured by repetitive behaviour, thought forms, and such, through brain ruts, as you think of them.

However, there are also a great many advantages to density.

For one, you are able to give of yourselves in a unique way. By transmuting negative energies through your bodies into positive energies, you are doing what some call "God's work." You are in fact, a very important mechanism, so to speak, through which the universe launders energy—like mob money—and increases or decreases the positive energy available in the universe. The more you align yourselves, body included, with positive energies, the more this transmuting and therefore increasing of the positive is advanced.

So there you have one: the amount of positive energy flow you are able to allow is the amount by which you service the Universal Spirit. Get it?

LILLY: Yes, I think so.

GOLYGA: Read it over later.

What we want to point out is that this can never be a masochistic, self-sacrificing behaviour. Since you and your body are part of the universe, any neglect, any harm, any negative thing you do to yourself, you also do to the universe. Your posture, fatigue, neglect of health have a direct and deleterious effect on all of us and everything there is.

LILLY: A tiny drop in the ocean but it can add to pollution sort of thing?

GOLYGA: No. It's more weighty and immediate. Because any neglect or negative action in connection with the self/body immediately affects a great number of things, both in your immediate circumstances and in the greater arena.

For example: you have ingested some harmful food—knowingly and with the self-negative attitude of "I don't care." Immediately, your energy changes. Unless you can be aware of that and turn it around, everything in your immediate surroundings is affected by that energy, causing reverberations in the way a stone dropped into a calm lake will cause ripples. At the same time, however, the ripples of disturbed energy cause others and so on and on.

If, for example, the ripple you first notice is met with neglect and "I don't care," you are setting up another cross-ripple, and the disturbance grows rapidly into a veritable storm.

There are reasons for all the storms experienced at this time, and it's not merely the direct outcome of Mother Earth changes. Disturbances have been gathering force for a long time in humanity's calendar, and when they come to a head as energy in the "natural" or "physical sphere," they are bound to be huge in the resulting ripples.

However, we are not doomsayers and gloomsayers here, not at all. Because while one stone causes ripples galore, one drop of essence causes the joy that heals.

Joy as an antidote is new to humanity, but a powerful tool and aspect of the universe. As such, Joy must be thoroughly explained in its function before this can be seen properly in its vast dimension and influence.

So the best way, again, is by example.

Take a moment's joy at the sound of a bird. The body as well as every other part of you is uplifted, so to speak, transformed for a brief moment into pure essence of positive energy. This moment, or drop of joy, also causes ripples. And these ripples join with every other moment and experience of joy that is floating around the universe—moments of joy not only experienced by humans but by every kind of living being, and all the universe is living beings. So there goes the drop of joy, joining all others, forming an ocean with a vast power, and all of it for good.

"A drop in the ocean" again? Too minuscule to give any sense of making a difference? Weigh it against a pebble and a ripple and, my dears, you would find—if you could weigh them both—that the drop of joy is infinitely more weighty and vastly more influential. How do we know? We who dwell in joy can tell you: every ripple felt or apprehended by us is so easily turned into joy that we have no hesitation in guessing its relative weight.

And you, my dears, have that same capacity, unexercised though it is. In but a moment, you can turn a negative bubble into one of joy merely by wishing it so.
LILLY: Never experience anything negative? How is that possible. How about the death of a loved one, say?

GOLYGA: You may perceive death as negative, but is it?

LILLY: I perceive my loss as negative.

GOLYGA: But is it loss? Or is it a transformation of the relationship to another plane?

LILLY: It's loss. Trust me: when you want somebody present in body and he is not, it's loss.

GOLYGA: It is also a doorway then to other realms. Because if you truly feel such a loss, you will want to reconnect at whatever point this is possible, and therefore you will expand your experience of available realms. And very soon, instead of loss, you will experience gain.

LILLY: So the process of transmuting is the painful part?

GOLYGA: Yes, it's not always easy, but it is always to be devoutly sought. It is futile pain that is most painful, is it not?

LILLY: I suppose. Tell me again how to go about turning a pebble into a drop of joy.

GOYGA: Yes, let us take another example or way of expressing the same process: you are not to think for a moment that your energy is not our concern. Please, simply type and think later, for this next part.

We have always wondered about the inability of humans to see this transition from negative to positive more clearly, and now we have had a recent infusion of understanding of it. We are now aware there is almost a wall between the negative and the positive in the minds of humans, when, in fact, there is no such wall. There is an elusive line that separates the two and often the permeability is so great that humans are not even sure whether a given energy is positive or negative. That's how close it can be in the real state of things. So please remember that and be always aware of how closely related are negative and positive energies and how easy, therefore, it is to turn one into the other. A mere thought can do it. A mere moment's joy—a drop in the ocean—can turn something around. And once that is done, the forward thrust of the positive energy carries with it the gathering power of all other drops.

Let us point out once again that the wall you posit between the positive and the negative does not exist. There is a fluid relationship between the two, and an easy transmuting is possible once you know that. Try it—you might understand it best experientially.

221

GOLYGA: *And now, dear Lilly, we will close. We'll return to this subject again and we recommend you look at these notes, because if you can begin to apply this knowledge right now, you'll fare so much better in the next days of much company and activity. All right?*
LILLY: *Thank you very very much. Yes.*
GOLYGA: *We love you, we care for you, we are your ever-loving large component.*
LILLY: *And teacher, friend, guide, and more.*
GOLYGA: *Yes, and more. Until soon, this is your Beeswax.*

* * *

GOLYGA: *Yes, we are finally at work on the very last parts to be added to the book, and lo!—you are eager and ready for another book, right?*
LILLY: *Right, yes. Though I would like first to tie up loose ends and get this one entirely finished.*
GOLYGA: *And so we shall. Starting right now.*

When we last saw our beloved characters, they were all more or less expecting to go on adventuring and delighting in their escapades for some time to come. The baby/youth was growing day by day, and not only physically—in fact, at times he was downright minuscule, having developed some interest in microbes and such. Our one and only Golyga was happy to observe his offspring, as he was wont to call him, become more and more interesting every day while Golyga was ever engaged in the machinations of joy and how to spread it around. Lillykins was busily doing rescue work though not without taking time off for simple joyfulness and fun with her partner, and her brother Hylie was making mischief, his preferred mode of causing thought to arise and be fruitful. The one character who felt neglected and even disrespected was the snake scientist. After having been billed as a major character early in the book, he felt he should have been given more to do in this saga and, feeling miffed, he was looking around for somebody to poison. Oh yes, he was perfectly capable of poisoning out of sheer pique and raging ego. So here he was, ambling balefully down the road, looking everywhere for somebody to poison. Somebody who had something to do with the saga preferably, but if not, then anybody at all. Just to let out some of the accumulated poison.

As the snake scientist came rounding round a bush, a bushy tail caught his eye and he said to himself, Aha! Somebody is likely to be attached to that bushy tail, and I'll be able to poison that somebody. Just come up behind him or her, and *whap...*

The snake scientist kept going, came closer and closer to the bushy tail, and suddenly stopped dead in his tracks. That bushy tail was not attached to anything! It wasn't part of anybody. It was just a bushy tail, suspended above the road by no visible means, gently wafting in the breeze issuing from the open mouth of snake scientist.

Finally, the snake scientist was able to pull together enough brain cells to say something: Er, excuse me. I'm not quite sure about how to address you, but, er, can you hear me?

Snake scientist heard a giggle. A tiny but unmistakable giggle, coming from the bushy tail. Or did it? There was nothing to show the snake scientist that the giggle proceeded from the tail itself. Nothing indicated a different movement, colour, direction, density—nothing at all had changed on the bushy tail. So what was going on?

The snake scientist repeated his question: Excuse me, can you hear me?

Something or other repeated the giggle.

Snake scientist said: Is that you giggling, oh Bushy Tail?

The giggling grew louder and more intense. Almost a laugh, or perhaps guffaw would better describe it.

Well, now snake scientist was getting impatient and even affronted. No co-operation here, he could see that. Nothing and nobody to be helpful in this quest for information.

Oh well, he sighed. Nothing has changed. As usual, it's an uphill battle to find facts and information and nobody co-operating at all. Just a lot of willy-nilly behaviour by all and sundry and nobody following the rules of science with their straightforward indications of how to pattern your behaviour according to what or who you are, etc., etc. (A snake scientist, once started, can go on and on complaining about the limitations of the universe in following scientific rules and patterns.)

Suddenly, there was a huge noise. An absolutely frightening rumbling roaring noise that duly frightened the snake scientist right out of his skin (and ever since, snake scientists have been known to shed skins regularly, as you know), and once out of his skin, snake scientist looked for something to shelter his vulnerable body and found a hollow in the ground just beneath the bushy tail. That's when he realized the roaring rumble was coming directly from the bushy tail! How horrible: here he was, right under the noise, no explanations possible for the suspended tail or the noise, and he himself vulnerable to the point of nakedness, totally at sea, so to speak, as far as any facts, information, or scientific knowledge was concerned.

Snake scientist put down his head and wept.

As he wept bitter tears of fear, of disappointment and failure, of futility and all those other things that make snake scientists weep, slowly, little by little his poison drained out of him with the tears. Bit by bit, it dripped out and away, and slowly, slowly, the snake scientist, naked and weary from crying, also began to feel cleansed.

He raised his head and looked around to see colours both bright and beautiful. And instead of asking himself what exactly was making those colours so beautiful and whether he could produce them just so in a lab, the snake scientist—much too weary for questions—simply sat and looked, in wonder and awe, at the beauty all around him.

The horrible noise, he found, had stopped some time before, when he was still crying with fear. The bushy tail was still suspended above him, making for a rather pleasant shelter. And all the questions the snake scientist had wanted to ask of the bushy tail or about the horrible noise waited somewhere way off in the distance. Waiting to pounce, it's true, but held at bay for as long as the sense of wonder and the joy of beauty suffused our snake scientist.

And when he did start asking questions again—you knew he would; none of a scientific bent of mind can stop asking questions for long—he did it in quite a different way and with a different tone of voice, for evermore. Respect was in it, and also, forevermore, a sense of wonder and the joy of beauty.

LILLY: And that would be the end of today's session, I suspect?
GOLYGA: Yes, indeed.
LILLY: Thank you. Can you tell me where it goes? At the very end?

GOLYGA: Very close to the end. We'll do a few more sessions to round things out, and one of them will be for the very end of this book. Okay?

LILLY: Okay. How am I doing with the ordering of the manuscript?

GOLYGA: Very well. You can actually start the new print-out any time because you can repaginate whenever changes occur—whether because you have found something to change or because more material came in. Go over it all slowly enough so you can do spell checks and use different fonts for our dialogues, etc.

LILLY: What about quotation marks for dialogue of characters?

GOLYGA: No, better start a new line with each speech instead.

LILLY: Next session, can you answer some of the questions I've jotted down?

GOLYGA: Okay, read them over before the session and we'll do that. For today, this is it, okay?

* * *

GOLYGA: Yes, my dear, we would like to add this segment to the book:

In recent times there has been much talk about the millennium—as written in the Christian calendar. By the time you, dear reader, have this book in your hands, it will be clear what has and has not come about as the result of the numbers involved—whether on a calendar or on computer screens.

We would like to point out that numbers are abstract and symbolic both, and that interpreting numbers is not actually at its height in the human realm. The Mayans, for one, had a better grasp of the nature of numbers, and other times and peoples did, too. As for science, it has taken a long time for scientists to understand that numbers are inventions based on theory and they have only symbolic relations to reality.

"Only" is suggested because scientists tend to take numbers as too real. Especially statistical enumerations. It may well be that ninety-nine per cent of people react in one particular way, but it may also be that the one per cent who react differently are, in fact, the significant ones to watch and understand. And so on.

Altogether, we would like to suggest that numerical approaches to reality must be highly evolved to be useful, and in the general tone of things as they are on Earth, most of you had better pay attention to other venues of understanding. Study not the quantity of existence but the quality. Be concerned not with the "most" but with the unique. Be open for surprises and revelations from the tiniest source and give up your infatuation with masses and amassing.

GOLYGA: Ha! We can hear Lilly thinking. Preaching now. How uncouth.
LILLY: I was thinking no such thing. Well yes, I was thinking "preachy," but in the nicest way.
GOLYGA: Very funny. But you are right. We have been rather preachy today. We have a reason...

All this millennium talk is drawing fear energy into the Earth's atmosphere at a great rate, and we seek to disperse it before it blows up unnecessary catastrophes. As we dictated the above ideas to you, they have a chance to travel in the atmosphere and disseminate among people pondering the millennium without merely swallowing the media hype or the fearmonger's. Among them, by the way, the nicest, most innocent of people, who are merely worried or "concerned" and are, unbeknownst to themselves, increasing the likelihood of nasty stuff going down.

LILLY: Is there anything I can do to counter that negative energy besides telling people I am shifting to a different calendar until this madness is over?
GOLYGA: Actually, keep telling people you plan, with your friends, to celebrate life with dancing and music. That will engender more positive energy than anything else. For your party, as well.
LILLY: All right.

*** *

GOLYGA: Yes, we are here, we care for you, we want to work with you, and so here we go:
 Yesterday, when you said you intended to work today, you said it with gleeful anticipation and we are happy you did. We, too, feel joy when we work together because the service involved is important and will help many people. We are also glad to be with you because we know our work together is always a spur to you, Lilly dear,

226

to continue your advance on the path. And so we decided to devise an episode for us today that reinforces the twofold purpose of serving and enjoying.

Once upon a time, a long time ago, there was a very large, adventurous elephant. This elephant decided to travel and see the world. He had heard of King Babar, another travelling elephant, and decided to follow in his footsteps but do him one better: be aware of all the creatures he encountered everywhere and learn from them.

Off he went, first to the planet Earth, where he nearly met his death at the hands of tusk poachers. This did not appeal to our elephant, so he went off to another planet and tried his luck there.

Sure enough, this was a peaceful place and the inhabitant creatures were not out to kill anybody.

The elephant rented a room in a pyramid and settled in to learn a thing or two. Next thing he knew, ten years had passed and he was married and had three elephant children, and his wife, who was a shrew and a nag, kicked him out for being lazy and sitting around contemplating his navel.

When what our elephant had actually been doing was to study the philosophical questions of the universe: who am I, what is the universe made of, and so on. Kicked out, he decided to study yet another part of the world and took himself off to a distant planet full of little Jibbertigibbers.

Jibbertigibbers, in case you don't know, are tiny flying people who resemble humans except for their small size and their large wings. Think hummingbird but human-shaped and no big beak. Something like that. Maybe we could mention tiny fairies, but they were not generally of the pretty female variety. Rather, there were many bearded men, kick-ass teenagers, etc., etc.

The elephant was enjoying himself enormously, studying the mores and habits and ways of thinking of the Jibbertigibbers. What he discovered quite soon and was astounded by was their ability to speak all languages on their planet. In other words, every Jibbertigibber could speak at least four hundred languages. And that despite the size of their tiny heads and presumably equally tiny brains.

The elephant couldn't figure it out.

He tried and tried but he could come up with no explanation. So he decided to seek the wisest of the Jibbertigibbers and ask him the question: How is it possible that Jibbertigibbers, despite their tiny brains, can speak four hundred languages?

A simple plan and it might have worked well indeed, if there had been such a thing as a wisest Jibbertigibber. But the moment one Jibbertigibber learned something, he or she immediately shared this knowledge with everyone else, and so all the Jibbertigibbers, each one of them, had the same degree of knowledge. No wisest of anything anywhere.

Amazing, thought the elephant. If I could introduce this habit, this development or evolutionary step, every creature everywhere could benefit from the knowledge anyone had anywhere!

The elephant stopped the next Jibbertigibber he saw and told him about his good idea.

The Jibbertigibber looked at him uncomprehendingly. Couldn't grasp the first thing the elephant was saying.

Why can't you understand me? asked the elephant. You speak my language, don't you?

Well yes, said the Jibbertigibber. The language is no problem. But you're not making any sense with it. How would it be possible for a Jibbertigibber to learn something that doesn't make sense on this planet? Like this "going to war" you told us about one day, or this "producing food that makes some people rich and all the people who eat it sick." What do you call it? Genetically engineered food? Or how about that other planet, where you were supposed to be doing doing doing and never contemplating. How are we supposed to understand that? I heard you tell about it. I heard you tell lots of things. I could understand the words, all right, but you were not making any sense to us.

The elephant nodded his head. He understood now that even if everyone everywhere could learn all the languages in the world, it was no solution to anything. What was needed was a context, a way of thinking, a philosophical underpinning, an ethical system, a common spiritual goal, an ideal to strive for, and a big bag of chips to eat while contemplating these lofty ideas.

All right, said the elephant to himself. In that case, I was definitely on the right track when contemplating the eternal questions. And no one is going to tell me differently. And with that, the elephant took himself back to the planet where his shrewish wife and his three elephant children still lived.

Here, he said to his wife. You can holler and nag all you want. Contemplation is important work, and I intend to do it. I'm not saying I won't chop wood or won't take out the garbage—without being told. I am saying that, henceforth, contemplation is not to be equated with laziness and you are not to bother me when I'm engaged in it.

His shrewish wife smiled a big smile. Thanks for telling me what you're doing when you're just sitting there ignoring me, she said. I always thought you were showing me how boring I was and how I wouldn't understand anything you told me and so you didn't bother telling me what you were thinking about and—

No, no, no, you've got it all wrong, the elephant said to his wife. I was trying to come up with answers before I told you and made a fool of myself, not knowing much about anything important.

The elephant and his wife smiled at each other and began talking and even thinking together on a regular basis.

The three children, meantime, grew up, and wherever they went, they took with them the habits of contemplation and communication. They were fine specimens and of great help to many others they encountered.

Meantime, the elephant and his wife—who was a Termigan, by the way, a combination of termite and permigan: very clever, very sharp teeth, and a great sense of humour when not upset by being ignored—decided to set out on a cruise and learn what they could. They were hoping to find, finally, what the universe was made of.

Off they sailed on the great seas they found to be water, and soon came to a great island in the sky where they disembarked and found, to their dismay, that no air was available for breathing here.

Not air then, said the elephant. The universe is not made of air, we can now know that much.

His wife laughed at him. It's not made of cream cheese either. That way we'll be dead before we find out anything. Let's get out of here and sail on until we find something likely to tell us what we want to know.

On they sailed, the two of them. On and on. As they went, they began to enjoy the sailing so much that sometimes they forgot why they were doing it and just sailed and sailed. Afterwards, they'd say to themselves: Well, I guess we needed a break. But now we'd better get back to questing for answers.

And on they sailed. And enjoyed the travelling. And forgot everything else for longer and longer periods of time. Feeling quite guilty when one or the other of them remembered they were supposed to be looking for answers.

Finally, on one fine day of sailing, the wife turned to the elephant and said: All this travelling to find answers. Maybe we never will. Maybe we should just enjoy the travelling, and if we run across answers, hallelujah, and if we don't, at least we won't have wasted all this wonderful sailing but will have enjoyed it!

The elephant was not the most flexible of creatures at the best of times, but even he had to stop and think about what his wife said.

We could, he replied after due thought, posit an X in place of an answer. If X equals an answer—

I never liked algebra, said his wife. Call it the Great Mystery instead of X, would you please?

Alright, said the elephant. We'll call it the Great Mystery.

Anyway, if we posit that as the answer, to be replaced by more precise knowledge as it becomes available—*if* it becomes available—we can go ahead and sail to our hearts' content, afloat in the Seas of the Great Mystery and enjoying every minute of it.

Phew, said his wife. It took a while but we finally got you there. Good. Now we can really go to it and sail away on the seas of joy.

Which is what they did and are still doing to this day.

* * *

GOLYGA: *Yes, my dear, we are here, we are ready to work and glad you set your intention. We'll make it a rather short session today for the sake of your energy and it will read like this:*

Once upon a time, Golyga had just returned from one of his many journeys into the wild blue yonder, when he ran across a lovely flower in full bloom, right at the crossroads. Golyga stopped to contemplate the beauty of the flower, never noticing that it emitted a rather harsh fragrance. A stink, actually.

By the time Golyga came out of his entranced state, he was covered and engulfed in stink and so he went screaming off in search of a stream, a river, a lake, an ocean—anything to rid himself of the horrible smell.

But Golyga found nothing of the kind. Howling with frustration, he hurled himself into a tiny trickle of a stream coming down the mountainside and, after his bruises and various abrasions became too painful, raised himself up once again from the pebbles and trickle of water and sniffed himself all over.

Much better, he said. Not entirely gone, but definitely better. Phew. What a relief.

Golyga then returned to the crossroads, intending to find out why that flower made such a stink and why it took him so long to notice it—too long, in fact, for his own good.

He arrived at the crossroads and searched all around—as if flowers play hide-and-seek or go for little walks in the countryside—but he found no flower. None at all—stink or no stink.

Well, what in the... Golyga said, looking none too intelligent. I just can't believe...

But in the end he had to believe that, in fact, he had seen a flower, been be-stunked by it, and now the flower was gone. Vanished without trace.

Shaking his head, Golyga made his way up the right side of the fork until he came to the great rock upon which he liked to sit while contemplating the mysteries of life. And there he sat and contemplated, getting not one bit closer to an answer because, really, he said to himself: What exactly was the *question* here?

How can you be so beautiful and yet stink like that?

How can you be here one moment and gone soon after, without a trace?

How come I noticed nothing about the smell until it was too late?

What exactly is the question I want answered?

And just as he was about to add more questions to the list, getting increasingly involved in the mysterious and flailing about in his mental maze—just then his old friend the Heron came swooping down and landed right beside Golyga's rock.

Ah, said the Heron. Thinking, I see.

Golyga nodded, then shook his head. It's getting me nowhere fast, he said. I'm trying to circumnavigate with questions a subject that is not open to logic. It is open to awe and wonder, of course—everything is open to that, but as for answers in a logical cause-and-effect manner, forget it. Nothing happening.

The Heron was mystified. In that case, he asked, why sit here and turn grey in the face? Why not go straight to awe and wonder?

Why indeed, said Golyga, and he jumped up from the rock, stretched his neck and legs until he resembled the Heron, and took off. Thank you, he called back to the Heron. Thanks for the reminder. Want to join me in some aweing and wondering?

The Heron shook his head. Why go from one place to another if it's awe and wonder you're after? Why not just open you eyes and ears and, not to forget, your sense of smell, and your heart, right where you are?

The Heron stepped up on the rock and surveyed the horizon. Yep, he thought. I think I'll just stay right here awhile, to awe and wonder.

* * *

GOLYGA: *And so we resume our tales with a short instalment for the day. Once your energy improves again, we'll do some marathon sessions so we can tie up some loose ends. After all, we've left quite a few of them dangling. Never fear, Lilly dear, nothing shall be left in an unsatisfactory condition according to the lights of readers, editors, or other cerebral entities. On the other hand, nothing shall be left in a closed state with no hope of future developments or exciting adventures. What we might consider is a kind of serial—episodic but with a decided direction and purpose. What do you think?*

LILLY: *Sounds fine. Are you still thinking this tale will be published?*

GOLYGA: *Yes, I most certainly am. After all, why pick a professional published writer for a channel if we're intending the whole thing for the drawer! Or do you suppose the lessons hidden in our tale are for your eyes only? Would be useful to you alone? Not so.*

But let's get on with our little tale-telling for the day...

When Golyga saw that the great Heron he once knew was flying around and around, trying to get his attention in order to communicate with him, he stopped what he was doing—whatever it was—and called on the Heron to come and talk with him.

The great Heron descended and deftly settled himself in the shade of a bush. From there he spoke to Golyga: You have now seen much of what the universe has to offer, Golyga—what do you think of its chances for survival, given that the creatures populating the planet Earth seem determined to sink not only their own planet but their whole solar system with it.

Golyga thought for about two seconds and said: Why worry? If they go, there are millions and billions of others to take their place.

But each creature, whether planet or ant, is unique, you know that. Not replaceable by any other. Are you still so sanguine about losing the millions and billions of beings on planet Earth, the planet itself, and many with it?

Golyga said: Well, *sanguine* isn't exactly the word I would use. Nor would I use the word *lose*. For *sanguine*, substitute *resigned*, and for *lose*, substitute *transform*.

All right then, said the great Heron. Let's do that. Are you resigned to have the planet Earth and all its creatures as well as other vast entities of the solar system transformed into a lower vibration than it is able to maintain at present with the help of those creatures who are working, evolving, transforming energy as best they can into higher vibrations?

Vibrations, vibrations, said Golyga. What a very abstract concept, unless you happen to have experience of it in yourself. And how many people do?

Everybody does, said the great Heron. Every single living thing. And all things are living. It's simply a matter of growing conscious of the vibrations and of maintaining that consciousness for longer and longer periods, and then none of us need be "resigned" about the planet or any of its creatures.

And how do you propose bringing about this state of consciousness in the creatures of the planet Earth?

Oh, listen to yourself, said the great Heron. Pontificating with the tone of a doubting Thomas, when you know perfectly well it's being brought about as we speak, you and I, by the delightful consciousness of Lilly dear. And by her many co-conspirators on the path. And by her attempts to grow and move along the path and sweep along with her all manner of energies that were once of low vibrations—or "negative," as she would term them—and are now increasingly higher in their vibrations, and Lilly dear increasingly conscious of them even in her daily activities and tasks.

So then this whole discussion is academic, is it? No need to worry at all about the planet Earth and its creatures, let alone other entities in the solar system.

You know better than that, said the great Heron. There is certainly cause to worry when entities such as yourself indulge in sarcastic tones and snippy comments.

Sorry, said Golyga. It's part of my character in this tale of adventure we're concocting.

So you say, said the great Heron. It sounds more like the sort of flippant teaching nobody enjoys, so watch it.

Golyga was crestfallen and showed it. And then the great Heron let out a great heron- cackle—which sounds, in case you've never heard it, like a turkey trying to sing opera—and then he said: Ha, pulling your tale feathers, I was.

And off he flew, cackling grotesquely, while Golyga stared after him, chewing on his moustache.

A moustache, you say?

Yes, yes, why not? Many suddenly sprout a macho moustache when cackled at by great herons. You might like to remember that, the next time you come across male creatures in danger of be-cackling.

And so we leave Golyga for the day, moustache and all, and give some thought to the great Heron's affliction: that awful cackle voice. Or perhaps we shall give thought to nothing at all for a while and just breathe, conscious of vibration in all its myriad forms and what manner of thought will raise them.

* * *

GOLYGA: *Yes, we are ready and able and willing and enjoying the thought of working together, but we do have one exceptional request: that you remember to rest*

afterwards. There is much energy flowing through you at this moment and throughout our sessions together, and your body needs time to adjust and to bridge back toward the usual amount of energy flow. If you take off immediately after working with us, without that period for adjustment, you will find your body deteriorating from the sheer porousness of its makeup. After we finish our work, you need to rest every part of you, holding still and holding quiet, until the adjustment is made. You will feel when it's done, and it shouldn't take more than ten minutes or so in your time. Watch for a shift inside yourself to know when the transition is completed. All right?
LILLY: All right. Yes, thank you.

Now then: when there is energy work of any kind going on—and this applies not only to channelling for this type of work but also for healing-energy channelling, for simple transactions between living creatures on Earth, for energy exchanges with forces of nature—energy exchange can have a positive effect or a deleterious one, depending on the sender(s) and receiver(s) involved.

Intention is one aspect of the exchange and influences a great deal of what happens. For example: if you intend to receive positive energy from a force of nature, set your intention and you will. If you fail to set your intention, you'll receive a mixed bag, depending on what and where and such elements on either side. As for energy exchange with people, it is even more important to set your intention to receive only positive energy and, at the same time, be receptive to it, indeed.

Being unaware while engaged in any kind of energy exchange with people can be both a lost opportunity and, sometimes, downright dangerous. Take, for example, your energy exchange with Ann, in Mexico. If you had been aware from the beginning, you would have sensed clearly that the exchange was sucking on your positive energy while depleting you and was also bombarding you with negative energy. Hence your health, already jeopardized by your physical environment, was further debilitated. And that was unnecessary debilitation.

Then there is the energy exchange between entities such as ourselves and humans. You, dear Lilly, are now an expert at bringing in energies from beyond the veil—yes, we can hear you balking at the term, but the fact is you can open yourself up and receive our energies almost at will. You are less adept at bringing in healing energy for your physical body but, thank goodness, MarTee, as you call him, is ever vigilant, and whenever there is the slightest chink of an opening for healing energy, he's there in a flash to do his healing work.

Thank you, MarTee.

Yes, and the ability to send your energy is improving, too. To send love and healing energy more powerfully, you need only practise.

And now we come to the crux of today's session: energy work is of paramount importance at this time precisely because time is running out for the present state of energy vibrations on Earth. The present state has gone on for a very long time, Earth time, and humans have evolved to be at ease with the current state. The changes experienced by the planet will have a strong effect on the vibrational states of everything and everyone there. Only those who can adjust to new vibrational states will be able to continue in their bodies as incarnate entities and only those able to amass energy information at the experiential level will make the transition with ease.

This is not news to you, Lilly, but how many people have watched or read Awakening to Zero Point? There will have to be many more avenues of reaching people with this information and with the wherewithal to make the transition with ease, so we urge you to both work with us regularly until this book is done and also with yourself and the energies, as per our suggestions.

Here is an exercise anyone can do and everyone can benefit from:

Still your mind—in whichever way works for you—and begin to follow your breath. After a few moments, start to "send" your breath. In other words, as you breathe out, intentionally "send" your breath to something or someone chosen. It might be a flower, a person, a world situation, an entity beyond the veil. The point is: with your breath flowing out, energy is sent. And, intended as it is, its force is far stronger than you would assume.

For the second part of this exercise: on the in-breath, receive with intention energy from a chosen source. This, too, can be a plant, a person, a rock, a lake, an entity beyond the veil—anything at all. Set your intention to receive energy from the chosen one and be sure to include in your intention-setting the word *positive*.

Positive energy is LOVE, you see, and since everything everywhere has energy, or *is* energy, everything everywhere is or has LOVE.

We also suggest you begin and end your day with a few moments of this energy work—rather than planning what to wear tomorrow or what to say to so-and-so, do the energy work that takes you to the core of your intention. You want to wear something that will have a certain effect—on others or yourself—and instead of planning the details of what that should be, try breathing with intention—sending or receiving or both—addressing the situation from that direction. You will find your life flowing smoothly, your energy improving steadily, and your love life, in the broadest sense, fulfilling you in the most delightful way. Get it?

LILLY: Got it, thank you, Beeswax.
GOLYGA: One more quick word, Lilly dear: we appreciate that you are not flinging yourself in all directions, keeping busy. Your dedication to our work is most delightfully noted and we are proud to be working with you.
LILLY: Thank you, Beeswax. I appreciate your appreciation.
GOLYGA: Now remember to rest and enjoy, and then go and enjoy!

* * *

Once upon a time, there was a young woman who loved to ski, run, fly (in her dreams), and climb mountains. She loved the feeling of movement in her body—of every kind.

It came to pass that this young woman—we'll call her Elizabeth, for no particular reason—had a fall and was hurt so badly she was paralyzed and could barely move a finger. Elizabeth was depressed by this turn of events and, since no one could help her or even promise improvement, she seriously considered taking her own life and ending the misery with which she was now living twenty-four hours a day.

Then something happened in her life that thoroughly changed her mind and her attitude toward life: she fell in love.

How, you'll ask yourself, is that going to help somebody in her condition? Hardly likely, you'll say, that the love will be returned, is it?

But it was. Elizabeth fell in love with a frog—a bright green one, with lovely buggy eyes—and the frog loved her right back, feeling sure that it was Elizabeth who was meant to kiss him and turn him into a prince.

As it happened, however, Elizabeth was not the kissing type. She was more likely to hug, hum a lovely tune for the frog, stroke his dry skin, or just look deeply into his buggy eyes. Kissing didn't actually occur to her, and so, to the frog's eternal disappointment, he remained a frog—albeit a beloved one.

One day, just as Elizabeth was returning from one of the many physiotherapy sessions that seemed to do her no good at all, the frog was playing hide-and-seek—all unbeknownst to Elizabeth—and hiding right under the wheelchair Elizabeth used around the house. The one with the motor and telephone and every other gadget known to humans for the alleviation of suffering and isolation of its handicapped population. (Those who could afford it, that is, or who could somehow hook up with a sponsor or patron.)

So Elizabeth was being lowered into her wheelchair, settled in with everything close by, and then left to her lonely afternoon—or so they thought, those nice people who picked her up and returned her after physio.

Must be hard, they said, spending so much time alone, not able to do much of anything...

How wrong they were.

Ever since the arrival of the frog that fine spring day, Elizabeth had been busy—getting on the internet to research her frog and his needs and gathering more and more information about frogs—the mythology of frogs, the biology and variations of frog—she even had a collection of songs about frogs. Pretty soon she was an expert on frogs and, come evening time, she regularly set herself down, frog in lap, to tell him of his ancestors, his relations—mythical and real—and his many appearances in people's dreams... On and on, Elizabeth would talk to her frog while the frog...well, he wasn't actually listening all that much...found all this frog stuff a bit boring, being convinced he was a prince himself, but he enjoyed her tranquil tones, her soft hand on his neck and back, her warm breath, and above all the hope that she would, one day, lift him to her lips and kiss him into princedom.

So the years passed. The frog was getting old and downright testy when he thought of all the wasted years he'd spent as a frog already and even wondered whether there was any point in becoming a prince so late in life. Still, he mused—better a few last years as a prince than no prince at all.

One day, just at the beginning of spring again, Elizabeth experienced a miracle recovery. She suddenly felt a tingling and whooshing in her body she had not felt before, and observed a pinkish hue spreading over her limbs and neck. She started moving her fingers, then her toes, her ankles, her wrists, her neck, her eyebrows, her torso. She was cured and she was ecstatic.

As you can imagine, this changed everything in her life and, therefore, everything in the frog's life. Suddenly, he was abandoned to his own devices because Elizabeth was too busy leading a catch-up life and being active every waking moment.

She almost, in truth, forgot about the love of her life, the frog. He who had been everything to her languished in solitude and sadness, and Elizabeth hardly noticed his absence when he crawled more and more often under the bed and stayed there for hours at a time.

Finally, one day when there was a light drizzle out and the frog had had it with hanging out under the bed, he decided to leave Elizabeth. Old though he was, he hadn't entirely given up hope of becoming a prince, and since Elizabeth was no longer paying attention—let alone lavishing love on him—he knew he had better seek his goal elsewhere.

The frog set out early the next morning, enjoying the dew and the freshness of the morning air, and started hopping down the road.

Suddenly, he heard a huffing, puffing sound behind him.

He looked around, and there was Elizabeth, jogging down the road, huffing and puffing because jogging was still a major effort to her long-lax limbs, but she was determined and puffing down this road every morning at this time.

Now, here in the middle of the road, she saw…the love of her life. Her frog!

For a second, the frog didn't know whether she was going to run past him, maybe even kick dirt in his face, or whether she was going to stop and talk to him.

Elizabeth did neither.

She scooped up her frog—her long-loved neglected frog, and she hugged him and apologized to him and promised she'd make it up to him, and then she…kissed him! Just held him up in front of her lips, puckered up, and kissed him right on his mouth.

They say it was the shock that killed him. Perhaps the disappointment at not turning into a prince on the spot. But Elizabeth knew better. She saw the smile on his face when she put him down again, and she saw him slowly fading, fading from view right before her eyes, and she saw a wafting misty shape floating off into the distance. Elizabeth knew that her beloved frog had indeed ceased being a frog and, somewhere in the universe, was now a prince.

Thank you, she called out after the disappearing mist. Thank you for never giving up hope. Thank you for depending on my love for such a long long time. Thank you for reminding me that love, above all else, has the power to transform, to give health and joy to all those open to it. And thank you for knowing that the love of a good frog, too, is Love.

Elizabeth didn't mourn the passing of her frog—she rejoiced for him, for his becoming a prince, and she rejoiced for herself: having known the love of a good frog, she was now ready to meet and receive love of every kind—and that, my dears, is a lot of love!

GOLYGA: *And so we resume our work together and bring into existence an entire new episode of our endeavour. Into existence on the Earth plane, that is, because this episode, as well as every other one, exists in its entirety on several other planes.*
LILLY: *Several?*

GOLYGA: *Yes. We have already brought these episodes into being on our own plane—some time ago, according to Earth calculations—because we were waiting for somebody's readiness. Not necessarily yours, Lilly dear, but somebody who was ready, able, and willing to undertake the work and able to sustain it on an ongoing basis. We also had already brought the work into existence in another sphere, that of the imaging-and-relating, brought to you courtesy of various entities not in the realm of words and verbal messages. There are messages akin to ours in the Earth's upheavals, in the way the Earth's creatures behave and change and, yes, die out, and there are messages also in the development of larger and larger groups of humans who heed the call to take care of Mother Earth and her creatures and beware of living mindlessly without thought to the future. All these messages are encoded and sent in so many ways that we can only point to the above few and encourage you all to seek out their various modes as you go through your days.*

These, our verbalized messages in the guise of stories and episodes of a book, are but one of the avenues of learning, and they serve most efficiently for those more educated and verbally inclined. Others with a more visual way of apprehending might get the same "news" by way of television, although the danger there is that doomsday anxieties will overtake positive attitudes and action. Never mind—it will all come out in the wash, as they say, and we'll be happy to continue our work in whatever form is useful. This one, our joint venture into book-writing, is certainly going to reach more people than any one lecturer or soothsayer or naysayer would. And so, here is the next episode...

Once upon a time, humanity was in trouble. Yes, this isn't the first time humans had faced the possibility of extinction. At that other time, there were climatic conditions that were extreme and no technology to help people out, there were wars and the danger of whole groups killing each other, and there were attacks from the world of disease-spirits.

I can see/hear/feel a gasp in reaction to the notion of "disease-spirits," so I will explain: these are spirits that bring disease to people not as a matter of punishment, of malign intent, or of simple nastiness that gets spread from person to person. No, these spirits are charged with the task of strengthening the stock, so to speak, by culling the herd. By bringing disease to large numbers of people and letting succumb those who will, while the stronger, more resistant types strengthen the stock of the species. Not a new concept, but perhaps not welcome as an explanation for humans. Though it has been used for years as the way herds of caribou, for example, are culled by the wolf. That wolf, we say, is akin to a disease spirit. A different form, but the intent is the same.

At this time, in the human herd, there are new diseases and old ones resurfacing that cull the physically weaker members in order to leave the stronger, because in the times to come, the stronger will be put on their mettle to make it through.

LILLY: I thought spiritual attunement was enough to see us through the shift of the ages.
GOLYGA: You were wrong. Spiritual attunement is necessary, and so is physical survival on the planet. Otherwise, the "school for scandal" is over. We are introducing levity to take the doom and gloom out of this scenario. Remember, please, that survival on this planet is not the only possible survival. So those who are "culled" live on, often in joy and happiness far beyond any possible on Earth, and rather than seeing them as victim, try seeing them as those who "have it easy." The survivors, you see, are in for a rough ride on Earth, unless they can raise their vibrations. And here comes the spiritual work: our task with this book is to help accomplish that. Get it?
LILLY: Got it. Thanks for reminding me that getting "culled" is no punishment.
GOLYGA: All right then. Bring on the next exercise, Lilly dear.
LILLY: I don't know what the next exercise is!
GOLYGA: You've just completed it. Did you not, only yesterday, resume communication with your mother, though she is on this side of the veil. and did you not endeavour and succeed in clearing the lines between you of unfinished business, unexpressed emotions, unsaid words?
LILLY: Yes, I did.
GOLYGA: Well, that's the one we recommend to all those of our readers who can undertake this exercise.

There are many ways of undertaking it, of course. Whether in direct communication with the spirit of the departed—from the Earth plane—or whether through the aid of a medium, channeller, or spiritual therapist, or whether through engaging in dream work or rituals or shamanic journeys, or through meditation and offers made in goodwill. Whatever your avenue of choice, the aim of the exercise is to clear the lines with those who were in close relationships with you and are now passed on to another plane.

Do not assume greater wisdom from those departed humans than they are capable of—there are widely different degrees of understanding among those on our side, much as there are on yours, but do assume their willingness to clear unfinished business. And to protect yourself from those in the world of spirit who have not yet cleared negative intentions, simply evoke the Light of Love as a protective shield. We can recommend the following evocation: *Surround me, oh Light of Love, and protect me from Random Energies, from Beings of Low Vibrations, and from Spirits that bring suffering to no avail.*

This evocation, said before and after each attempt at the exercise, will protect you, increase the love in your energy field, and improve your life in many other ways.

So: contemplate, those of you who are not in the habit of working across the veil, what you can do to accomplish the goal of this work— the best method for you at your present stage. Then begin by saying the evocation, aloud if you can, and do the exercise for as long as your concentration holds. Since it might involve emotional outbursts in the form of tears, utterances, etc., you had better choose your time and location wisely, but neither is restricted to a therapist's room, and no harm will come to you if you repeat the evocation before and after each occasion.

Also, if you feel overwhelmed or have any strange sensations that are actively unpleasant and seem to come from outside yourself, do the evocation again right then and there and feel the sensations abate.

One more word of caution: don't start talking to all and sundry about the conversation you had with your dear departed. Too many people perceive such endeavours as a mark of insanity or, at least, screwiness. So unless you know like-minded seekers, be content with the growth and peace that will result from this exercise.

In future, perhaps we can give examples of the value of this work in the lives of humans on the Earth plane and we will certainly explain the value of this work in the realms of spirit. For now, we have rattled on long enough and so we say to you: Bon chance, fruitful journeys, and until soon, all the Beeswax you might want.

LILLY: Is it useful, other methods being unavailable or unfamiliar, to have dialogues with the departed in one's imagination?

Absolutely. And perhaps we have been too exclusive in our list of methods altogether because, of course, there are many more. Perhaps it would be useful, in fact, to make a complete list. On the other hand, that could take months—it is an almost infinite list, given the infinite variety of human experience, and so we will, instead, suggest you each seek out whatever is likely to work for you.

Be alert and aware, and opportunities will arise in your lives for just the work and exercises we mentioned, in whatever form. Okay?

LILLY: Thank you, Beeswax.
GOLYGA: Until soon, Lilly dear. And good work.

* * *

GOLYGA: Hello, my dear, and let's get right to it, shall we? We have an interesting session in store for you personally as well as for the book and its readers.

Once upon a time, there was a young shaman's apprentice who, though not young in years, was new to the world of spirit. At least as far as his conscious life was concerned. You see, he had spent most of his time tilling the soil of mundane life with success and satisfaction and had only recently come up against the mysteries in a way that pushed him into trying to answer questions he had never seriously entertained before.

The young/old man approached the great mysteries with a skeptical eye but nevertheless delved seriously into books and other sources of knowledge such as research would allow, and then he sat back and expected wisdom and answers to come raining down on him. However, neither did, and he felt more confused than ever and in no position to answer anything at all to himself.

All right then, he thought, I'll accept that these are mysteries, I won't try to fathom them with my rational mind, I'll just sit and believe that these things are not answerable, period.

However, no sooner had he said this to himself than a bird appeared on his left shoulder and laughed raucously into his ear.

Hey! said the young/old man. What are you and what are you up to?

Just having a bit of fun at your expense, said the bird. Just enjoying a cackle. You must admit it's a pretty funny sight, a young/old man like you giving up on knowing the mysteries because they can't be fathomed with the rational mind. Haven't you ever heard of knowing with your gut? Your spirit? Your heart?

Well, actually no, said the man. I have never heard of such knowing. Although "gut feelings" are acknowledged in some circles, generally female, the rest—what were they? heart knowledge and spirit knowledge?—well, I've just never heard of them.

In that case, we'll have to do something about you, said the bird, and he flew off the man's shoulder and onto the nearest fence post. From there he surveyed the man with a cocked head and beady eye and thought out loud: Never heard of such things as heart knowledge and spirit knowledge. My, my. Can you believe it, in this day and age. With all the opportunities available to people who seek knowledge. Well, better figure out what to do about this…

The bird looked up and down and around and spotted something he figured might be helpful. He hopped down off the fence post and onto the ground, and picked up a tiny pebble. This he brought to the man, dropping it right into his lap.

Lift it, said the bird. Touch it. Feel it. Weigh it in your hand. Lick it, if you like. Stroke it. Listen to it, too. And then tell me what you have learned.

The man did all the bird told him to do. A tiny pebble, he said. What more can be said about it? It's sort of roundish, whitish, fairly smooth, not very pretty, but it does have tiny spots of something in it, tiny greenish spots. Now, I wonder how they got in there? And I wonder if they have a taste?

The man licked the pebble. He couldn't taste anything, but since he'd lifted it already, he held it up to his ear, and he heard the pebble speak:

Yes, green specks. You've got that right. And the way I got those is a story all its own. Want to hear it?

The man was too intrigued to fathom the amazing fact that a tiny pebble had just spoken to him. Tell me, he said to the pebble. How did you get those green specks?

Well, it happened like this, said the pebble. I was peacefully lying on a beach, sunning myself, getting whiter and whiter, as pebbles will do, when suddenly a great white heron passed by overhead. He saw me

245

lying there, glistening and sweating with pleasure, and came swooping down, picked me up in his beak, and took me to the nest of his lady love.

A gift for you, he said to his lady love, and laid me at her feet. The lady love looked down, way down, at the little pebble at her feet, and because I wasn't in the sun, and certainly wasn't glistening with pleasure anymore, she disdained the gift and told the great white heron to get that thing out of here.

The great white heron became furious, picked me up in his beak, and flung me as far as he could. So there I was, sailing through the air from way on high, wondering where in the world I was going to land and rather enjoying the outing, I must say, when suddenly I was snatched up by a mosquito. Yes, you heard me right, a mosquito. A giant one, obviously, and freshly nourished by the blood of some poor human tourist on the beach.

The mosquito held me gently and lovingly and took me to the nearest rock. There it set me down and sat down beside me and sang me a song. Lovely, it was. About green grapes and blue rivers, and clouds all silvery and feathery and bright.

Swat!

Right in the middle of the singing, down came a huge hand and bashed the mosquito to death, right in front of my eyes. Blood spattered everywhere. I was covered with it and looked like a solid drop of blood beside the corpse of the squashed mosquito.

Oh look, a little red pebble, said the voice of a child, and the child's hand picked me up and carried me down the beach to his parents.

Throw it back, said the mother. You don't know where that pebble's been.

Oh, let him play with it, said the father. I used to play with stones and pebbles when I was a boy.

And look where it got you, said the mother, snatching me out of the boy's hand. But I'd had it by then of getting snatched up by everybody who just happened along, be it great white heron or mosquito or boy. I slipped out the side of the mother's hand and skipped away, rolling into the sand and hiding there.

The boy looked for me for a long time until his parents called him to come back to the hotel, and even then he vowed he'd look for me again the next day. Sure enough, first thing in the morning, there he was again, a little boy with pail and shovel, wearing a baseball cap with a large visor to protect him from the sun, and there was I, lying in the sand, hiding. Well, pretty soon the boy was coming closer and closer to where I hid, and I was trying to decide whether to let him find me and see what happened next or keep on hiding, when the boy stepped on me. Accidentally, of course, but he put his green-sandal-clad foot right on top of me, and that's how I came to have green specks on me.

How about that for a story, eh what?

The man who had been listening with great attention was disappointed.

All that, and in the end it was just green rubber off a beach sandal? he asked. That isn't really very interesting, I would say.

It's interesting to me, said the pebble. It was the beginning of a whole new life for me, a white pebble turned white-pebble-with-green-specks. You would be amazed how different I feel. How different the world looks, in fact, now that I am a green-specked white pebble.

The man couldn't see it. How different could it be? It was still just a little pebble, for heaven's sake. It didn't turn into an elephant or a rhino or a bird or anything.

Ha! said the pebble. That's how much you know. When I was just a white pebble, would you have picked me up and licked me and listened to me telling you a whole story?

Well, sure, said the man. Why not?

Well, when's the last time you licked a pebble and listened to it tell you a story?

Actually, I've never done that, said the man.

Aha! said the pebble. So how do you know my green specks aren't the real reason you picked me up and listened to me?

The man was getting impatient with this nonsense but he had no real answer for the pebble. He couldn't, in fact, believe he was arguing with a pebble.

What has come over me? he asked himself. I'm sitting here, talking to a stone! And how did all this begin, anyway? Oh, I remember: a bird was talking to me, telling me about other ways of knowing besides the rational-mind way, and next thing I knew, I'm arguing with a pebble. There must be some connection, but what is it?

The man stared down at the pebble in his hand. He looked up, to ask the bird some questions, but the bird was gone. And the next time he looked down at his hand, so was the pebble. Not a trace left, and maybe the whole thing had been a dream. Maybe he had fallen asleep here and dreamt the entire thing?

The man shook his head, trying to clear his thinking of the follies of talking birds and pebbles, and as he shook his head, something fell out of his ear and tumbled right into his hand. It was the pebble.

But…no, it wasn't. This was a different pebble. A white one, without one speck of green.

The man looked at the pebble. Ordinary-looking, quite small, nothing interesting about it at all. Not even one speck of green or anything else. So the man flung the pebble away, got up, brushed off his trousers, and lo!—the bird was on his left shoulder, laughing to beat the band.

Now what are you laughing about? said the man, no longer even amazed to find himself speaking to a bird. What's so funny this time?

You, of course, gasped the bird. Can you imagine anything funnier than a man who will speak to a pebble with green specks but won't either speak or listen to a pebble without green specks, and he still maintains he is a rational being who knows about things by way of reason and that other ways of knowing are not part of his life? Did your rational mind tell you that only white pebbles with green specks can talk? Did your rational mind tell you to listen to me, a bird? Who and what exactly is listening to me right now?

The man had to admit there was sense to this question. Logic told him that birds don't speak English. But here he was listening and replying to this bird, and no doubt about it.

All right, said the man. I'll concede that there are other ways of knowing. What exactly am I doing right now, hearing and understanding a bird talking to me?

Oh, lovely, said the bird, starting to laugh again. Now he wants to understand other ways of knowing with his rational mind. Go ahead, read more books, do more research, see where that gets you. And when you're all done reading and figuring and making sense out of nothing, then come back here, pick up a pebble, and lick it. Okay?

The man watched as the bird flapped his wings and took off—flying up and up until he was a speck, a little green speck in the blue sky. And then he was gone.

The man sat and pondered for a while, letting his mind drift aimlessly because it seemed to have been cast off its mooring. Then he got up, started walking, and every so often he picked up a pebble, held it up to his eye, licked it, then stuck it in his ear. And every so often, he smiled a great big smile.

LILLY: Thank you, Beeswax. Lesson well taken. I seem to be looking for corroboration and validation in books, not trusting experiential knowledge or giving it its appropriate weight.
GOLYGA: You've got it, my dear. Now go lick pebbles!

* * *

GOLYGA: Hello, my dear, your eagerness notwithstanding, we will have a shorter session today than last time. Not because your energy is flagging, but because the work calls for a concentrated segment that needs rather more space for digesting and internalizing and, for some readers, engagement in exercises. So we'll do a pithy, condensed segment today and later we'll pick the episode that best serves to illustrate the information in it.

"Once upon a time" is not our mode of storytelling today; rather, it is a form of exhortations.

Do not believe for a moment that you are unaffected by the events that denote the upheavals of Mother Nature, of the planet Earth, of species and living beings of every kind. Humans are not exempt from the effects of these events, and no amount of ignoring them or berating them or even bringing environmental action to bear on them will protect humans from participation in those events. You may not be living in an area prone to earthquakes or floods or tornadoes, and yet your physical body will feel the effects of those "natural disasters," as they are called. Every such event has energetic consequences that humans as well as all other beings on Earth feel at some level—whether conscious or not. There is no way of escaping these effects, just as there is no way of escaping the effects on Earth and all its inhabitants of the moon, the planets, the stars.

Not that most people are even aware of the effects of the moon on their energy field. In fact, most are blithely unaware of the constant flux and symbiotic condition in which they live. The mind, designed to be a categorizing tool, simply does not encompass the experience of the subtler energies and influences, and only those who are able to open to them and apprehend them with tools other than the mind become cognizant of their true condition on Earth.

So, we repeat: every human is influenced and affected by the events occurring on the planet, and many of the after-effects of these events are not seen as connected but nevertheless influence every person alive.

Now: what can we do about it and why are you even telling us that?

To take the second part of the question first: we are telling you that because there is something you can do about it that would be beneficial to you, and we recommend you do the exercises we are going to outline for you to prevent deleterious effects resulting from the upheavals and chaotic energies engulfing you at an increasing rate.

Here is what you can do: every time you hear about one of nature's "unusual" events, or see mention of one, or hear talk of one, or think about one as a result of anything at all, use this as an opportunity to help yourself avoid the worst of the fallout from these events. Pause for a moment in whatever you are doing—a split second is all it takes—and be conscious of the energy flow in your body. Then take a deep breath or two and give yourself a protective shield by surrounding yourself with light.

Whether you visualize light or verbally call on light or feel the sensation of warmth all around your body—take that moment to become conscious of yourself as body, then surround that body with light.

That's the exercise, and if you practise it diligently, you will feel an increased strength in yourselves. Those of you especially sensitive to energies and their influences, such as you, Lilly dear, will benefit the most and soonest. Others may find it less obviously evident and might have to take it on faith that the exercise is giving them protection from unwanted effects of the Earth's upheavals.

They might want to look at the matter thus: Mother Earth is struggling with the ill effects of many abuses while undergoing a major change in her life in the natural process of things. Combine those two and there are bound to be chaotic energies and great upheavals. Humans are in no way separate from Mother Earth. They are *of* her, completely entwined and infused with her energies.

There is no escaping that fact while in body, so learn to engage consciously in the process of energy exchange in order to make it the most beneficial exchange you can for yourselves and—this is bound to be news to many—for Mother Earth as well. For as you call on light to surround your own little body, you call on light to surround that tiny part of Mother Earth energy that is you. And if enough of you are engaged in calling light to surround you, that much more light energy— which is love—will be available for Mother Earth and her self-healing.

Get it? All those of you who engage in this exercise are workers in the field of light, of "environmental protection," of self-protection, of bringing health to Mother Earth.

To repeat: whenever anything reminds you of the upheavals undergone by Mother Earth, pause, become aware of the energies in your body, and surround yourself with light.

GOLYGA: And that's it for today, Lilly dear. You are indeed a dear, setting your intention so clearly for work and making your own energies available for it. Remember to rest, and then lick the pebbles and enjoy!
LILLY: Thank you, Beeswax.

* * *

GOLYGA: All right then.

Once upon a time, there were the two delightful creatures we have already met, namely snake scientist and the Blue Blob.

Now, snake scientist had always been interested in—nay, obsessed with—the nature of the Blue Blob and had tried time and again to capture it so he might dissect it and find out its true nature. But every time the Blue Blob came near snake scientist, it would start quivering and shaking with silent laughter—so much so that it couldn't remain on the ground for long and had to float off to give itself room to properly vent its vast amusement.

What was so funny about snake scientist's wish to discover Blue Blob's true nature?

Why, nothing. Nothing at all. It's the method by which snake scientist hoped to make his discoveries that was so ridiculous, according to Blue Blob.

The "true nature" of anything at all, Blue Blob knew well, is not discovered by dissecting but by inclusion. Include context, all relevant information about all related phenomena, and pretty soon you are including everything in the universe and asking the true nature of the universe—is that not so? The air breathed, the waters and soil, the creatures all around, the emotional relations to everything and anything, the perceptions that influence... On and on, until truly everything in and of the universe must be included.

So then the question becomes "What is the true nature of the universe?" and that is something snake scientist also asks himself almost daily. You see, snake scientist is also a bit of a philosopher. A bit of a trickster, too—he was overly fond, some believe, of turning around and poisoning the very things he was studying by his paranoid conviction that something or other was out to get him—a cloud, seeds blowing in the air, sound riding the waves—anything at all could set him off and thinking: That's just what I needed. No sooner do I come close to discovering the nature of anything and somebody or something is running interference, trying to keep me ignorant. Never realizing, poor snake scientist, that he really had to include the so-called interference as part of the phenomenon.

So now, let's just have a look at snake scientist and Blue Blob in action during one of their encounters.

Snake scientist was slithering along the ground, having a philosophical thought about first this and then that, and suddenly he was surrounded by a great clap of thunder.

Snake scientist stopped cold.

How was he to incorporate that into his understanding of

anything? How was he to include the energy, the sound, the results, the various reactions everywhere to this clap of thunder without going mad with all the details to be coordinated and enumerated and cross-referenced? A computer would help, of course, but even then, snake scientist was sure, the end result could never include everything. Because, of course, even as he would be tabulating and cross-referencing, etc., etc., everything would be changing at the very same time! Flux being one aspect of everything alive and everything being alive.

No, more than ever snake scientist was convinced that it was Blue Blob he had to study if he wanted to learn about the true nature of anything.

So off he went, looking for Blue Blob. For eons and millennia and even longer, snake scientist searched the universe far and wide and found no Blue Blob. Not even anything resembling Blue Blob. Because Blue Blob, as it happened, had changed colour and shape and was, for a while, visible only as a high-hatted pussycat.

GOLYGA: Thank you, Lilly for not refusing that trite image. It is the very familiarity of "the cat in the hat" we want to evoke and subvert.

As a high-hatted pussycat, the former Blue Blob was able to go and come anywhere on Earth where children enjoyed books and could bring much joy and laughter to thousands. And, if snake scientist only knew, that was the very essence of Blue Blob: joy and laughter. And that being so, before anyone knew it, children everywhere, including the baby, who Golyga and Lillykins had been trying to educate, knew the essence and true nature of Blue Blob. And, without lecturing or studying or otherwise getting heavy about it, the children were spreading this joy and laughter and contributing more than anyone on Earth to the creation of the Joyous Kingdom.

Now, obviously snake scientist had no idea that every time he ran into a laughing child, a singing child, a skipping child, he had the best opportunity in the world to study the nature of Blue Blob. Far from it. He thought such children a nuisance, troublesome and time-consuming, and tried his best to avoid the pesky creatures.

And so, gradually, snake scientist became more and more glum and more and more frustrated and, as he realized, no closer at all to knowing the true nature of Blue Blob.

Well, one day, feeling thoroughly fed up, snake scientist decided to give it all up. Give up study, give up philosophy—just give it all up. He curled up his body on a rock and lay there in the sunshine, convinced his life had been a great failure and he would never amount to anything. (Odd phrase that, isn't it?) And as he lay in the sun, despondent and then asleep and dreaming, it so happened that Blue Blob came back into Blue Blob form and saw snake scientist lying there.

Blue Blob hovered above the sleeper, who looked defeated and almost decrepit, and he pitied snake scientist and wished he could just get out of his old skin and start life afresh, with new perceptions and perspectives and attitudes.

Well, no sooner wished for than it happened. Snake began to shed his skin; he rubbed and rubbed and slithered and slid, until he had left behind an empty shell and was freshly glistening in a new skin.

Oh, my goodness, said snake. Look at me. Aren't I wonderful! I think I'll have to study myself for a while, I'm such a wonderful, amazing creature. Now where shall I begin? Which end? Or maybe the middle? Or should I try to find out what I'm made of in my own Personal Being? Oh, dear. Much to do, much to study. Better get started or I'll never learn enough.

Blue Blob listened to all this, gave a great sigh, and took off for the wild blue yonder.

Snake scientist saw Blue Blob for the first time in eons, saw he had missed the opportunity to get to know his nature, and suddenly snake sat back on his hindquarters and sighed, too.

And shook his head from side to side. (Scaring some berry pickers half to death because they thought snake was threatening them.)

No, no, no, thought snake. I'm going about this all wrong. I just know I am. I seem to have blown a chance at change and I want it back, so I am going to lie here, curled in the sun, until something happens to show me what I am to do next.

GOLYGA: And that is where we are going to leave snake scientist for today. Halfway between Sturm und Drang and the truly receptive state that allows all knowledge to enter.

* * *

We are happy to see you eager to continue and we feel certain our sessions will now continue on a regular basis. Today we hope to convey to you the first part of our message with full inscription and attention to the purpose to which it will be put by various readers. There is no point in pretending that everyone will receive this message in like frame of mind or that each reader will do the work or be inspired to share the information. However, as we said before: if you read it, you'll change. And if you read it and do even some of the work, the trajectory of ideas will carry you further than expected. It's not a matter of the time involved; the results of any work are measured not in quantitative units but in a leapfrogging of energies heading into the future on a wild and wonderful journey. All right, then…

This first section will deal with expectations humans have of the coming events and era. None of which are quite correct in their assumptions because they do not include yours truly or other entities working on behalf of the planet Earth and its inhabitants.

Why are we doing this? Altruistic motives being suspect, we won't try to convince you that we do it out of sheer holiness. We'll tell you the part you are more likely to give credence to, namely our interest in the experiment, which is the planet Earth. It's a rather large order to explain this experiment, but we shall try:

In order to make manifest the extensions of all thought, dense energy called "material" was postulated. This energy has qualities that Beings of Light, for example, do not exhibit. Whether we want to is another thing, but the fact is that people—humans—on Earth are able to experience matter and its various qualities in a way we cannot. Thus we can observe and learn about matter, about denser energies, and become more adept at the possibilities of that state.

LILLY: Are you trying to say that billions of years of manifesting matter are a mere experiment, and it's taking you this long to learn what you want to learn?

255

GOLYGA: Not quite.

There have been changes and shifts all along, and the resultant changes in the experiments and their outcomes. And while all this studying is going on, you understand, people are evolving and changing, as is the planet Earth, and all the time a transmutation of matter to light is ongoing, and all those tired of being subjects of the experiments need only grow into lighter energy and can leave the state of being in body forever.

So as you see, humans come into being on the planet to help with the experiments and they sign on, so to speak, to be the guinea pigs. They also assist enormously throughout all the stages of their evolution to show the various possibilities of matter and manifestation in dense energies.

Now, as the shift of the ages comes near, there will be a drastic change—temporary but long in human terms—which will necessitate rapid changes in the density of energy manifested on Earth. All those able to transmute enough of their energy, enough density, to a lighter energy will have smoother sailing than those who cling to the densest of matter in their beingness. This has been said by others, including Gregg Braden, as you know, and he has also demonstrated, to the satisfaction of some, how this is to be achieved. We aim to give a more detailed and specific course of action to bring about this transmutation in all those who care to engage in the work.

Lest you begin to worry that this work will be arduous and onerous, let us assure you, every one of you, that it will be nothing of the sort. It will be a kind of humming accompaniment to your days and hours of living. A very cheerful note because every little advance will bring you increased joy, increased awareness of yourself as a Being of Light, and increased abilities to shape your universe.

To speak for a moment of this "shaping your universe": manifesting on the planet Earth takes the course of Thought—Intention—Action—Surrender. An example: say you want a new car. (Mundane, we know, dear Lilly, but it happens.) Say you even *need* a new car. Such is the thought: I need a new car.

Then comes the intention to find one, or to earn the money to buy one, or to choose one, or any of the steps involved between the thought and doing something about it. Action means doing something about it, even if it's only looking at cars with a more discerning eye. And whatever other little step can be taken to make the thought and the intention have a concrete result.

Then, and this is the hard one for most humans, comes Surrender. Give the intention over to the universal energy and let it provide. Stay alert to every little sign from the universe that it is working on your behalf—such as reports on cars in consumer shows, something a friend heard, etc., etc. See every little car-related thing as a sign from the universe and thank it for working on your behalf. And surrender onto it the machinations necessary to manifest the car. Or any other—less mundane—desired outcome.

As you can see, your world will change drastically if you live with this attitude toward what you want. Meantime, you are engaged in living life to the fullest, perhaps doing some of the work out of this book, bringing joy and delight to all beings on your path, and generally having a whale of a time.

What about working, earning money, you say? Go ahead. It's part of life in body, isn't it? We are not suggesting you stop earning a living, because we know you can't stop eating and continue in body. We are saying, don't sweat it for anything beyond the necessities—simply think it, intend it, take a step or so toward it, surrender the "how" of it.

All this is not new either, though some of you may come to it for the first time.

Let us do one more little thing today: a preview of the work you might be asked to do: go about your day today appreciating all there is in it that can be appreciated. And if you can, list those things—whether right away or later, whether on paper or on your computer or in any other way, making the list somehow concrete or visual. And when we say all there is "that can be appreciated," we include every part of you that is working all right, from body parts to mental or emotional ones, every little thing in your day that comes from others, whatever brings you an iota of joy or comfort or delight.

Every time you find yourself having forgotten to go on with the appreciations, don't try to recapture the time you skipped; simply begin from the moment of NOW and go on from there. And then, at the end of that day, note what kind of day you had. That's all.

We count on your preferring a wonderful day to a miserable one as motivation to continue appreciations on a regular basis—though we do concede that you will need reminders of this "work" for a while to come. We'll give those reminders, too. And so you need not fret or grow tense, because gradually, the habit of appreciating will replace the habit of complaining, or of worry, or of fearful anticipation, and will become a self-perpetuating growing heap of joy in which you'll find yourself immersed for much of your time.

GOLYGA: Sound good? Try it—you'll be amazed at the swiftness of results coming in. And enjoy!

* * *

GOLYGA: We are pleased to be welcome and working. A short session again because the emotional climate on the anniversary of your mother's death last year might be difficult to penetrate for long. However, "short session" does not mean "less valuable." Short session means: a work-related segment. Something for the reader to do, get their teeth into, chew over for a while, allow to become part of their life. So:

Once upon a time there was a very old woman who loved to knit. As she grew older yet and more frail, she was unable to knit any longer—her eyesight was failing, her hands arthritic, even the strength to lift needles and wool was fading. So now the old woman had to decide: what to do instead with all the hours of rhythmic soothing activity she had enjoyed in the past. There was little she could do in the physical realm to fill those hours in a satisfactory way. There was, in fact, nothing she could think of to do instead.

One day, the old woman was sitting in front of her door, enjoying the morning sunshine but also ruminating on how to fill the hours of the day, when she heard a bird. The bird was singing lustily and loudly, sitting on a branch not far from the old woman's door.

Wish I was a bird, said the old woman to herself. Wish I could sit and sing all day long.

And then she realized something: there was no reason on Earth why she couldn't do just that! Sing! Loudly and lustily, or quietly under her breath, or even silently, in her head.

Singing had been one of her joys in early years—as a child and young woman, she always sang when going about her activities, and though later she was no longer actually singing out loud, there were many times when she went about her duties with a song in her head.

Sing! she told herself. Sing, old woman! And since there is none to hear you, sing aloud and with gusto, when you can.

And that's exactly what she did, the old woman who was getting too old to do much. She sang. Often, she sang silently in her head because she was too tired to sing out loud, but since it was singing out loud that had tired her, she was perfectly happy and satisfied with singing silently the rest of the time.

The hours of the day flew by and the old woman was busy—singing—and wasn't bored or lonely for a moment. When she ran out of songs she knew, she began making up new ones, to herself. She sang about her life, about the life of all the people she had known in her long years, and about everyone else who ran across her ken, such as the bird perched in the tree singing on the day she rediscovered her own singing.

In fact, the old woman began and ended her days with a song of appreciation for the bird whose gift of singing had descended on her just when she needed it. And pretty soon, she was singing motley songs of appreciation for all the gifts she had received during her lifetime, and the more she sang out her appreciations, the more of them she discovered in herself. Until every breath she drew became an appreciation of air, of her own lungs' ability to breathe, of life itself.

Now, one day, as the old woman was sitting in her doorway, singing at the top of her voice, a lark came by. Larks being songbirds much praised and lauded for their singing, they have developed a rather solid little ego, and this lark in particular had been decorated by some human with a small band around his neck, to mark him, as he thought, a Songbird Supreme. He felt that, in birdland, he was akin to a Nobel Prize winner for song and he didn't take it kindly when any old old woman sat around singing at the top of her voice.

Hey! said the lark to the old woman. Who the hell do you think you are, singing away as if you're made for it? Shouldn't you be sitting and knitting or something? Thinking about all the things you did wrong in your life, regretting most of what you did or didn't do? Shouldn't you be putting the fear of god into little people and passing on lots of old sayings, both superstitions and pearls of wisdom, so long as they're old? What do you think you're doing, opening your mouth and your throat and singing away for all the world like an old bird?

The old woman had listened to everything the lark sang, but since she didn't speak lark language, all she heard was singing. And, being lark singing, it was of course beautiful, so the old woman was delighted and appreciative and sang in her best and loudest voice all the appreciation she felt for her little singer companion.

The lark, thoroughly disgusted, flew away, and the old woman never knew that he had been—rather than a beautiful messenger from the world of song—an ego-infested, collar-wearing loudmouth, not much liked in his own world because he was always telling others, from high above, what they should or should not do.

Thank you, called the old woman after the lark. Thank you for your beautiful song. Here, let me sing my thank-you again. And the old woman once again opened her mouth and her throat and sang and sang and sang.

Somebody told us that on her deathbed, many years later, they saw one of her fingers moving, moving, rhythmically tapping tiny little taps, and they thought: Well, we know what she is doing inside herself. She's singing!

So at the old woman's funeral, everyone there—and there were many—agreed that the proper way to say goodbye to the old woman was to sing her on her way, and a marvellous chorus was heard across the land, as all those voices rose in song, and pretty soon the birds and everyone else who heard the singing joined in and celebrated life with fully opened mouth and throat. Singing, singing, singing appreciations and woes, and all their best and worst feelings and doings and living, filling the air and the heavens with their song of life.

Meantime, the old woman, on the other side of the veil, had run into the lark, and here they both spoke the same language.

Thanks, said the old woman, for the gift of your beautiful singing.

You're welcome, said the lark, having forgotten that his mean-minded ego had once told the old woman not to sing. Let's sing together, shall we?

And they did, the lark and the old woman, singing their joy and their appreciation together as they flew about and around, needing neither rest nor respite.

And once in a while, the old woman, looking down at the goings-on on Earth, would indulge in repeating an old saying: We have come to hear the angels sing but we are not going to be persuaded that our own song is negligible.

GOLYGA: You say this is not an old saying you ever heard? And, anyway, it's too long? Okay, we'll try again: Angel or not, sing like one! That's it for today and, until soon, have a happy song.

✳ ✳ ✳

GOLYGA: Yes, we are here and glad to be here; we care for you, we are ready to work. Are you?
LILLY: Yes, I am.
GOLYA: Then take down as follows, without monitoring, please: When we come in to talk to you, Lilly dear, we are always in awe of your willingness to put aside your own tasks, personality, and other endeavours of the psyche to assist us in our task of writing this book. We are also glad you are willing to do so because as we work together and you do the exercises and follow the suggestions and precepts we introduce, you grow and grow into a shining light of mammoth proportions. At times, we know, this doesn't feel like the right description of your state, but trust us, you are indeed a shining light.

Now on with the book...

As Golyga often said to his mate Lillykins: Omigosh, look what's gone and happened now!

It's not something we mentioned before because it doesn't sound as erudite and lofty as Golyga likes to hear himself portrayed, but the fact is, he said it often.

And every time he did, Lillykins answered something like: What in the world are you talking about now? What have you seen, discovered, unearthed to make you sit there and say something as profound as that?

Lillykins, you see, was fond of the satiric and the deft verbal putdown. But then, as soon as she heard what Golyga was so awe-inspired by, she'd have to concede that yes, indeed, it was yet another instance of ohmigosh.

For example: one fine day, Golyga and Lillykins were wandering around in the bush. On this planet where they wandered on that day, the bush was green emeralds growing on red swatches of cloth, bound together with silver strands of pearls and held aloft by feathery clouds.

So as they wandered, they were high above ground level and could see far and wide.

Golyga thought he had spotted a spotted cow and was ohmigoshing away, and Lillykins had to agree with him: an awesome sight among the bush was this spotted cow. And then both of them came closer and saw it was really a dragon.

Not the ash-breathing dragon but the regular kind: multicoloured and fierce-looking and not very forthcoming in the way of small talk or chatting.

Get out of my way, said the dragon, who huffed a few flames and puffed some smoke. Get out of my way or I'll barbecue you on the spot.

Hm, said Golyga. I wonder what it would feel like to get barbecued. Want to try it, Lillykins?

Lillykins thought about it and said: Well, if I could be sure a good sauce was available for when we're done, I wouldn't mind trying it, but since we can be sure of no such thing, let's first get some sauce and then try it.

The dragon listened to this exchange and by now his great maw was hanging open, little flames dribbling to the ground. The dragon had never heard anyone be quite so casual and nonchalant about the prospect of getting barbecued. It made him curious, and a curious dragon is not a dragon to be trifled with.

Here, he said. You two. What are you on about then? (The dragon was from the South of London in the area called the Milky Way and had never lost his peculiar inflections, though he had spent millennia tooting up and down the Milky Way, scaring and barbecuing anything in his path.)

Golyga and Lillykins found these very same inflections rather charming, especially in a fire-breathing dragon, so they decided to let him off the hook of his own habits and tape loops.

Here's the drill, said Golyga. You let Lillykins ride on your back twice up and down the Milky Way, and I'll let you have a delicious secret. How does that sound?

The dragon thought about this proposition. A delicious secret sounded exciting, and the dragon, if he were to be honest, was getting really bored with his eternal trekking and scaring and barbecuing.

All right then, he said. Hop on, you.

Lillykins hopped on, and off the two of them went, galloping up and down the Milky Way, with Lillykins yelling loudly into the ether, enjoying every moment.

As soon as they returned to where Golyga sat waiting, chewing on a piece of barbecued spare rib, the dragon wanted to hear the delicious secret.

Take this, said Golyga, and handed him the leftover part of the spare rib. Smell it, taste it, enjoy it.

The dragon did all that and then asked again: So, what was this delicious secret you were promising me?

You just ate it, said Golyga. You ate it and enjoyed it and so you've already received the delicious secret, haven't you?

The dragon was about to holler and breathe fierce fire and devastation but when he stopped to take a deep breath he had to admit that Golyga was right. What he had was a secret—unknown to him, whatever that taste was he had ingested so thoughtlessly. It had been delicious, all right, but what was it? What *was* it?

The dragon started begging Golyga to tell him what it was he had eaten, but Golyga just kept shaking his head, saying: It was your delicious secret. If I tell you what it was other than that, it is no longer a secret, and I'll have broken my promise, don't you see?

The dragon looked so disconsolate that Lillykins wanted to take pity on him and tell him what it was he had eaten, but Golyga kept shaking his head.

Think about it, Lillykins, he said, whispering to her alone. If we tell him, he'll go back to his own old ways in a flash, same old habits, same old boring barbecuing everything in his path. If we don't tell him, he'll stay awake and alert to every experience that comes his way, always searching for the answer to the secret. He'll be alive in every fibre of his being instead of slumbering through life and he'll learn a great deal along the way.

Lillykins had to agree. Indeed, she said, you are right, Golyga. And I can see quite clearly why and how you brought this about. But what made you say "ohmigosh" in the first place this time around?

Golyga laughed.

Oh my, he said. You have hung on to that question all this time and have not yet figured it out? I guess that will be *my* delicious secret then, for you to find out. Watch me, study me, pay full attention to me and you will come across marvellous surprises and all manner of delicious secrets, and I, why I will bask in your attention.

Lillykins was annoyed but what could she do? Nothing for it but to pay attention to everything Golyga said, did, and experienced. And as she did so, lo and behold, her attention sharpened her wits and she noted that everything in her path looked brighter and breathed more fully and seemed much much more interesting than ever before.

Lillykins told Golyga what had happened with her ever since she began paying close attention to every little thing.

This time Golyga didn't say a word. He gave her a long warm hug and, before she could ask about the reasons for that hug, he swept her off her feet, popped her onto his shoulders, and carried her off to an entirely new place to engage her attention. (Golyga, you see, had by now begun to feel rather uncomfortable under all that close scrutiny and needed some time out.)

Here you go, Golyga said to Lillykins. Practise paying attention here for a while. To anything and everything. I'll be back anon.

Off went Golyga, and before long, he returned, and here is what he found: Lillykins walking about, saying over and over again: Omigosh, will you look at that, will you just have a gander at this, and smell that, over there, and omigosh, will you just believe the marvel of this and the wonder of that!

On and on went Lillykins, and Golyga watched and listened and grinned from ear to ear, and when he felt he wanted some of that omigosh of Lillykins' to pour over him again, why, he just lay down in her path, right under her nose, and Lillykins looked at every bit of him, saying, Omigosh, look at this little finger and how it works and at that hair in his ear and how it wafts when I blow on it and— Well, you get the idea.

Omigosh was the word of the hour and day and year and lifetime, and a marvellous wonderful time was had by all.

LILLY: Is that it for today?

GOLYGA: Yes, it is. Good on you, Lilly dear, for your skill, your effort, your enjoyment of this session after so long a hiatus.

LILLY: I'm happy to be working together again.

GOLYGA: We know that, and we feel the same way. Of course, we're also happy we are soon coming to the end of this particular book and can look forward to starting new work with you.

LILLY: Really? Another book?

GOLYGA: Yes, another book. Though we intend to wait until this one is off your desk, so to speak, and taking flight. Which will come sooner than you think.

LILLY: I'm glad to hear we won't have to say goodbye.

GOLYGA: No need to worry about that. We'll be together for a long long time. Now, remember to rest, do the chakrah breathing, the thought-form work with breathing, and then enjoy, enjoy, enjoy the rest of the day and life.

* * *

GOLYGA: Yes, we are here and ready to resume our work together. We are pleased to see you, Lilly dear, paying close attention to energy and not falling into your earlier habit of pushing the river. Today is therefore an auspicious day for the resumption of our work, because your energy will sustain a goodly instalment. Here we go...

Once upon a time, there were three trees, all of them of a very lofty stature and great presence. A tiny frog, sitting under one of the trees, thought to himself that he would really like to do something grand and lofty in his life and so he decided to climb each of the trees in turn and become the most famous frog in the world.

Up he went, climbing the first of the trees, up and up and up, until the altitude made him dizzy and he had to pause and rest.

This, he said to himself, isn't merely a matter of will and endurance, but also a matter of physical ability, of stamina, and of the makeup of my rather fragile body. It seems to be responding to the air and altitude as though I have entered a different world than the one I usually live in.

Ha! said the tree on which the frog sat. You noticed, did you? Not only the air but the very atmosphere you breathe in this lofty environment is different, and so your fragile body ought to take notice and make adjustments all along the way. Stop simply climbing and pushing yourself to get higher and higher, take note and accommodate yourself to the changed condition or you will pay a great price for your endeavour.

The frog sat and thought. Should he perhaps abandon this project entirely? Was he made for climbing huge lofty trees? Ought he perhaps to stick to swampy places and be content?

The tree heard the frog's thoughts.

You can do that, it said. You can stay put and enjoy life. Until, that is, the swamp changes. Yes, yes, it's true, even swamps do change, and right now, everything is changing rapidly, so why not the swamp as well? Face it, frog, the best way to engage life at this time is to flow with changes, to be cognizant of them, to adjust to whatever they bring in the way of the new. For example. Difficulty in breathing? Begin exercising your breath. With full awareness, take in air and push it out, and soon, you'll see, breathing will again be possible in an automatic way. A different way, mind you, but unimpeded by the assault of new conditions.

The frog tried it. Sitting high above the ground, in the fork of a branch, he breathed in and breathed out, and after a while, lo!—his breathing became easy again, even at this altitude, and he felt ready to continue his climb.

Wait a minute, said the tree. Your body may be ready to continue upward, but what about the rest of you?

Whatever do you mean? asked the frog, never having been a particularly tuned-in frog when it came to emotions or spiritual awareness. What else, he asked, am I supposed to be doing before I can climb higher?

Well, said the tree. Look at yourself. You're a tiny green thing, usually close to the ground and clinging except for little hops, and here you are, leaving your security, your usual milieu, your every familiar thing, setting out on an adventure so huge you can't even see the end of it, and yet you have given no thought to preparing for this change.

How do I prepare? said the frog. I might scare myself right off if I think about it. So what to do?

By now the frog realized that the tree had answers for him, and he listened with great attention, albeit with some skepticism because frogs do not shed their natural suspiciousness just like that.

The tree told him to sit down again and hold his breath.

The frog was puzzled. Didn't you just tell me to breathe deeply and consciously, in and out, to adjust to this altitude and change of environment? Now I'm supposed to stop breathing altogether?

Not altogether, said the tree. You couldn't do that if you tried. No, I want you to hold your breath for a count of three, then let it out with a great big whoosh. Lilly dear calls this dolphin breath, and she can vouch for its efficacy in ridding herself of useless old emotions. So go ahead, little frog, and try it.

The frog took a deep breath—well, as deep as possible with his tiny lungs—and held it. Then he whooshed out the breath so fast and so hard, he almost fell off the tree. Oh gee, he yelled. I could have broken my neck, I could have fallen to the ground and broken every bone in my body, I could have got speared on a branch and been stuck there like a pig for roasting, I could have—

There now, said the tree. That's out of the way. The fears of falling were bound to come up sooner or later during your climb, so you can be clear of those right off. And any other fears that come up can be cleared in the very same way.

Now, as for your spiritual development during this climb, you had better pay close attention because all the breathing or holding of breath will be useless unless you develop your spiritual muscles immediately.

How in the world do I do that? asked the frightened frog. You see, he had no spiritual muscles at all, the poor little thing. He'd never even heard of them. He'd just come across these three tall trees one fine day and decided it would be grand to climb them and become an important frog. Now here was all this work to be done: making his body adjust, preparing himself emotionally, and now—what was that again? Spiritual muscles?

The tree nodded, making the frog quite nervous with all the motion involved, so the frog started holding his breath and whooshing it out again. The tree laughed and shook, and the frog clung and whooshed his breath, and pretty soon that little frog was totally exhausted. Just lying flat on the branch, hoping for somebody to come along to help him out of this horrible mess he'd gotten himself into.

Well, there you have it, said the tree to the frog. The beginnings of spiritual growth.

The frog looked around. What growth? Where? Certainly nothing on his body.

Don't make me laugh again, said the tree, or you'll be whooshing all night. No, the first part of spiritual growth is to go deep into the question of "How alone am I?" Am I connected to anything at all outside myself? Is there a source of energy that is intelligent and connected to me or do I stand alone on my own two or four feet, able to count on nothing and nobody except my own know-how?

Well, I don't know, said the frog. Never thought about it much. I'm part of a frog family, of course, and we do help each other out here and there, but then we kind of lose track of each other and that's that. Everybody on his own. Except I hear them at night, of course. Knew they were around. That sort of connected—is that what you meant?

The tree giggled. Now, I don't know whether you've ever heard a tall and lofty tree giggle.

The frog certainly never had—because he'd never expected to hear it—and so hearing this tree giggle, he almost fell off again in surprise.

Hang on, giggled the tree. You have an even bigger surprise coming, so hang on tight. And watch the sky, please.

The frog looked up at the sky. Suddenly, he saw a host of little winged frogs floating across it, perched on white clouds, playing harps.

The tree watched the frog's mouth open wide in amazement and giggled again. Why not frog angels? he said. Or frog clouds, for that matter.

The little frog, watching the sky, saw the clouds take on the shape of frogs and was even more amazed.

Are you doing all that? he asked the tree. Are you some kind of magic-maker tree?

No, said the tree. Nothing magic about it. It's knowing how to direct one's energy and open one's beliefs to the wonders of what is possible, and, finally, to be able to enter fully into the Great Mystery without reservations by the skeptical mind.

And is that what you call "spiritual development"? asked the frog. If that's the case, I want some of that.

It's some of the fallout of spiritual growth, said the tree. And if you "want some of that," you had better start developing some of those muscles.

I'll do it, I'll do it, said the frog, who started flexing his puny forearms. I'll work out all day long, if I have to.

The tree shook and shook with laughter at the sight of that little frog and his high ambitions, but it was kindly laughter and soon he had more to tell the frog.

Stop twitching your arms, he said. It'll get you nowhere spiritual fast. Practise this instead: look at everything you see, everywhere and anytime, with eyes of wonder. Be filled with a sense of awe at every little thing and soon you'll be able to dwell in the wondrousness of life. We'll discuss the next step when you get that far.

Right, said the frog. Let me see now. Where shall I start? Okay, here it is. I'll start with the branch I'm sitting on. Hey! Look at that! I never knew that bark was alive. And has all those little grooves full of other living things in it. And has a smell, and a sound, and a pulse, and everything. And hey! Look at this—a tiny little mite is doing push-ups underneath that leaf, and its mother is brushing her mite hair! Goodness, at this rate I'll never get to see and wonder at all there is. Let me peer into the sky again and see the big stuff.

The frog looked up and there in the sky were three seagulls, circling around and around, swooping and climbing as though they had an invisible connection to each other, or maybe were dancing a dance they'd rehearsed for years. The frog became fascinated and filled with wonder and awe. And the more he watched and wondered, the more came into his ken until, after a while, he entirely forgot why he was sitting in the fork of that tree and what the purpose of his climb was. All he could feel was the sheer sense of awe and amazement at the world about him.

And that, dear reader, is where we will leave the little frog for today.

LILLY: Thank you for sticking with me through the interruptions.
GOLYGA: No problem for us, as you can see. We do appreciate that you don't jump away for every phone call or such distraction, but as you saw we can handle interruptions. We also want to commend you on your ability to stay with the connection after being pulled into everyday matters such as a phone call—long-distance at that—from your elder son. Have the decency now to remember that energy-flow adjustments must be made, and we want you to make our work in that line easier by lying down for the short duration of this adjustment. "Have the decency," my dear, was not in any way censorious—it is, after all, for your own protection. "Have the decency" meant and means "be decent to yourself." All right?
LILLY: It's an accusatory phrase in our language, suggesting the recipient might opt for not having decency.
GOLYGA: Yes, we can see that. Let us rephrase then: be decent to yourself now, Lilly dear, and rest for the energy adjustment phase. All right?
LILLY: Yes, thank you. Will do. Until soon, Beeswax.

* * *

GOLYGA: Yes, my dear, we are here; we care for you as always and are glad to be working together. Your recent growth spurt, as you call it, brings us joy galore, and we are going to watch you light up the world in ever increasing circles wherever you go. Now…

As we have been telling you for some time, the book is near completion. However, some essential parts are missing. We did think that humans would be able to deduce the teachings without difficulties from the events and adventures we brought to them, but we have recently become convinced that the more direct approach, in combination with the adventure tales of teaching, would be best. Those who "get the message" in the stories can always skip the more direct teachings.

As you know, many segments already exist on the page that do direct teaching, summarizing the stories' messages and so on. Now we come to the themes not yet fully elucidated.

Once upon a time, there was a great frog story that set all its readers to chuckling and was obvious in its message to some. Others thought of it as simply a lovely, funny, delightful, inventive, and entertaining tale and left it at that. We want to make sure nobody can just "leave it at that" and so we are going to put an addendum on the frog story. To wit:

There comes a time in everyone's life when a door opens on the infinite. Many people ignore it. Many even ignore it more than once or twice. They go merrily or not so merrily about their business and assume they can do so to the end of their days, which, they assume, lie somewhere in the distant future—even if they're ninety-five and feeble. Well, to be truthful, not many make it to ninety-five without noting the open door and peeking through it.

Peeking through it, what is the first thing you see?

It matters not. Whatever may lie there, the first thing you see will elicit a sense of wonder, awe, amazement. Whichever marvels of the universe will be revealed to the first glimpse through that door to the infinite, they will change the one peeking through.

Now, some people immediately slam shut that same door and try to go on with their lives as though they had never even seen such a door, let alone looked through it.

They try, we say, but they do not succeed.

After that one short glimpse, they are inevitably changed and discomfited by ordinary everyday life as they used to know it. Until, one fine day, they again glimpse that open door, peek through it, and, once more, marvel at the wonder of what they see.

The next thing that happens is this: being a changed person—new of eye, so to speak—they now begin to notice all manner of things around and to see them all with an increasing sense of wonder. Gradually, the entire world seems a wondrous place, and soon there are distinct signs of growing wings on those eyes of wonder. A marvellous feeling of life-as-adventure that brings about changes in the experience of life that bring further awe and amazement, and so on and on.

How to recognize the door that is ajar and affords a glimpse of the infinite? Why, keep your eyes peeled. Keep your senses receptive. Keep your attention honed. All of the above will, sooner or later, lead you to that door. Recognizing it is easy. Though it comes in many forms and shapes, every one of them has about it an aura, a feel, a shimmering invitation to look more closely. Every one of them has in it the sound of *ahhh* and the light of the magical hues you see when the sun is low in the sky and the world is bathed in a deep, rich, full light. You'll recognize it by your own heart beating to get your attention, or your breath insisting on expanding your chest, or the sudden sounds of birds.

Do not believe for a moment that you must first clear your emotional baggage to be worthy of glimpsing that door. Or that you must first devote your time to earning this or that, for your family or yourself, or that you must grow wise and strong and able to withstand with equanimity what life is throwing your way. None of those are prerequisites. You can, in fact, be a snivelling wreck of a human, bringing complaints and taking umbrage and generally behaving as though the world has stepped on your toes—whatever. You can be anyone at any time and yet find that door ajar and beckoning. And then?

It may be curiosity that leads you to take a closer look—as it did with Lilly dear. Or the challenge of the unknown, or the desire to acquire new experience. Whatever brings you close enough to peek through that door is fine. Just fine. Because once you have seen, you will change. Perhaps not overnight. Perhaps not for a lifetime or even two. But you will change and be glad of it and look back on that first glimpse through the open door with an awe and wonder that will be yours from that moment on.

Are you getting impatient yet to encounter that door? Can hardly wait to look through and be awash in amazement?

Well, no need to wait for it to appear from nowhere. You can conjure it. All you need to do is develop spiritual muscle. Remember our frog? All the climbing and the fright and the entire adventure led him to this: a sense of wonder and awe is the first requisite for developing spiritual muscle.

So there you are: happens you see that door and look through it, and you'll develop a sense of wonder and awe equalling the beginning of spiritual muscle.

Happens you don't see that door and want to? Develop a sense of wonder and awe and develop spiritual muscle, and that door will appear. And then who knows what wonders you will see!

LILLY: Is that it for today?
GOLYGA: Yes, my dear. Make sure you rest well. And thank you for the excellent clear channel, without editor or monitor for most of it, and with appreciation when you did catch what was coming through.
LILLY: Thank you. And for the elegant writing. Until soon?
GOLYGA: Certainly. All the best on your transition to the city. Exciting new things developing for you there, so be of good cheer.
LILLY: Thank you, Beeswax.
GOLYGA: Beeswax and more. We have with us another Entity, called Abracadabra Hallelujah Jehosepath Kinkyberry.
LILLY: Welcome.
GOLYGA: Enough fooling around. Rest and enjoy the day!

* * *

Have you thought of this one: bring your own little-girl self along wherever you go and hold her by the hand for comfort when she wants it, and enjoy her antics and frolicking when she's in the mood? It's not a new thought, as you know, but it certainly is one to bring you joy and comfort both day and night, if you but remember to do it whenever you feel lonely or restless or bored or deserted by friends and family or upset by people at work, or any other situation where you want someone with you. If the situation is distressing to the child in you, comfort her. If it is an opportunity for fun, let her have her joyous way. Either way, you both benefit.

Yes, I say "both" because your child-self lives on inside you, and much of what she's about informs your present self so you are restricted by her lacks—of love, of comfort, of anything at all—and you respond to everything in your daily life with those same lacks/restrictions built in. Take her along and reassure her that the lacks are a matter of the past because you can now give her all the love and comfort she needs, and she is allowed to play and be joyful whenever the opportunity arises, and you will find yourself richly endowed with an addition to your life that will amaze you.

After all the work I did, we hear Lilly saying, to alleviate the after-effects of trauma in my childhood? Now I'm supposed to drag the kid-me around still? When do I get to be an adult who fully enjoys being an adult and isn't hampered by having to drag along a little girl?

LILLY: I object. This is Lilly speaking. Those are not my words or thoughts—well, not the last part, anyway.
GOLYGA: Yes, we know. We were teasing. This is ground you have covered, but you never fully had the benefit of having your little girl along because you didn't do it enough. Not often enough and regularly enough to incorporate into your adult self both the comfort and the joy of a loved child. You are beloved and you don't know it, and today's meditation, when you led your little girl by the hand, can be a regular source of love and comfort in your life. Not only during meditation. Take your little girl along on country walks, into the internet—yes, we do see that coming—and everywhere else you possibly can. Get used to having her delightful presence around and with you and you'll soon incorporate all her best qualities while also giving yourself—through her—the love and comfort and sense of safety you need, want, and enjoy.
LILLY: Thank you, I'll do that.

Here is a summary:

Whenever about to undertake the next part of your day, ask yourself: Would my little girl like to come along for this?

If the answer is yes, take her by the hand and lead her into it with you. And if it's appropriate, allow her free reign of her joy and curiosity.

And now, my dear, we would like to suggest a way of incorporating the above into our project. As you know, we have been preparing this book for a while. We are almost ready for the next stage—arranging and putting in order its various parts and segments. However, there are some more loops and holes to deal with first, so the next few sessions will seem rather disjointed and disorganized.

Trust us, please, to know how it will all fit together and allow us to be all over the map, so to speak, until all the holes are filled.

Aren't you glad this isn't your job to accomplish?

LILLY: Yes, there is a wonderful feeling of ease and discovery for me.

GOLYGA: We are pleased to hear it and happy to be working with you. As for a time frame, you'll find that the book is closer to completion than you think. We'll finish it this summer, and when you go to New Mexico, you can take it with you—unless a publisher comes along before then.

LILLY: Is this really you speaking or is it my mind replaying something I have thought, or is it sounding familiar because you've put the thought into my mind before?

GOLYGA: Good question. Here is the answer:

As we have told you once before, in brief, you are not so separate and divided and apart from us as you think. Nor are we all separate and divided to the extent that you perceive us to be. For example: the entity you call MarTee is one of us as we speak to you now, and when you are sitting on the porch, talking to MarTee, there are trailing beams of light energy that connect him to us and thus us to you.

There are also connections and interlapping between us and every light-body around you, whether it be entities from our side of the veil or beings-in-body. We are interflowing, so to speak, and that is why we are constantly in communication these days—with you perceiving our voices sometimes as yours and sometimes as ours, depending on your judgment of yourself.

By that we mean that whenever something smart comes along, you tend to assign it to us. In fact, such knowledge is part of your own understanding by now. It does partake of our light and we are glad this is so.

Try to feel the "us" of our communication and try to stop denigrating yourself and placing yourself in some lower-than position. You couldn't understand or communicate with us if we were on so different a plane as you perceive us to be. Be assured that "your Larger Self—"higher" gives the erroneous impression of a hierarchy—is entirely capable of anything and everything we can do or know.

LILLY: I like thinking there are wiser beings than I am from whom I can learn and who can protect me and help me.

GOLYGA: We said nothing to the contrary. We are saying that your Larger Self is part of that source of wisdom and loving care. We are saying that you can avail yourself of these gifts, knowing that you yourself are part of the Entity bringing you these gifts.

LILLY: *Okay. As long as you are not saying I am to do without you, to do it all myself.*

GOLYGA: *Your Self and our Selves are so intertwined, my dear, we can only be torn apart by a horrendous effort on your part to shut the us-part out of your life. We are family in the tightest sense, if you want to think of it like that. We are ONE.*

LILLY: *Thank you. Are there times when MarTee and I can get together just the two of us?*

GOLYGA: *Yes. There is a shield, a cocoon he can place around the two of you, and he sometimes does. We encourage anything that increases your ability to love— whether yourself, others, anything, and anybody—and we know whatever goes on between you is love.*

By the way, you, too, can shield yourself and be private in your mind or body. Simply state the desire with your thoughts and you are entirely unobserved by any consciousness until you release the state. There is nothing wrong with that either. It's a state many humans find necessary because of the built-in sense of guilt, or of "pulling myself up by the bootstraps," or of shame, or of delight in secrecy. Whatever the reason, feel free to avail yourself of the shield any time you please and don't think for a moment we are insulted or upset or put off. When you want to be in communication again, think it or say it. The opening will instantly be re-established.

We want to give you one more word of advice, Lilly dear. When you begin to think of the cottage and being alone up there, make sure your fears of yesteryear don't inform those thoughts. When fear comes up, take your little girl by the hand and show her all the delights she will encounter there, and reassure her again and again that you will take care of her. Okay?

LILLY: *Yes, thank you for the reminder.*

GOLYGA: *And now, rest and enjoy the day, my dear. And be assured that our work is ongoing.*

LILLY: *Thank you, Beeswax. Until soon.*

***

GOLYGA: *Yes, we are here, we love you and care for you and are glad to be talking with you today. We have plans. Lest you think we're not sure what you have in mind for today, let us assure you: the journeying is a good idea. But not today. Today, we suggest a session of channelling for the book. What say you?*

LILLY: I say fine.
GOLYGA: Then we shall start right now...

Once upon a time, a rapt young listener at the bosom of Mother Earth heard the singing heart inside and said to himself: That's a song I would like to learn.

He listened some more and pretty soon he could hum the melody to himself. However, he couldn't understand the words. He couldn't even guess what language they were in. So, intently though he listened, he made no progress at all on the lyrics.

One fine day as he lay there, ear pressed to the ground, fingers gripping some tufts of grass, deep in concentration, he heard a bird laughing out loud just above his head. (Have you noticed how birds tend to come through our tales, laughing at the foibles displayed therein?)

The young listener straightened up and looked at the bird. Listen, he said. You may find this funny, sitting as you do on your high branch, able to sing and fly and all. Me, I have to learn how to do these things, so don't give me that laughing bird trip. It's hard work being human, and you're not helping at all, making fun of me.

Whoa, said the bird. Where do you get this "making fun of"? I was just having a laugh, that's all. It's a damned funny sight, to me, seeing a human pressing ear to ground, trying to learn a song. Why not sit up and look at the sunshine and flowers and make up a song?

The young listener thought about that. Well, okay, he admitted. That would be fun, too. But I want more than fun here. I want to learn the specific song of Mother Earth, you see.

I see, said the bird. And what have you learned so far?

Well, said the young listener: that she sings a different song every time I listen. That I don't understand the words in any of them. And that I am going to go crazy trying.

The young listener stood up and, disgusted with his own inability to grasp the lyrics of the songs of Mother Earth, was about to stalk off, never to try again.

The bird again said: Whoa. Not so fast. Maybe I can help you decipher the words of these songs. Let me just have a quick listen.

The bird flew down from his branch and pressed his little ear to the ground. Oh goody, he said right away. There's a big fat worm moving around in there. Let me just… The bird pecked away a few crumbs of earth, found a hole, and *zip zip*, pulled out a big fat worm. Then he flew off into the tree, deposited that worm in a nest and returned.

Now, where were we? he said. Ah yes. And bent his ear again to listen to Mother Earth. 'I hear it now, he said. A low humming melody—quite lovely, isn't it?—and what's that?

The little bird screwed up his tiny face, he was listening so hard, trying to catch the lyrics. But it was obvious by his face that he was getting none of them.

Ah well, sighed the young listener, disappointed and resigned. He hadn't really believed a bird would understand what he himself had not been able to decipher.

Hold it, said the bird, sitting up straight and wobbling a bit from the suddenness of his move.

I hear something very strange and deep down there, inside that song. Not words, you see. There aren't really any of those. But there are overtones and undertones and harmonics and all manner of sounds inside the sound of Mother Earth's song. It's no use even trying to hear words, there are none. There are so many sounds inside the sound, however, that you can listen all your life and never get bored. Try it, try just listening to as many sounds as you can hear. Go ahead, try it.

Well, the young listener tried it. He glued his ear to the ground and listened. And he grew enraptured. Mesmerized. Ecstatic. He was so taken out of himself by the sounds he heard—more and more and more of them—that he forgot to eat, to sleep, to speak to anyone, or even to brush his teeth.

Pretty soon, he was a dirty messy skeletal figure lying on the ground, and people came to see him there out of curiosity about this strange man and his strange doings. Pretty soon there was a camera crew and a reporter, trying to get the young listener to answer a few questions, but the young listener didn't listen to the questions. He was busy and exalted as ever, listening to Mother Earth and her song of many sounds.

And so the story ends: he is there listening still, and hardly anyone but the bird and a few other creatures of the wild have any idea what it is he is doing.

So what do you think of that?

LILLY: Are you asking me?
GOLYGA: Yes, What do you think?
LILLY: As a writer, it makes me a bit uncomfortable with the lack of ending, resolution, something more. As a learner, it makes sense on several levels.
GOLYGA: All right then, we'll indulge the writer and add an ending, shall we?
LILLY: If you like.
GOLYGA: We like. Readers might prefer it also. So here is the rest of it now…

One day the young listener—who was no longer as young as he once was—heard a new sound coming from Mother Earth. Inside the song she sang was a new note. A gurgling, burbling kind of note.

The listener kept his attention on that note and pretty soon he realized it was growing stronger. It was, in fact, almost as loud now as Mother Earth's song, yet it blended in perfectly and augmented it and enriched it, too.

Wonderful, thought the listener, ecstatic again. I simply can't get enough of listening to these wonderful sounds. I'll never get enough of it.

Just then, a young girl came out of the forest and, seeing the listener lying on the ground, she thought he might be ill.

Can I help you? she asked. She had obviously never heard of the listener and his strange ways. Can I get you some food, or help getting up, or a blanket for your bones—er, I mean body?

The listener gestured with his hands: No, no thanks. (He didn't shake his head because that would mean removing his ear from the marvellous sounds.)

The young girl was intrigued. She could tell now that he was listening to something inside the ground and so she lay down beside him and pressed her ear to the ground. And she heard the same marvellous song sung by Mother Earth.

Wonderful, wonderful, she thought, and listened for quite a while.

Then she got up, dusted off her skirt, and said: Well, I'll be going now. I have work to do.

The listener was astonished that anyone who had heard that marvellous song could just get up and leave. What work, he said, could be important enough to leave off listening to the wondrous sounds of Mother Earth's song?

Oh, said the young girl. I won't stop listening to that. I'll keep right on listening to it any time I want to. It's the same song we carry in our hearts, after all.

And off she went, humming and smiling at the world.

The listener sat up. He was so astonished that he actually lifted his ear off the ground and sat up, staring after the young girl.

The same song we carry in our heart? Had he heard that right? Could she be telling the truth? Oh me, oh my, said the listener. I better check that out pronto.

And he did. Closed his eyes and listened as hard as he could to his heart. At first he heard only its rhythm. A wonderful, regular reassuring beat. Then he heard the tone of it: deep and resonating. And as he listened more and more closely, he began hearing songs. Wide-ranging and various, they were songs of joy and songs of tears, songs of every conceivable kind, all emerging from his very own heart.

Well, after that the listener had no need to stay put lying on the ground. Off he went, out into his life, and wherever he was, he listened to the songs of his heart.

GOLYGA: How is that now?
LILLY: Even better.
GOLYGA: Good, then we'll leave it at this for today.
LILLY: Could I ask you a question?
GOLYGA: Of course.
LILLY: I had a strong signal earlier that I should be paying attention to something. Was it the publisher of the Hilarion book?
GOLYGA: No, it was the writer/channel we want you to get in touch with.
LILLY: Through his publisher, I guess. All right.
GOLYGA: That's it for today, my dear. Rest awhile. And we'll see you again soon.

* * *

GOLYGA: We are going to do something new today, since you, dear Lilly, seem determined to have no editor present during this session but to take down anything coming along without even listening in. Here we go...

Once upon a time, there were other people, other planets, other worlds. There were people on Earth, too, before the coming of the apes. Evolution is never so straight a line as scientists seem determined to persuade people, and given the advent of science as religion, it has been hard to persuade humans otherwise, but there were, indeed, a race of people on this planet that was advanced and delighted in many things even today's Earth population has yet to achieve.

However, there was one major flaw in existence at that time: the Earth was cooling rapidly and humans had no way of studying the effects of reduced warmth and succumbed rapidly to all kinds of effects and after-effects of the disappearance of sustaining sunshine and warmth.

So they died out. Not, however, before leaving a legacy: an imprint of their existence, which can be found until this day, if only people knew what to look for. Atlantis, another civilization lost to present-day earthlings, was able to leave behind rather more evidence of its existence, and even that is not enough to convince most people.

The previously mentioned group or period of population left its mark not in the earth or water but in the air. In the energy flows that come and go around the planet rather than on it or inside it.

They left coded energy they hoped would benefit future generations of the planet's inhabitants. Since they thought of themselves as humans and were advanced in the uses of energy for all manner of achievements in manifestation, it is no surprise to learn they left their legacy in that domain. However, to retrieve and understand their messages, it is necessary to achieve a certain control and access to energy forms other than those so far achieved by humans on the planet at this time.

We are not going to endeavour to teach or prepare either Lilly or anyone else for this work of discovery until a certain level of energy work has been achieved in other realms of that vast subject—energy—so you can all relax about possible burdens laid on your shoulders. We do want to titillate you with the knowledge that there is, just around the corner—or shall we say up two layers and around the circle—a body of evidence of former occupation of the planet as well as a great deal of useful information about manipulating energy and manifesting it in material form.

What you are all invited to do with this in the meantime is to become ever more aware of what is around you, what is possible, what is imaginable. You see, the expansion of awareness and perception is the first necessary step toward acquiring and contacting the aforementioned codes. Every little step forward by even one person soon has the effect of making that energy-knowledge available to ever larger numbers and thus prepare someone or other for the next step.

Acceleration is the catchword of the day, as you know, and in no area is it more evident and widespread than in energy work. Be assured, every little new perception, thought, awareness moves great gobs of it forward. "It" being the body of knowledge available as a trampoline, so to speak, and jump-off point for the next lot of adventurers in the vaster realms.

Now imagine this, dear Lilly. Imagine yourself walking along in the forest one day and encountering a life form you have never seen before nor heard of from any source whatever. What would your first reaction be?

LILLY: Probably fear.

Right you are, and honest, too. Yes, fear. And so would most people react to such a being with fear. Exceptions are small children who have neither come into the world with it nor been taught fear, people who spend their time in realms that have no place in consensus reality—in other words, people considered crazy—and those on Earth who came from other places with the knowledge already imbedded that there are sources and manifestations other than those regularly encountered on the planet.

These last mentioned are emissaries from other manifested bombardments of energy, and they can impart much knowledge to those humans who are earthbound during their time in body.

However, these beings are restricted to communicating in various ways that are not easily recognized as useful. Poets, for example. And why are they so restricted? Because everyday human language does not lend itself to communication of the material they address. Shamans are others who can, through the language of energy, symbol, ritual, song, etc., convey such knowledge to some degree and be understood. Now comes a third group, comprised of those among you who have learned to channel. Be warned: not every entity channelled conveys useful or even accurate information, but you can easily sort the true messengers from the spurious by looking at the content of their material. Does it convey useful, positive information or merely ramble like a drunken sailor who hasn't yet got his land legs after six months at sea? Most of you will easily be able to tell one from the other, so we'll leave that for now.

Other sources of useful energy and information about other realms will open up as the time comes closer when more and more people are open to receiving knowledge in alternate ways than the academic, scientific, etc., etc.

As you are probably aware, channellers are proliferating as we speak. Not every one of them is able to stay clear for the long haul. Many channel only personal guidance. Others concentrate on the study of ongoing theoretical developments or on play of the imagination. Some, like Lilly dear, do all of the above and, as well, put their time and energy at our disposal to produce a useful book for many others. We want to assure Lilly that this service is not only appreciated now, by us, but will be helpful and appreciated by many, for many years to come.

GOLYGA: We close for the day with our appreciation and our assurance of ongoing work and delight, and are, forever yours, Beeswax and Co.
LILLY: Thank you, Beeswax. Is that it for today?
GOLYGA: Yes, my dear. Until soon!
LILLY: Excuse me, Beeswax, but at the beginning of this session, there is some material that is not clear to me as I read it over.
GOLYGA: You are a delight, my dear. Let's go over it and correct it right now.

...

LILLY: Done. Is it okay now?
GOLYGA: Yes, it'll do. It conveys enough of what we mean, and other segments will elucidate further. Though, as you probably have guessed, Lilly dear, this material may come at the very end to entice the reader to think big and varied and to entice you, Lilly dear, to be ready to do another book with us.
LILLY: I'll be delighted, I'm sure.

* * *

Once upon a time, there was a woman named Lilly dear who became, through a sequence of events and lifetimes, ready, able, and willing to be the channel for a book. We were thrilled, of course, because, since she was a writer already and her style and elegance of mind were pleasing to us, we had great hopes for our collaboration on this project. However, the end result of our work together far exceeded our hopes. We are pleased to tell you, dear reader, that the entire project and our work on it together was accomplished with mutual delight and much enjoyment of the material included. Also, the additional benefit that accrued from the fact that Lilly dear undertook to learn, practise, and undergo the lessons and exercises was a bonus. We had hoped for such but could hardly expect it since many channels are content to simply produce the material without engaging it in their own lives. And so we want to thank Lilly dear, and we want to express the hope and the wish that we might work together again in the future. Please be assured that there is evidence aplenty of the need for more books and more work in the service of educating earthlings, and that it is still our contention that an entertaining tale is the best vehicle for such lessons as are needed and useful.

* * *

As we have come to see more and more clearly, another book will follow this one soonest. That is, Lilly dear willing, we shall begin working on it as soon as this one has begun its physical journey toward publication.

Meantime, we recommend that you, dear reader, keep the present volume nearby and handy in order that you might refresh your memory on any points relevant to your lives ongoing. Keep us in mind, coming and going through your days, and keep in mind also that we wish you well and that we are happy to have been your companions.

We look forward to more time in the future, as they say where you are (this entire sentence is both mysterious and hilarious where we are, but we'll let it stand).

* * *

Epilogue

We have come to the end of this endeavour and we are happy to say it has been accomplished with joy, ease (for the most part), and much application of our best energies all around.

We now want to assure you that the adventures of Golyga, Lillykins, Baby/Youth, Hylu, and all the other characters we have met in this book are not over. There will be other adventures, other times, other learning in the future—speaking in Earth terms—and we have already designed, devised, and composed such a continuation.

You see: Golyga the shape-shifting genius has become enamoured of the story-telling he is engaged in and is thrilled with the idea of collaborating on another book with Lilly. So this is not goodbye; it is rather: so long. See you soon.

However, this book has come to its timely end and we wish all of you—readers, Lilly dear, publishers—the very best of everything until we meet again.

Be joyful, be open-hearted, be a growing Light until we come together once more. And in the meantime: bon voyage.

Yours as always, Beeswax.

THE END

CPSIA information can be obtained
at www.ICGtesting.com
Printed in the USA
BVHW030656131120
593123BV00017B/124